Woolf

BLOOMSBURY GUIDES FOR THE PERPLEXED

Bloomsbury's Guides for the Perplexed are clear, concise and accessible introductions to thinkers, writers and subjects that students and readers can find especially challenging – or indeed downright bewildering. Concentrating specifically on what it is that makes the subject difficult to grasp, these books explain and explore key themes and ideas, guiding the reader towards a thorough understanding of demanding material.

Other titles available in the series include:

Woolf

KATHRYN SIMPSON

Bloomsbury Academic
An imprint of Bloomsbury Publishing Plc

B L O O M S B U R Y
LONDON · OXFORD · NEW YORK · NEW DELHI · SYDNEY

Bloomsbury Academic

An imprint of Bloomsbury Publishing Plc

50 Bedford Square   1385 Broadway
London   New York
WC1B 3DP   NY 10018
UK   USA

www.bloomsbury.com

**BLOOMSBURY and the Diana logo are trademarks of Bloomsbury
Publishing Plc**

First published 2016

© Kathryn Simpson, 2016

British Library Cataloguing-in-Publication Data
A catalogue record for this book is available from the British Library.

ISBN: HB: 978-1-4411-6902-0
PB: 978-1-4411-9122-9
ePDF: 978-1-4725-9067-1
ePub: 978-1-4725-9068-8

Library of Congress Cataloging-in-Publication Data
A catalog record for this book is available from the Library of Congress.

Series: Guides for the Perplexed

Typeset by Integra Software Services Pvt. Ltd.
Printed and bound in Great Britain

For lovely B.

CONTENTS

ACKNOWLEDGEMENTS

First, thanks must go to the editorial and production staff at Bloomsbury Academic for their initial enthusiasm for this project and for their on-going positive encouragement and patience, namely David Avital and Mark Richardson. Many thanks also to Rajakumari Ganessin and Balaji Kasirajan at Integra.

Second, many, many thanks to friends, family and colleagues for their love, care, support and friendship.

Finally, all my love and thanks to B., without whom none of this would have been possible.

LIST OF ABBREVIATIONS

Introduction

Virginia Woolf is now an iconic figure in our culture. She is best known as a novelist, but also as a prolific essayist, reviewer and a writer of short fiction. She is recognized as a feminist, socialist and pacifist, as a central figure of the Bloomsbury Group, as part of the fabric of Englishness as well as a national commodity to be exploited and exported.[1] As critics explore her work in ever more diverse ways it is also clear that she was in many ways a 'cultural magpie', her thinking and writing critically engaging with a vast range of new ideas and modern phenomena emerging in her contemporary period – from avant-garde movements in the visual arts, developments in cinema and photography, experience of new technologies such as the telephone, gramophone, broadcast radio and the motor-car, to philosophical ideas, psychoanalysis and the 'new physics'. The exciting and challenging possibilities these new experiences created also shaped and informed Woolf's literary experiments and aesthetics suggesting as they did new ways of perceiving, experiencing and representing reality and the self. Woolf also lived in a period of dramatic social, political and economic change, all of which impacted on her writing in significant ways. She saw the rise of the Labour Party, successes in feminist politics and the achievement of female suffrage, developments in mass industrialization and the of expansion commodity culture, as well as significant changes in the empire and in the international sphere resulting in war. She is, as the plethora of critical assessments demonstrates, an inherently complex and contradictory figure, as much the subject of controversies as a promoter of them.

Critic Brenda Silver has demonstrated that there are now innumerable 'versions' of Virginia Woolf in circulation, produced by the many and various ways in which readers, taking wildly different perspectives on her and her work, have interpreted and constructed her. These sometimes impassioned and clashing versions, Silver suggests, are a result of the powerful responses Woolf's writings provoke, leading readers to feel intimately connected to her work and her life. These many versions are a testimony to the lasting influence of Woolf's writing, but also highlight the many 'Woolfs' we have to negotiate as readers of her work, 'Woolfs' that are multiple, varying, contradictory and still emerging. This makes it impossible to limit her cultural meaning and to arrive at hard and fast interpretations of her writing. Yet given that Woolf asserts (in many different ways) that 'nothing was simply one thing' (*TTL* 177) and that acceptance of both/and rather than either/or is the only way to live and be, it would seem that acceptance of diversity, plurality, contradiction and an on-going fluidity of interpretation is what we need to aim for as readers of her work.

Woolf and the modernist canon

Although Woolf and her work are now unquestionably recognized as belonging to 'modernism', her position in the modernist canon has not always been so secure. The retrospective delineation of modernism as an artistic and cultural movement, begun in the 1950s, constructed it as male dominated, masculine in values and ethos, gender blind and middle class. It was the 'Men of 1914' (Ezra Pound, T. S. Eliot, Wyndham Lewis and James Joyce) whose work was seen as definitive and 'canonical'. As Bonnie Kime Scott notes in her ground-breaking study, *The Gender of Modernism*, 'Typically, both the authors of the original [modernist] manifestos and the literary historians of modernism took as their norm a small set of its male participants, who were quoted, anthologized, taught, and consecrated as geniuses' (Scott 1990: 2). Growing out of a male-dominated academic context, early critical views of Woolf saw her as asexual and apolitical, a feminine or 'lady' writer of exquisite works and also as a weak woman subject to nervous illness. These are views that subsequent criticism has done much to correct.

Feminist criticism of the 1970s and 1980s opened the doors for recuperating 'lost' and forgotten women writers and for challenging the gender politics of the canonical male modernists and the critics defining such a canon. Feminist readings alongside other critical approaches (such as post-colonial, queer and class-focussed criticism) consider Woolf's work in a wide range of ways that draw attention to the political as well as aesthetic dimensions of her writing and thought. However, critical assessments also take on board the tensions running through modernist literature generally – between the radical nature of the literary experiment and the embracing of 'the new' and conservative, even sexist, politics and views. Even the most forward thinking writers were not immune to the anxieties generated by the social and political changes of the early decades of the twentieth century in relation to gender roles, class and sexual identities and the disruption of established hierarchies of all kinds. Like that of her contemporaries, Woolf's writing simultaneously embraces change even as it registers anxieties and stumbling blocks and her work can be seen to foreground processes of transition.

Woolf's writings – a wider view

Woolf's novels are still the primary focus of critical assessments of her work but the critical scope is now significantly extended to encompass Woolf's successful and prolific publication as a reviewer and essayist. She wrote over 500 pieces during the course of her lifetime, spanning writing from the Renaissance to her present day. Her first foray into the world of the literary professional was the publication of a review in 1904 in the clerical newspaper, the *Guardian*, and she became well respected and well-known in this capacity with articles published in important journals, such as the *Times Literary Supplement*, the *Nation and Athenaeum*, the *Criterion* and *Scrutiny* (see Rosenburg and Dubino 1997: 1–2). This work played a significant role in extending her knowledge and understanding of contemporary writing and of the political and philosophical ideas in circulation, but also in developing a wider audience for her own fiction, creating opportunities to connect with what Woolf called the 'common reader'. The huge project that Andrew McNeillie began in 1986 to publish all of Woolf's critical writings has given readers and critics access to a plethora of Woolf's writings and this in turn has altered and exponentially expanded the critical landscape of Woolf studies. Woolf's non-fiction is now seen as valuable in its own right as well as in informing critical assessments of her fiction (see Lee 2000). Similarly, there has been a more recent surge of critical interest in her shorter fiction. Although Woolf published only one collection of short stories in her lifetime, *Monday or Tuesday* (1921), she wrote and published shorter fiction throughout her career. While her shorter fiction has often been treated as a kind of 'testing ground' for ideas and literary experiments more fully developed in her longer works, this extensive and protean body of work is now considered to be fundamental to her emergence as a modernist writer and of value in its own right (see Benzel and Hoberman 2004). The publication of Woolf's diaries and letters has also broadened and complicated our understanding of her as an individual woman, a writer and a political thinker. The information and insights gleaned from her personal writings would, we might assume, go some way to 'explaining' this complex figure. However, this is far from the case and these fascinating writings open up many new avenues for exploration of Woolf's work.[2]

Woolf's life

Understanding Woolf's literary innovation, her attitudes and politics depends in part on understanding her perspectives on the past and on her own Victorian upbringing in a patriarchal family. In her essay 'How It Strikes a Contemporary' (1925)[3], she discusses the critical reception of contemporary fiction and reflects on the necessity of marking a separation from the past given the vast changes that have taken place in every aspect of experience:

> We are sharply cut off from our predecessors. A shift in the scale – the war, the sudden slip of masses held in place for ages – has shaken the fabric from top to bottom…No age can have been more rich than ours in writers determined to give expression to the differences which separate them from the past and not to the resemblances which connect them with it. (*E4* 238)

While it is tempting to think of Woolf and other modernists making a break completely with the past to 'make it new', Woolf's relationship to the past, and specifically to her own past, involves both a sense of connection as well as separation. This is seen very clearly in her feelings for her mother who died in 1895 when Woolf was thirteen. This led to the first of Woolf's major breakdowns and her grief was compounded by the sudden death of her older half sister, Stella, two years later. Her loss had a profound and life-long effect on Woolf even though she rejected her mother as a role model for womanhood, conforming as Julia Stephen did to Victorian ideals of femininity summed up in the phrase taken from the title of Coventry Patmore's mid-century poem celebrating marriage, 'The Angel in the House'. More recent critics take a nuanced view of Woolf's personal and political engagements with the Victorian period (see, for example, Jane de Gay 1999; Emily Blair 2007; Steve Ellis 2007). Woolf clearly felt the need to resist the detrimental impact of the social 'machinery', the pressures exerted on her as a middle-class woman to conform to cultural expectations. As she explained in her memoir, 'A Sketch of the Past', 'the machine into which our rebellious bodies were inserted in 1900 not only held us tight in its framework, but bit into us with innumerable sharp teeth' (*MOB* 166). Throughout her life Woolf challenged the dominant ideologies of gender, sexuality, race and class that shaped the Victorian period and persisted into the twentieth century, as she also engaged critically with the political contributions of members of her own family who played prominent roles in the building of Victorian society. Yet Woolf, her outlook, her literary and intellectual aspirations, and her political views are inevitably shaped in sometimes complex and highly problematic ways by her experience and her response to this experience. She may be able to stand back and, to a certain extent, create a critical distance from which to assess and represent the past, but she is also inextricably connected it and her writing articulates some of the complexities in understanding these connections. See 'Woolf's (perplexing) politics' below for discussion of gender, sexuality, class, empire and antisemitism.

Bloomsbury

Following the death of her father, Leslie Stephen, in 1904, Woolf (then Virginia Stephen) and her siblings set up a new home at 46 Gordon Square in Bloomsbury. Leaving behind the claustrophobic respectability of Hyde Park Gate in Kensington, Woolf entered not only a new geographical area of London (a more dubious, Bohemian and cosmopolitan milieu) but also a new space in which she could engage in the political life and pursue her profession as a writer (see Jean Moorcroft Wilson 1987; Anna Snaith 2000: 24–30).

Although the Stephens still had a cook and servants, Woolf records the emancipation and newness that her new living arrangements signified: 'Everything was going to be new; everything was going to be different. Everything was on trial' (*MOB* 201). Woolf also entered a new social, intellectual and cultural space as Gordon Square became a meeting place for Thoby Stephen's Cambridge friends (including the writers E. M. Forster and Lytton Strachey, the economist John Maynard Keynes and Leonard Woolf) and what became known as the 'Bloomsbury Group' developed. The group included contemporary artists – Woolf's sister, Vanessa Bell, Bell's lover, the artist Duncan Grant, the artist and critic Roger Fry as well as Vanessa's husband, the writer and art critic Clive Bell, amongst others. The group is frequently criticized for its elitism and the predominance of male figures has led to accusations of sexism and even misogyny. However, Woolf flourished in this liberal and lively political and artistic context in which she could debate a wide range of issues. It not only afforded her the necessary ingredients of intellectual, social, political and creative stimulation for her success as a professional writer, but also provided support, encouragement as well as critique. Woolf's early short story 'Phyllis and Rosamund' (c. 1906) conveys the importance of the uninhibited nature of Bloomsbury 'talk'. Her female characters, visitors to a Bloomsbury party, are startled yet thrilled by the 'hot and serious' combative debate about art they hear there (*CSF* 24). This open, frank, 'new, but unquestionably genuine' talk is part of a lively atmosphere of 'merrymaking' for the 'feasters' and proves a stark contrast to the staid and conventional conversation that dominates their ordinary lives (*CSF* 25, 26). This (semi-autobiographical) story seems to confirm that for Woolf the transition to membership of this radical group, her proximity to the various feminist societies based in Bloomsbury itself and 'the symbolic power' of independent living in Bloomsbury were felt to be powerfully liberating (Snaith 2000: 29).

Cultural contexts and influences

Woolf's cultural experience was rich and extensive and this can be seen to have informed the development of her literary aesthetics and new modes of representation. Woolf engaged with new developments in technology and critics have explored the ways in which modern phenomena from the motorcar to the gramophone can open up new avenues for exploring and understanding her work. Significantly, she lived in a period of innovation across the arts and her friendships and associations brought her into contact with a range of new and experimental artistic forms and visual cultures. The influence of painting on her aesthetic and formal development is well documented, particularly the influence of Roger Fry's ideas about Post-Impressionist art and his aesthetic theory of what Clive Bell in *Art* (1914) termed 'significant form' (8). These theories argue that artistic expression should not be mimetic but should find an equivalent in form to convey the sense and emotion of what is represented. In this popular critical art book, Bell explained significant form as the way that art, by certain arrangements of line and colour, can provoke our aesthetic emotions. Fry's formalist exposition on the work of the Post-Impressionists, especially Cezanne, resonates with Woolf's own quest to find new forms of representation. In *Vision and Design*, Fry explains that Post-Impressionists 'do not seek to imitate form, but to create form; not to imitate life, but to find an equivalent for life' (167). In her biography of Fry, Woolf celebrated his encouragement of pleasure in 'the disinterested life, the life of the spirit ..."all those human faculties and activities which are over and above our mere existence as living organisms"' (1979: 205). Woolf's discussions with and writings about the artist Walter Sickert were also influential, as was the work of Woolf's sister, Vanessa Bell. Woolf was inspired by her sister's paintings and influenced by their discussions about art. Bell designed the dust jackets for Woolf's novels, and they worked as co-creators on texts such as 'Kew Gardens' that combined text and woodcut illustrations. See Gillespie (1998) for detailed discussion of the mutual inspiration between them.

There is now a growing body of criticism that focusses on Woolf's interest in and experience of photography and the cinema, interests that grew out of her family experience (Woolf's great-aunt, Julia Margaret Cameron, was a renowned photographer) and from her own engagements with visual representation. As a teenager Woolf took and developed her own photographs and 'By the time she entered womanhood ... photography was a constant presence in Woolf's life and a constant reflection of her evolving visual consciousness' (Humm 2012: 296). As Maggie Humm suggests, Woolf's experience as a photographer and her knowledge and understanding of 'photographic techniques, including framing, space and distance, would unconsciously shape her fictional use of frames' (297). Her own photograph albums were arranged with a disregard for chronology and, as with her fiction, the photographic 'narrative' is organized according to other principles (Humm 2012: 296, 298). Photographs also have a key role to play in Woolf's experiments with character and contribute to the ideas about identity, perspective and multiple modes of expression in *Flush*, *Orlando* and *Three Guineas*. Woolf also enjoyed the new developments in, and intellectual debates about, the cinema which flourished in the early decades of the century and which were discussed in specialist periodicals (such as *Close Up*) as well as in reviews in the popular media (Humm 2012: 292–3). Many critics have identified cinematic qualities in Woolf's literary method and the influence of cinema on Woolf's writing was noted by one of her earliest critics and biographers, Winifred Holtby, in *Virginia Woolf: A Critical Memoir* (1932). Holtby devotes a whole chapter to the 'Cinematograph' and considers Woolf's narrative techniques to be cinematic in her early experimental story, 'Kew Gardens', as well as *Jacob's Room*. Woolf viewed 'an eclectic range of films' and was involved, along with other Bloomsbury Group members, with the London Film Society which was formed in 1925 and which screened an 'innovative mixture of avant-garde and popular film' (Humm 2012: 292). In her essay, 'The Cinema' (1926), Woolf outlines what she sees as avant-garde cinema's capabilities in relation to narrative technique and to the representation of psychological states and new ideas about the apprehension of reality (see Chapter Three). As Humm states for Woolf, 'film is a new, dynamic, psychic, and cognitive process' (2012: 294) and informs her literary techniques.

Less frequently discussed is Woolf's fascination with dance (particularly ballet) and music and the influence of these art forms on her writing. Rishona Zimring argues persuasively for the importance of everyday 'social dance' that grew in popularity in Britain in the interwar period (2013: 3). Exploring the representations of dance in Woolf's fiction, she suggests that dance was influential as a means of exploring issues of sociability, identity and connections. She also considers Woolf's response (and that of other Bloomsbury Group members) to the sensational new form of ballet introduced into Britain by Sergei Diaghilev's Ballet Russes.

While the somewhat scandalous and eroticized performances provoked a sense of unease, they also signalled a sense of emotional liberation and physical exuberance. The effect was to open up a new and exciting creative sensibility, a modern aesthetic that inspired the work of painters in Woolf's circle, including Roger Fry and Vanessa Bell. Evelyn Haller notes, 'The idea of dance contributed to Woolf's visual milieu' (Haller 2010: 458) and the new forms of choreography she experienced can be seen to inform her own innovative literary techniques of movement through narrative that resisted the constraints of realist chronology. The skywriting aeroplane in *Mrs Dalloway*, for example, moves 'swiftly, freely' like 'a dancer' across the sky, simultaneously 'moving' the plot along too as it shifts narrative focus and location. Haller and Susan Jones note the 'choreographic form' of *The Waves* (Jones 2009: 73) and Woolf's sense of 'writing to a rhythm and not to a plot' (*L4* 204) suggests the influence of the Russian ballet. The place of rhythm in Woolf's creative processes and her experimental forms and aesthetics was also influenced by her life-long love of music. Critics have explored her appreciation of Mozart, Bach, Beethoven, Wagner and also her familiarity with more contemporary and avant-garde music (see Kelley 2010; Sutton 2012, 2013). As Woolf remarks in a letter, her creativity is inspired by music: 'I always think of my books as music before I write them' (*L6* 426). A number of critics are now exploring the role of music in relation to her experiments with modes of expression, formal structures, subjective perspectives and the articulation of political issues. As Joyce E. Kelley notes, Woolf's writing is 'infused with musical metaphor and meaning' (2010: 417) and music takes on significance in all of her novels, as well as in some of her short stories and essays (for example, 'A Simple Melody' and 'Street Music'). In her memoir, Woolf affirmed the centrality of music in her philosophy of life as collectively experienced: 'we are the words; we are the music; we are the thing itself' (*MOB* 81).

Woolf and her literary contemporaries

Woolf's privileged position at the centre of the Bloomsbury Group and as publisher of the Hogarth Press put her at the heart of a network of writers and artists whose ideas and experiments influenced each other. New works prompted responses – critical and creative – and fuelled rivalries as each writer worked to develop their own artistic forms. Woolf herself notes the influence on own writing of the Russian writer Anton Chekhov in her essay, 'Modern Fiction' (see Chapter One) and critics have explored this influence in detail (see Nena Skrbic 2004; Darya Protopopova 2012, for example). Woolf personally knew E. M. Forster and T. S. Eliot and set and printed *The Waste Land* at the Hogarth Press; she met Gertrude Stein and had a passionate affair with Vita Sackville-West. Her necessarily short-lived friendship with Mansfield (Mansfield died aged just thirty four in 1923) had a profound impact on Woolf for the rest of her life. She and Mansfield felt a personal and professional affinity and Woolf valued her relationship with Mansfield as 'priceless' (*D2* 45) (see Smith 1999; Simpson 2012). Woolf also knew Dorothy Richardson's work and, although she was critical of what she saw as the severely limited subject matter of her writing, she admired Richardson's creation of an innovative, woman-centred modernist style that Woolf referred to as 'the psychological sentence of the feminine gender' (*E3* 367). She recognized James Joyce as an exciting and innovative writer and discusses his work in her own influential essay, 'Modern Fiction' (see Chapter One). Privately, however, she described *Ulysses* as '[a]n illiterate, underbred book … the book of a self taught working man' (*D2* 189). Some of her comments about Mansfield took on a similar acerbic tone and Woolf accuses her of 'stink[ing] like a … civet cat that had taken to street walking' and disparaged what she saw as Mansfield's self-advertisement (*D1* 58). These attacks speak perhaps of Woolf's snobbery and elitism, but are also motivated by a sense of rivalry: she feared that Mansfield and Joyce could do what she strived to do only better. Angela Smith (1999) has identified a number of echoes of Mansfield's work across Woolf's *oeuvre* and similarities between Woolf's *Mrs Dalloway* and *Ulysses* have been critically explored. Woolf was reading *Ulysses* as she worked on her short story, 'Mrs Dalloway in Bond Street' which grew into *Mrs Dalloway* and there are some obvious parallels between the two novels, not least that both are set on a single day in a capital city and revolve around the perambulations of a small number of characters. A crucial difference, however, is Woolf's focus on the experience and consciousness of a central female character, so that we might read Woolf's novel as, in part, a revisionary response to Joyce from a woman's point of view. The similarities between Woolf's writing and that of her rivals also suggest the cross-fertilization of ideas as writers worked to devise new literary techniques, engaging creatively and competitively with each other. In 'How It Strikes a Contemporary', Woolf notes both the prevalent 'ungenerous distrust of contemporary genius' amongst those engaged in reading and critically assessing new literary works, but also the need to 'cherish' these fellow writers since they are attempting to convey modern experience and to build something new 'by common effort' (*E4* 234, 238).

Historical and cultural contexts

Woolf was writing during a period of great social, political and economic transition. The economic depressions across Britain, Europe and America in the late 1920s and 1930s and the rise of fascism and other right wing movements in Europe at that time had dramatic and devastating effects on individuals as well as communities. The First World War is often perceived as a watershed event heralding in unprecedented change in social relations and hierarchies and there is no doubt that the war and its aftermath played a key role in the reshaping of Britain in the immediate post-war period and beyond. It was a shocking and horrific experience, with massive loss of life, and led to a new scepticism towards established hierarchies and upper and middle-class authority and leadership. The circumstances of war, particularly after conscription began in 1916, led to a shake-up of the social order in terms of gender relations and expectations as women took the places of the men in the workforce, taking on 'men's jobs' as manual and clerical workers and as engineers. Although feminist campaigns had laid the foundations for women's suffrage, it was largely as a result of their war-time contributions that women over the age of thirty were granted the vote in the Representation of the People Act of 1918 (it was only in 1928 that the voting age for women was lowered to twenty-one) and were granted the freedom to enter all trades and professions with the Sex Disqualification (Removal) Act of 1919. However, in reality, the post-war period brought a backlash against women's new freedoms and rights as (more) equal citizens.

'On or about December 1910 human character changed'

As Woolf records in her essay, 'Mr Bennett and Mrs Brown', dramatic political and cultural changes were underway in the years leading up to war and she registers the disruption to all social hierarchies during this period: 'All human relations have shifted – those between masters and servants, husbands and wives, parents and children' (E3 422). She illustrates her perception of the effect of cultural and political changes through her example of the behaviour and experience of a domestic servant: 'The Victorian cook lived like a leviathan in the lower depths, formidable, silent, obscure, inscrutable; the Georgian cook is a creature of sunshine and fresh air; in and out of the drawing room, now to borrow the *Daily Herald*, now to ask advice about a hat' (E3 422). Typical of Woolf's approach, she demonstrates her awareness and understanding of the complexity of larger issues (political change in the realms of class and gender) through their impact on everyday experience. Finding new ways to represent experience in a cultural landscape reconfigured by historical, political and social change is a central preoccupation in Woolf's writing. There have been various explanations for the significance of this particular date but all speak in some way of Woolf's retrospective identification of this moment as 'the historical gateway to cultural change, cataclysm and catastrophe' (Goldman 2004: 38) inaugurating a destabilization of traditional structures of power and authority at all levels in society – artistic, cultural, political, institutional and economic.

1910 was a watershed year for institutional change at the level of monarchy as Edward VII died and George V acceded the throne. Woolf uses the distinction between these two monarchical eras to articulate what she stressed as a dramatic generational division between the outmoded 'Edwardians' and modern 'Georgians'. There was also considerable change in the political sphere during 1910 with general elections in January and December. In the previous year, the Chancellor of the Exchequer in Asquith's Liberal Government, David Lloyd George, had implemented a radical budget, referred to as the 'People's Budget', with the specific goal of redistributing wealth through the introduction of new taxes to fund welfare reforms to benefit the majority of British citizens. In fact, the social landscape in relation to class had begun to alter in the late nineteenth century with various moves to increase working-class unity. Most importantly the rise of the Independent Labour Party in 1893 and the Trades Union Congress, alongside legislative changes which loosened financial prohibitions on strikes and the introduction of salaries for Members of Parliament in 1911, facilitated working-class representation in government. Other changes around this time also instituted dramatic shifts in the balance of power, including the 1911 Parliamentary Act that restricted the power of the House of Lords to reject legislation approved by the House of Commons, and the National Insurance Bill which protected the working classes during periods of illness and unemployment.

However, protests against established class and gender power hierarchies in 1910 were heavily handled by the authorities. In November 1910, a Welsh miners' strike in Tonypandy that had become a riot was broken up by police and cavalry ordered by Winston Churchill (then Home Secretary); military support was also sent to quell riots in other parts of the Rhondda Valley. In the same month, the peaceful suffrage rally of the Women's Social and Political Union in London was similarly brutally broken up by police. In February 1910, Woolf took part in what has become known as the 'Dreadnought hoax'. She, with some of her siblings and friends, gained access to one of the most secure and celebrated of the navy's battleships, HMS Dreadnought. Disguised as the Emperor of Abyssinia and his entourage, their 'joke' has been read as an attack on both the institution of the military as well as on the forces of empire. 1910 was also a landmark year for avant-garde art. In November 1910, the first Post-Impressionist Art Exhibition called 'Manet and the Post-Impressionists' opened at the Grafton Galleries. This was arranged by Woolf's friend, Roger Fry, her sister, Vanessa Bell, and her husband, Leonard Woolf, and exhibited the work of late nineteenth century continental European artists (Cezanne, Seurat, Van Gogh and Gaugin). These art works employed what were, for many British viewers, shockingly new artistic methods and forms of representation, challenging not only a sense of artistic conventions but also the relationship between viewer and the work of art, instigating new ways of seeing and responding to art. We could say that 'On or about December 1910 human perception changed'.

Ways of reading Woolf – time and subjective selves

'On or about December 1910 human character changed' ('Mr Bennett and Mrs Brown')
'For nothing was simply one thing' (*To the Lighthouse*),
'life is not a series of gig lamps symmetrically arranged' ('Modern Fiction')

These three statements in many ways convey ideas fundamental to Woolf's writing and thinking about experience, the self and human consciousness that resonate throughout her writing and thinking. They chime closely with the philosophical debates in circulation at the time that were taken up by many modernist writers seeking to understand consciousness and to find new narrative methods to articulate modern experience. The ideas emerging in the work of French philosopher, Henri Bergson, and the Austrian psychoanalyst, Sigmund Freud, as well as the American philosopher, William James, were particularly influential. The idea that 'nothing' is 'one thing' holds true for Woolf's approach to everything – life, writing and politics. For her there are always a number of different, and often contradictory, ways of perceiving, understanding and responding to experience since this is based on a shifting subjective awareness and multiple levels of consciousness. Language, the medium through which we primarily conceive and communicate our sense of self and our understanding of the world, is in itself ambiguous, with words signifying a multiplicity of meanings and significances. As Woolf states in her essay, 'Craftsmanship' (broadcast on BBC radio in 1937), 'it is the nature of words to mean many things' (*E6* 94). The view that life is not simply a linear and chronological unfolding of experience, progressing systematically from one stage to another (as if walking past gig lamps in a row), is central to an understanding not only of the lives Woolf maps out for her characters, but also of a more profound sense of what constitutes the self. The work of James, Bergson, Freud and others prompted radically new understandings of the self – both the conscious self which exists in and responds to the material and cultural world, as well as the inner self, the semi-conscious or unconscious levels of self.

Woolf's approach to time in her declaration about the change in human character seems to be informed by these new ideas, particularly those of Bergson whose popularity soared in the period 1909–11 (Gillies 2003: 97). 1910 was a significant year in the translation and publication of two of Bergson's most influential books, *Time and Free Will* ([1889] 1910) and *Matter and Memory*, for which Bergson wrote a new introduction in 1910 ([1896] 1911). Woolf's phrase draws together contradictory ideas about time: the sense of a specific historical point is indicated by the declaration of the year '1910', but this certainty is undermined by the 'On or about' which suggests a more approximate, ambiguous experience of this moment. In tune with Bergson's ideas about the duality of conscious experience in relation to time, as articulated in *Time and Free Will*, it suggests that 'official' records of time work like clock time and at the level of the intellect (which Bergson calls *temps*); at this conscious level time is spatialized, segmented and organized into consecutive, contiguous 'units' which are thought of as being placed next to one another (as distinct periods – past, present and future). The more approximate 'On or about' resonates with the intuitive level of consciousness in Bergson's theory; at this level time is experienced subjectively, intensely and inconsistently as psychological time takes on the quality of an organic flow, expanding and contracting (Bergson calls this *durée*). For Bergson, subjective time is the more 'real' yet the flow of time has to be interrupted, 'broken into segments' and spatialized 'in order to explain, analyse, and even understand the nature of experience' (Gillies 2003: 102). The historical turning point that Woolf identifies in 1910, then, is actually part of a web of connections and contexts that are subjectively experienced so that this phrase also signals Woolf's awareness of how change in the wider world can impact at a more intimate, private level, bringing a new sense of what it is to be human. Life, experience and meaning are impossible to pin down in absolute terms and, like the effect of a drop of water hitting the smooth surface of a pond, seemingly endless possibilities for interpretation radiate out. Bergson's theories posit a duality of self and experience and this is articulated through his discussion of the intellect and intuition, clock and psychological time, voluntary and involuntary memory. These theories suggest that the self has a 'surface' that it presents to the world but more 'real' is what is experienced in the inner life, the rich, complex, constant flux of consciousness. His theories fuelled the growing interest in the early twentieth century in interiority and in multiple states of mind, ideas that were also hugely influenced by the emergence of new science of psychology, particularly the work of Sigmund Freud.

Woolf and Freud

Although Woolf claimed not to have read the work of Freud until shortly after she met him in 1939, after which she was 'gulping up Freud' (D5, 249), she was very much aware of his theories and their impact on the popular imagination as well as, to her dismay, the direct application of Freudian ideas to literary plots and approaches to characterization. In the 1920s, Freudian ideas became a kind of craze, and many of Woolf's close relatives and friends were directly involved in the dissemination and popularization of Freud's work. The Hogarth Press was the first to publish Freud's works in English (as part of the International Psychoanalytical Library, which also published the work of Freud's followers), a risky undertaking that required a significant financial outlay. Freud's writings were translated by two of the first professional psychoanalysts in Britain, James and Alix Strachey (James was the brother of Woolf's close friend Lytton Strachey); Woolf's brother, Adrian Stephen, and his wife, Karin, also trained to be psychoanalysts in the 1920s. In 1914, Leonard Woolf reviewed a translation of Freud's *The Psychopathology of Everyday Life*, referring also to the ideas in Freud's ground-breaking and popular text, *The Interpretation of Dreams* (Lee 1996: 197). Woolf's association with psychological research preceded the arrival of Freudian ideas in Britain: her father, Leslie Stephen, was also interested in these ideas and, would have been aware of new developments through his friendship with James Sully, professor at the University College London (UCL) and organizer of the inaugural meeting of the British Psychological Society (1901). Sully played a key role in developing research into psychology at UCL and wrote several of the first psychological textbooks. However, Woolf, along with other writers and artists, was publicly disparaging of Freudian ideas. Roger Fry and Clive Bell both vehemently attacked Freud's work for its associations of the artist (and artistic production) with neurosis. Woolf's fiction and other writings about the self and experience, however, explore a similar psychological territory so that some aspects of her fiction seem to readily invite a Freudian reading.

New physics

The early twentieth century was also a period of great scientific discovery, particularly in relation to physical matter and the perception and experience of the physical world. Discoveries in one area of physics led to rapid developments in other areas as scientists discovered new (often counter-intuitive) facts about 'reality' and theoretical ideas prompted further discoveries. The popularization of scientific ideas provided the general public not only with new ways of conceptualizing matter but also with a new vocabulary with which to discuss and imagine the world. As Michael Whitworth argues, the metaphors used to articulate new scientific discoveries infiltrated modernist literature and worked to shape ideas about narrative form and aesthetic formulations (2001). Woolf's interests covered a wide range of new scientific ideas as popularized in successful books, lectures and BBC Radio broadcasts and she was particularly drawn to the work of James Jeans who published *The Mysterious Universe* (1930). As critics have suggested, Woolf engaged with, adopted and adapted ideas from new scientific thinking to advance her own experiments in the literary field in relation to form and aesthetics (see Gillian Beer 1996; Michael Whitworth 2001; Holly Henry 2003).

The new scientific developments built on the significant discoveries made at the end of the nineteenth century, notably the development of X-rays by Wilhelm Roentgen, followed by Henri Becquerel's discovery of radioactivity and Marie and Pierre Curie's discovery of radium. In 1900, Max Planck produced his theory of 'quanta' which revealed that energy flows are not smooth but that energy is transmitted in pockets, or 'quanta'. In 1910, Ernest Rutherford's experiments split the nitrogen atom, making the discovery that the smallest unit of matter was actually largely composed of space with smaller elements (protons, neutrons and electrons) held together not by anything solid but by electrical energy. Building on this discovery, Niels Bohr advanced Planck's theory to discover that electrons move discontinuously, making a 'quantum leap', an abrupt movement between energy levels. Light energy was discovered to be different from other matter and Louis de Broglie made the discovery that electrons had the properties of waves and particles, and proposed the concept of wave-particle duality whereby the two aspects complement one another. Albert Einstein's theories of relativity were published just as Woolf began her professional career as a writer. He published two ground-breaking texts, 'Special Theory of Relativity' (1905) and *General Theory* (1916) which revolutionized thinking about time and space. He discovered that time does not move in a constant, regular manner but is variable and that physical matter, space and time are interconnected entities that impact on one another. These new scientific concepts and the language associated with them provided Woolf with a new stimulus for thinking beyond conventional epistemological frameworks for understanding the self and 'reality', and she readily adopted and adapted the ideas and metaphors for her own experiments with narrative space and time.

Woolf's (perplexing) politics

There are many controversies provoked by the contradictory nature of Woolf's political and personal views on certain issues – gender, class, empire, race – which generate confusion and uncertainty. Leonard Woolf's assessment of Woolf as 'the least political animal that has lived since Aristotle invented the definition' has, for some critics, been a confirmation of an idea of Woolf as elitist and aloof, cut off from the 'real' world of politics, economics and conflict. What is less frequently recorded is that Leonard goes on to state that Woolf was also 'highly sensitive to the atmosphere which surrounded her...therefore the last person who could ignore the political menaces under which we all lived' (Woolf 1967: 27). Woolf is now undoubtedly recognized as a political writer who critically and astutely engaged with complex issues and concerns in her fictional and non-fictional writings. She played an active role in political processes and recognition of her engagement in political organizations has also shed new light on her relation and attitude to her social, political and economic context. Although below I discuss the different elements of Woolf's political and at times controversial thought as discrete entities, it is important to keep in mind that there is always significant interconnection, synergy as well as conflict, between these different elements. As one critic asserts, 'race, gender and class are not distinct realms of experience, existing in splendid isolation from each other ... Rather, they come into existence *in and through* relation to each other – if in contradictory and conflictual ways' (McClintock 1995: 5). Indeed, it is sometimes the combination of political threads that leads Woolf's political views to be seen as puzzling and controversial.

Feminism and gender

Woolf is now perceived as the feminist 'mother' to which subsequent feminist writers, thinkers, activists and critics refer back as a point of reference for their own feminist politics. Yet, Woolf's feminist credentials are repeatedly called into question as critics debate not only her relative lack of involvement in *the* campaign for women's equality in the early part of the twentieth century – the campaign for women's suffrage – but also her ambivalence (and even hostility) towards such militant political feminism. She did support 'the cause' in a number of ways (including working for nearly a year for a suffrage group in 1910), and was surrounded by friends active in suffrage politics, such as Leonard Woolf and his sisters, the Strachey family and Ethyl Smyth (Park 2005: 119–20). The fact that she also created characters involved in suffrage campaigns (Mary Datchet in *Night and Day* and Rose Pargiter in *The Years*, for example) also indicates that her writing and thinking was informed by this aspect of feminist politics. Woolf's support for feminist campaigns is also registered in more subtle ways, in her use of 'feminist colourism' (the suffrage tricolour of purple, green and white/gold) for example, as Jane Goldman has persuasively demonstrated (Goldman 1998: 70). However, her injunction in *Three Guineas* to burn the word 'feminist' because it is 'a dead word, a corrupt word' also raises significant questions about her political stance and perspective (*TG* 117). As with much else about Woolf's thinking, this is complex, contradictory and, at times, confusing.

As noted above, in her now famous assertion that '[o]n or about December 1910 human character changed' Woolf specifically identified a woman's experience to convey the momentous cultural shift she detected. However, the somewhat idealized picture she paints of the experience of a cook's new freedom in relation to a greater sense of equality with her employer (she 'is a creature of sunshine and fresh air' (*E3* 422) seems overly optimistic, perhaps pointing to what Woolf freely admitted was a lack of information about working women's experience (see 'Introduction' to *Life as We Have Known It*). Although this choice of date may be related to the activities of the suffragettes in this year (see above), it also seems to wilfully ignore what for many feminists of the time was a landmark date of 1918, when female suffrage was achieved. This example serves to draw attention to two key elements of Woolf's engagement with gender issues and feminist politics that have become a source of controversy and confusion. Her concern with gender issues is almost entirely focussed on middle-class women's experience and, as discussed below, she expresses a reluctance to depict the working classes. It also points to the fact that she recoiled against the militancy of the suffragettes and was sceptical of what she saw as the narrowness of the women's suffrage campaign more generally. This said, Woolf's polemical feminist essays, *A Room of One's Own* and *Three Guineas*, are 'deeply rooted in the culture of suffrage' and the key political ideas she puts forward were already in circulation in newspapers, manifestos and memoirs at the time (Park 2005: 125).

In what has become a source of controversy for feminist critics who include all classes in their political focus, Woolf also attributes her ambivalence towards this political campaign in part to her own class position and her sense of distance from the material necessities working women demanded. In this sense, she felt herself to be 'a benevolent spectator' of the women's movement' (Woolf 1977: xxi). Such views have provoked hostility from some feminist critics, yet her inclusion of working-class female characters and their views is, at times, a significant part of the political outlook of her fiction. Woolf's attitude towards organized feminist politics and campaigns for equality is also complicated by her anxieties about women's loss of independence and their difference in view as they gain access to male-dominated institutions – the professions and education as well as the political realm. She expresses concern that women will be absorbed into these powerful institutions and take on the masculinist, patriarchal, patriotic, imperialist and capitalist values that underlie them. Suffrage and other political successes that achieve greater equality of opportunity for women were, for Woolf, only a small part of the battle. Her view that the word 'feminist' should be destroyed could mean that it is no longer needed – the specific goals of the feminist movement had been achieved by 1938 – but also suggests that such goals were always too narrow and not effective in bringing about the transformation in gendered relations and social structures Woolf saw as necessary.

Woolf's most sustained and strident feminist attacks are on what she saw as the underlying causes of inequality: the patriarchal ideological beliefs, cultural expectations and values that in subtle yet insidious ways reinforce and perpetuate inequalities between men and women. This works notably though the perpetuation of gender identities and roles that seem to endorse sexual hierarchies as natural and self-evident. In particular, she criticizes the social institution of marriage which she saw as perpetuating conventional (and stifling) domestic roles for women and which shores up impossible cultural ideals of femininity. In her essay 'Professions for Women', Woolf argues that the legacy of outmoded, specifically Victorian, ideals of femininity persist in the post-war period and work to circumscribe opportunities for women. This ideal is summed up in the much quoted phrase, 'The Angel in the House' and Woolf, feels compelled to kill this powerful metaphor and to defy the cultural assumptions of women's subordinate position in order to achieve the freedom to write. Woolf's essay humorously describes this event, 'whenever I felt the shadow of her wing or the radiance of her halo upon my page, I took up the inkpot and flung it at her. She died hard. Her fictitious nature was of great assistance to her. It is far harder to kill a phantom than a reality' (E6 481).

Woolf's feminism also operates through a focus on the power of language and her understanding of its plurality and mutability: words have 'mysterious properties' and 'it is their nature to change', as she states in her essay 'Craftsmanship' (E6 94, 97). Her writing interrogates the structures and politics of language, drawing attention to the operation of hierarchies and the power of images and symbolism. Importantly, her feminist perspective is articulated through literary innovations and experiments with form which revise the conventions of the male-dominated literary tradition to find different ways to articulate new ideas about modern women's experience. Such a focus is unsurprising since, as a woman writer in a male-dominated literary sphere, Woolf had to negotiate the social, political and material limitations imposed on women and rework and revise the cultural expectations placed on women to fulfil certain gender ideals. She did this by taking writing to be her profession and by challenging the limitations traditionally placed on women *through* her innovations in writing. Her early (1905) review of W. L. Courtney's *The Feminine Note in Fiction* contests his view that women's fiction has a detrimental effect on the 'art' of literature, arguing instead that it is new forms of fiction in which women's voices can be heard that 'will in due time' take on a 'permanent artistic shape' (*E1* 16). Throughout her career, she challenged the male-dominated literary tradition from which women writers are largely excluded or perceived as inferior, and in which fictional representations of women simply serve to confirm social, economic and political inequalities. However, Woolf's more oblique articulation of feminist politics presents challenges for the reader, leading at times to a sense of uncertainty in relation to Woolf's feminist views.

A *Room of One's Own* and *To the Lighthouse* will be the focus for discussion of these issues (see Chapter Five).

Sexuality

Another important dimension of Woolf's politics related to her thinking about gender identities and her feminist perspective is provided by a focus on issues of sexuality. Her criticism of marriage as a social institution which reinforces unequal gender roles is further complicated and strengthened by her representation of desire between women. As ever, there are different views about how Woolf's own sexuality and her representation of sexuality in her fiction can be conceptualized and discussed. This is in part due to a perplexing combination of personal details: Woolf was married and so seems to conform to heterocentric social expectations, but this does not preclude her homoerotic desires nor prohibit her same-sex relationships. She has been described as sexually frigid or afraid of sex and has also been described as a lesbian feminist, bisexual and queer.

There is no doubt that relationships with women played a central role in Woolf's life. These included her close relationship with her sister, Vanessa, and many passionate and sometimes sexual relationships with women friends, such as Madge Vaughan, Violet Dickinson, Ethyl Smyth, Katherine Mansfield, Ottoline

Morrell, and her most significant lesbian relationship with Vita Sackville-West. Woolf was also part of other social and intellectual networks through which she came to know a number of lesbians and bisexual women, such as Jane Harrison and Hope Mirrlees, Margaret Llewelyn Davies and Lilian Harris, Gertrude Stein and Alice B. Toklas. As a member of the Bloomsbury Group, she was immersed in a liberal atmosphere which was profoundly at odds with dominant heterosexual norms and sexuality was seen and experienced as far more diverse than in the wider social world. Many of her close friends were gay or bisexual (the artist, Duncan Grant, the economist, John Maynard Keynes and the novelist, E. M. Forster). If, as some critics have argued, this Bloomsbury context was also oppressively male-dominated, misogynistic and phobic in its attitudes to desires between women (see especially, Marcus 1987), others have argued that Woolf's friendships with gay men provided her with support and were 'of vital importance to her construction of relationships between women' (Vanita 1997: 165).

Looking at Woolf's writing itself there is a contrast in the ways in which sexuality is discussed and represented. In her personal writings, there is a more overt acknowledgement and celebration of her desires for women, whereas her published texts tend to be more circumspect, guarded, tentative and indirect. Some attribute this to Woolf's fear of discovery and critics examining manuscript drafts of her fictional works have noted a degree of self-censorship as these were finally prepared for publication. Some also suggest that Woolf used strategies which encode lesbian desires in her fiction so as to speak only to an audience 'in the know', including 'metaphoric substitutions' (Cramer 1997: 123), allusion to famous literary lovers, eroticized language and suggestive gestures. As Woolf makes clear, she was keen to speak about women's desires and sexual experiences, but was also keenly aware of the cultural taboos around and social stigma attached to so-called 'sexual deviants'.

This difference between Woolf's public and private writings has been perceived as in keeping with her cultural context. As Patricia Cramer notes, 'women of Woolf's generation enjoyed an unprecedented flourishing of lesbian visibility and culture in their private lives', and moved in social circles which were open to same-sex love and with connections to 'lesbian subcultures extending beyond [Woolf's] immediate circle of friends' (1997: 119). However, this was at odds with the cultural shifts in the wider public world.

Woolf lived in an era in which homosexual and lesbian identities were theorized and categorized in scientific and medical discourses as psychological disorders such as 'arrested development' or 'perversion' (in Freudian terms), or as 'sexual inversion' or the 'third sex' (in the discourse of sexologists such as Havelock Ellis and Richard von Krafft-Ebing). Such theories intended to legitimize non-heterosexual identities arguing that homosexuality was congenital and so not 'unnatural'. However, Woolf was critical of all theories and discourses which attempt to rigidly define and categorize.

Her writing also offers a scathing criticism of the detrimental effects and inadequacies of theories that attempt to encapsulate and delimit the diversity of women's desires. The trial of *The Well of Loneliness* (1928) written by Woolf's contemporary, Radclyffe Hall, highlighted what Woolf saw as the dangers of categorization. Hall drew on the theories of inversion in her representation of her central lesbian character, Stephen Gordon, yet despite this 'legitimation' of women's same-sex desire according to sexological frameworks, Hall's novel was prosecuted for obscenity, banned by the courts and Hall was castigated in the press. Although Woolf was prepared to testify in defence of the novel at the trial, it was to defend the right of artistic freedom rather than specifically to defend Hall's novel itself. Woolf was herself aware of the threats of censorship and her own novel containing a wildly sexually deviant character, *Orlando: A Biography*, came to the attention of the censor (Marshik 2006: 91). That her fantastical character is hard to define in terms of accepted gender or sexuality categories is perhaps the reason that it escaped censorship. Although her novel playfully makes reference to scientific debates and medical theories about gender and sexuality, it deliberately refuses to give any conclusive explanations for her character's change of sex and the implications of this. For the most part, Woolf's representations of homoerotic desires, as with her representation of experience and identity more generally, aim not to define and categorize, but rather to explore the multiple possibilities of relationships and the spectrum of desires and emotions. Orlando as a woman, for example, continues her sexual associations with women but also marries a man (though he is as sexually ambivalent as she) and has a child. Similarly, Clarissa Dalloway marries and has a daughter, though she maintains that a kiss from her friend Sally Seton when she was eighteen remains 'the most exquisite moment of her whole life' (*MD* 40). Clarissa's marriage allows her social success, but in many ways she forfeits the 'something infinitely precious' of her homoerotic desire for Sally. Here and in all her fiction, Woolf represents homoerotic desires largely in an indirect and richly metaphorical way. Clarissa's desires for women continue and the intensity of Clarissa's fleeting moments of homoerotic passion are conveyed through sensual metaphor and suggestive imagery. Such indirect and metaphorical representations clearly help to avoid censorship, but also convey the sense of a more expansive and complex idea of the emotional life and sexuality than the 'models' of desire available in Woolf's time.

This resistance to categorization and the refusal to conform to given definitions of sexed and gendered identities also has powerful political impact. Clarissa, for example, is placed in a liminal position on the borders of heterosexuality and homosexuality and this problematizes any notion of a clearly defined sexual identity for her. Woolf's other ambiguously sexed and gendered characters refuse to conform to the binary oppositions of gender and sexuality (either male or female, masculine or feminine, gay or straight) that organize relations between individuals in a heterosexual and patriarchal society. They embody contradiction, defying the cultural logic of either/or to embrace both/and. Woolf's fiction presents a challenge to the hierarchies of power and authority on which the social and symbolic order of society is founded and in doing so, brings all seemingly normative sexual identities into question.

Orlando: A Biography and *To the Lighthouse* will be the focus for discussion of these issues (see Chapter Five).

Class

Woolf had a very privileged upbringing in Hyde Park Gate, an upper middle-class household in the respectable area of South Kensington in London. With seven servants to attend to the needs of the eleven members of the family, the house was 'Crowded, shared, but also segregated, the house was a space divided between parents and children, men and women, masters and servants' (Light 2007: 9). The Stephen family were incredibly well connected both by family lines and through intellectual, political and artistic circles with some of the most influential families and figures of the nineteenth and early twentieth centuries. Many of these figures had an influence on Woolf's thinking but she also detached herself from these connections, preferring to see herself as an 'outsider' to the social and political establishment with which many of these figures were associated. As an upper middle-class woman writer she was aware of both her class privilege and gender disadvantage in a male dominated society and literary sphere.

Woolf has been criticized as elitist and snobbish by critics highlighting the middle-class bias in her writing and the apparent lack of interest in working-class issues and characters. One extreme critical view is that of John Carey, who castigates Woolf among other modernists, for her intellectual snobbery, seeing even Woolf's criticism of Arnold Bennett's conventional literary style as rooted in her class prejudice (see Chapter One). While other critical assessments focussed on class also indicate the limitations of Woolf's thinking, they take into account the complexities of Woolf's engagement with these issues, including the interconnection between Woolf's class attitudes and gender politics. Woolf's ambivalent attitude to class issues can be seen to be informed by her awareness of the contradictions in her own social and political position. At a personal level, Woolf was uneasy with the role of middle-class wife, efficiently managing household and servants (as her mother, Julia Stephen, had done in such an exemplary fashion) and often had fraught relations with her servants. She was very conscious of her securely upper-middle-class status and sense of superiority, but also recognized that her feminist freedoms as an intellectual and writer depended on the work of the lower classes, particularly the domestic work of female servants. As we see repeatedly in her fiction, working-class women are central to the life of middle-class households, physically and emotionally sustaining the middle-class families. In *The Waves* Mrs Constable, the nurse, squeezing water from a sponge at bath-time opens up the child Bernard's world of bodily sensation (*TW* 22, 98), Mrs Bast and Mrs McNab resurrect the family's holiday home in *To the Lighthouse*, and Lucy and Mrs Walker, the cook, in *Mrs Dalloway* enable Clarissa's party to succeed. As Clarissa reflects, servants contribute to the creation of 'exquisite moments' for which she feels indebted and must 'repay' (*MD* 34, 33).

Woolf's essay, 'Am I a Snob' (1936) is a good illustration of the complicated 'slipperiness' of Woolf's position and attitude. In her essay, she admits her penchant for titles and elegance and her disinterest in those outside her social circles, but she simultaneously mocks her own social and intellectual snobbery and effectively dismisses ideas of innate class superiority: 'The snob is a flutter-brained, hare-brained creature' (*MOB* 224) perpetually chasing the illusion of self-importance. While such admissions lay her views open to scrutiny and criticism, Woolf was also candid about issues of money and class. As Alex Zwerdling points out, Woolf did not shy away from probing the uncomfortable difficulties of class and money, and 'wrote about class and money with exceptional frankness at a time when these subjects were increasingly felt to be indecent' (1986: 88).

It is important to recognize that through her involvement with organizations whose aims were to bring about social and political reforms, Woolf gave practical support the working classes. Following her move to Bloomsbury, Woolf worked for the Workers Educational Association, teaching evening classes in literature at Morley College which offered non-vocational courses to men and women (1905–7). Later, she was involved in activities focussed on reforms for women and in particular gave her support (in terms of time, monetary and other donations, and in the use of her influence) to work that extended women's access to intellectual life, such as her support for The Women's Service Library, now The Women's Library, in London (Snaith 2003). She also sought to challenge and correct unequal access to literature (which she saw as a national asset that should be made accessible to all) via her commitment to the idea of the 'common reader'. She published two volumes of informal essays called *The Common Reader* (1925 and 1932) which confirm her role as 'an advocate for both democratic inclusiveness and intellectual education' (Cuddy-Keane 2003: 1). Melba Cuddy Keane refers to Woolf as a 'democratic highbrow' and discusses Woolf's attitude to class as part of what she refers to as the 'social project' underlying Woolf's writing and publications (2003: 13, 2). As publishers, the Woolfs also played an instrumental role in promoting the work of working-class writers and publishing materials which debated class issues, publishing work focussed on domestic industries (mining and manufacture) as well as on the wider concerns about the North/South political and economic divide (see Southworth 2010: 208). Alongside Leonard, Woolf also gave her support for working-class political reforms. She attended meetings of the Fabian Society and Labour Party Conferences, and was secretary for and hosted the Rodmell Labour Party at their home, Monk's House.

There is no doubt that Woolf's fiction demonstrates a middle-class bias and Woolf has been criticized for her unsympathetic representations of the working classes and for a lack of positive and fully developed working-class characters in her fiction. More recently, critics have noted that there are a surprising number of characters from the lower classes present in her fiction. In fact, we see a spectrum of social classes represented and this social variety is consolidated by reference to a range of London locations and communities, from the places of wealth and ease such as Chelsea and Mayfair to the 'low down' streets of the East End. Woolf's representations of working-class characters and places in some ways seem to confirm negative class-based stereotypes. More than this, though, such derogatory representations of the lower classes bring to the surface the tensions and anxieties underlying such prejudiced views, suggesting the precariousness of class-based identities reliant on markers of difference (money, education, cultural 'capital', taste and experience) which are, in Woolf's time, becoming increasingly blurred. Class distinctions are culturally constructed and working-class characters have the potential to destabilize the seeming security of middle-class life.

To the Lighthouse will be the focus for discussion of these ideas in Chapter Five.

Empire

Criticism of empire and the forces of imperialism permeates Woolf's work from her earliest novel to her last, recurring also in her essays, reviews and personal writings and she saw their damaging impact at home as well as abroad. Her anti-imperialist politics are, however, both complicated and enriched by other concerns (including her feminist politics) and by some contradictory (even racist) views. In 1884, the German chancellor, Otto von Bismarck, convened the Berlin Conference to formalize the competing European claims on Africa, known as the 'scramble for Africa'. Fourteen European delegates met (there were no Africans present) and Africa was partitioned according to the economic and political demands of the European nations, with no regard for existing boundaries and cultural groupings. This was a significant turning point in international relations and a consolidation of the power of European imperialism as a world system. Born in 1882, Woolf can be seen to be a child of this system, aware of and subject to the power and brutality of empire and the prevalent ideological belief in imperial dominance. She can also be seen to be a child of this system literally too, given that her family on both her father's and mother's side had long-standing involvements with the British Empire, playing key roles in the making and shaping of imperialist policy, as well as in criticizing and undermining imperialist ideologies (see Marcus 1992; Phillips 1994; Seshagiri 2009; Snaith 2012). Woolf's great-grandfather, James Stephen, was an abolitionist in the politically influential Clapham Sect. This group of evangelical reformers included William Wilberforce and produced the anti-slavery Foreign Slave Trade Bill (1806) which led to the Slave Trade Act (1807). Stephen's connection was also personal and he and Sarah Wilberforce were married (Lee 1996: 59). Woolf's grandfather, Sir James Stephen, became one of the most influential colonial administrators of the nineteenth century and, as Counsel to the Colonial Office and Board of Trade as well as Permanent Undersecretary to the Colonies (Lee 1996: 60), played a key role in building the British Empire. He also married a member of the Clapham Sect, Jane Venn, and followed through his family's commitment to achieving emancipation in the colonies, playing an instrumental role in the implementation of the Slavery Abolition Act (1833). Woolf's uncle, James Fitzjames Stephen, also played a central role in facilitating the governance of India and one of his daughters, Dorothea Stephen, worked as a Christian missionary and religious teacher in India and published a book, *Studies in Indian Thought* (1919). Woolf's father, Leslie Stephen, continued this history of involvement in empire in his role as editor of the *Dictionary of National Biography*, where he 'immortalized England's nation-builders' (Seshagiri 2009: 304). Woolf's maternal line was equally involved in empire. Her great grandfather, James Pattle, was a member of the Bengal Civil Service and the Pattle family had connections, via marriage, to highly influential Anglo-Indian administrators and 'collected around them a huge circle of Anglo-Indian, literary, artistic, and political friends' (Lee 1996: 89). Woolf's mother, Julia Prinsep Jackson, was born in Bengal, then part of British-ruled India. Woolf's family life, then, was completely immersed in empire: 'Colonial society, attitudes and traditions were embedded in the fabric of Julia Jackson's maternal ancestry, just as the legal history of colonial government ran as the main thread through the Stephen family tree' (Lee 1996: 87).

While Woolf's anti-imperialist politics may have been galvanized by what she saw as her family's complicity in colonial and imperialist oppression, her position is made complex not only by her familiarity with the vivid personalities and stories of her close relations, but also by what could be seen as her own economic complicity. Her Anglo-Indian Aunt Caroline Emilia Stephen bequeathed Woolf a legacy of £2,500 in 1909 that augmented her inheritance from her father and ensured that Woolf had the financial security that allowed her the freedom to write. Her marriage in 1912 to Leonard Woolf, newly resigned from his successful role as a colonial civil servant in Ceylon (Sri Lanka), might also suggest a compromise of her anti-imperialist politics. However, Woolf's writing against empire in defiance of any sense of loyalty to the source of her bequest, and Leonard's career as a political writer and leading anti-imperialist clearly signals their critical stance. Amongst other roles, Leonard worked as Secretary of the Labour Party's Advisory Committee on Imperial Questions in 1924. He wrote extensively about imperialism and international politics and Woolf was closely involved with Leonard's research, notably for his *Empire and Commerce in Africa* (1920), which she read and re-read (Phillips 1994: viii; Snaith 2012: 207). The Woolfs' decision to publish colonial writers and anti-imperialist books, the 'key works of the decolonization movement' including those written by C. L. R. James and Leonard Barnes (Esty 2003: 250, n. 75) and Mulk Raj Anand (Snaith 2012: 208) at their Hogarth Press signals their political commitment and their attempts to influence public opinion. Reading manuscripts and her personal contacts with writers also provided Woolf with information that helped to inform and shape her representations of empire and its connections to other areas of experience (Phillips 1994: xxxiv).

In significant ways, Woolf's political critique of empire differed from that of Leonard – not only in the sense that she took a less obviously activist role, but importantly because her anti-imperialist views were closely bound up with her feminist politics. Woolf saw the colonial exercise of power as inseparable from patriarchal power hierarchies oppressing women in the domestic realm: both colonial and patriarchal systems (social, economic and political) perceive women and colonials as being in need of control and as objects for exchange and exploitation. Her attacks on British colonialism (on individuals as well as ideological systems) are simultaneous with her attacks on patriarchal structures – the two systems complementing each other to maintain oppressive power dynamics at home and aboard. As Snaith argues, 'Woolf's writing prefigures many of the feminist debates of recent decades to do with the intersection of racial and gender identities' (2012: 208).

These political intersections, as well as some of the contradictions in Woolf's critical stance on empire, will be explored in Chapter Six, with particular reference to Woolf's first novel, *The Voyage Out* (1915).

Antisemitism and Jewishness

One of the more troubling aspects of Woolf's writing surrounds her representations of and attitudes to Jews and Jewishness. The antisemitic aspects of her work seem at odds with her political stance, with the feminist, pacifist and socialist dimensions of her political perspective being premised on ideas of tolerance and an undermining of power hierarchies. Antisemitism also seems incongruous with her personal circumstances, married as she was for thirty years to Leonard Woolf, a secular Jew. Put simply by one critic, 'There can be no straightforward account of attitudes toward Jewishness in the work of Virginia Woolf' (Schröder 2003: 298).

These contradictions can be seen as symptomatic of a wider cultural confusion about the figure of the Jew in this period. At the turn of the twentieth century, there were a number of conflicting ideas about Jewish identity and attempts to conceptualize and categorize Jewish people drew on a range of discourses and bodies of knowledge, including racial, medical, eugenicist and social evolutionary discourses. The Jewish people were identified as an ancient race, as mythical 'Wandering Jews', as timeless outcasts, and as the eternal scapegoat for all of society's ills. Jews also became a particular focus and topic of discussion in this period due to the influx of East European Jews between 1880 and 1914 (approximately 120,000). This immigration disrupted the already established Anglo-Jewish community in London and added further complexity to issues of identity and belonging, giving rise to the

perceived sense of the 'problem' of the Jew in British society. As
critics note, 'Jews were popularly perceived as being "un-British"
or a threat to British culture' (Lassner and Spiro 2013: 64). The
Conservative Government's proposal of an 'Aliens Bill' in 1905,
'which refused entry to diseased, pauper, or criminal "aliens"',
was in part a response to the immigration of Jews to poorer urban
areas such as the East End of London (Whitworth 2005: 70). Later,
'Common attitudes towards Jews as corrupt or overly powerful'
also had an impact, 'affect[ing] government policies towards
Jewish refugees escaping Nazism and British acceptance of Jewish
immigrants' (Lassner and Spiro 2013: 64). Yet Jews were also
perceived to be the group best suited to adapt to the newly modern
world, as critic Maren Tova Linett suggests, 'Jews were often
viewed as moderns *par excellence*. Like modernity itself, they were
seen as cosmopolitan, rootless, and urban' (2007: 80). In particular,
given the long-term association of Jews with financial matters and
commerce, they were also seen to be able to adjust to the new
economic climate which involved an intensification of capitalism
and which had an impact on all aspects of life.

The Jew is a recurrent figure in the work of many avant-garde
and modernist writers. Jewish characters are variously represented
on a spectrum from the starkly antisemitic representations found
in the work of T. S. Eliot, Ezra Pound and Wyndham Lewis, to the
more positive depictions in James Joyce (notably Leopold Bloom in
Ulysses) and in Sylvia Townsend Warner (notably Minna in *Summer
Will Show*), as well as in the writing of Stevie Smith and the work
of Amy Levy, an Anglo-Jewish novelist and poet. Jewish characters
can be found in a number Woolf's fictional texts, sometimes echoing
negative Jewish stereotypes but also demonstrating a more positive
approach to Jewish culture. In Woolf's writing of the mid-late 1930s,
her representations of Jews and attitudes to Jewishness become more
complex and contradictory, and her engagement with these issues is
bound up both with antisemitism as well as with attacks on fascism.
In this period, there was a renewed public awareness of Jewishness
as the European crisis mounted and Woolf was increasingly aware
of the rise in power and popularity of fascism in Germany, Spain
and Italy and of violence towards Jews. She was also well aware
of the rise of fascism at home as the activities of Oswald Mosley's
British Union of Fascists (B.U.F., founded in 1932) reached a peak
in the period 1934–6. These activities culminated in the issuing of

a Public Order Act in 1936 which banned political marches and which aimed to protect East End Jews from the B.U.F.

Given this context and the Woolfs' awareness of increasing violence towards Jews especially in Nazi Germany, their inclusion of Germany as one of their holiday destinations in 1935 is likely to strike us as bizarre to say the least. The Woolfs were clearly aware of the risk involved and went armed with a letter from Prince Bismarck at the London Embassy and were warned to avoid Nazi demonstrations. Nevertheless, finding themselves driving down a street festooned with antisemitic banners and lined with cheering Nazi supporters awaiting Goering provided Woolf with an alarming first-hand experience that made her aware of the complex, powerful and dangerous responses fascism elicits. In particular, this experience demonstrated the power of propaganda to galvanize a mass response, and the danger of what she describes as the 'docile hysterical crowd' whose 'stupid mass feeling' of racial hatred fuelled by fascist brainwashing was 'masked by good temper', as she records in her diary (D4 311). In this period, Woolf's revulsion and battle against fascism intensifies, as *Three Guineas* attests, but she is also increasingly aware of the fears, anxieties and misconceptions that underlie racist and antisemitic attitudes, and of how racism and antisemitism can be fuelled and provoked. While her representations of Jews and antisemitic attitudes may in part be attributed to her own racism and prejudice, what is also clear is that she is able to reflect on this complex situation and does so in order to provoke her readers to think so that they do not simply conform unquestioningly with the unthinking masses.

Chapter Six will explore Woolf's engagement with these complex and perplexing issues in relation to her representation of Jewishness in *Between the Acts*, *The Years* and 'The Duchess and the Jeweller'.

CHAPTER ONE

Woolf's Modernism

This chapter will consider the historical, cultural and political context in which Woolf developed her 'modern fiction'. This entailed a radical departure from the literary conventions of realism and also involved a reconception of the reader's role from a passive recipient to more active participant in the creative process. Woolf wrote many essays in which she put forward her views on literary traditions and innovations and two of her most well-known modernist 'manifesto-essays' will be discussed here: 'Mr Bennett and Mrs Brown' (1924) and 'Modern Fiction' (1925). This chapter will also discuss the role of the reader in 'How Should One Read a Book?' (1926). Woolf's story, 'The Lady in the Looking-Glass: A Reflection' (1929) seems to echo the ideas Woolf put forward in her essays, reiterating her critique of realism through the form and style of this fictional text.

Context

The early decades of the twentieth century marked a period of significant and rapid cultural change. The horrors of the First World War and the concomitant loss of faith in the leaders of the war means that it is often perceived as a 'watershed' event, heralding in a disruption of the cultural order and a scepticism towards authority. However, lived experience was also profoundly affected by the political changes taking place in relation to class, with the formation of the Labour Party, and gender, with the success of the women's suffrage campaign, alongside changes in the economic, scientific and intellectual realms. Established power hierarchies were destabilized and the social consensus that had confirmed the belief in European and Western culture as unquestionably rational, civilized and superior was shattered. As Woolf states in her essay, 'The Narrow Bridge of Art'[1], her contemporary period 'is an age clearly when we are not fast anchored where we are; things are moving around us; we are moving ourselves' (*E4* 429). It was this sense of a changing political, material and intellectual landscape with which modernist writers engaged and aimed to represent in their fiction.

Woolf's modernist aesthetics and literary practices continued to evolve over the course of her writing career and many of her essays and reviews (as well as her letters and diaries) explore and critically assess new possibilities for fictional form and experimental techniques. Her own writing can be seen to have been influenced by the work of other writers (such as Chekhov and her British contemporaries), by new developments in the visual arts (particularly Post-Impressionist art and photography), music, dance, as well as new technologies and modern phenomena (such as the motor-car, cinema, telephone, typewriter, gramophone and radio). She was influenced by philosophical thought and new scientific discoveries, as well as by new understandings of the mind in relation to perception, cognition and experience (as articulated in the theories of William James, Henri Bergson and Sigmund Freud). Many of these modern phenomena emerged during the second half of the nineteenth century and we can trace the beginnings of early modernist forms and techniques from this point. While for many these cultural changes and modernist responses were perceived as shocking, incomprehensible and as a source of crisis and anxiety, for others they were seen as an opening for new possibilities.

Manifestos

It seems unsurprising, then, that manifestos proliferated at this time, embracing 'the new' in a variety of ways, evoking and promoting visions of the future and signalling a desire for change. Manifestos articulate a vision of the future that is different from the present. As Laura Winkiel defines it, the manifesto is '[s]hort, spirited, and straddling the boundary between theory and practice, [it] communicates an experience of crisis and a conceptual break with the past. As its urgent tone pushes ongoing debates and practices to new realms of possibility, it seizes the present moment in order to intervene in history' (2008: 1). The two essays discussed in this chapter function as manifestos in this sense. They advocate a break with literary conventions associated with the past and urge the development of new literary aesthetics and forms. However, Woolf was sceptical of forms of writing, such as manifestos and propaganda, that sought to *impose* ideas, views and values on others, and she became increasingly critical and hostile about such forms of writing in the 1930s when fascist propaganda posed what she saw as a dangerous threat to democratic principles. Her own 1930s essay-manifesto, *Three Guineas*, revises formal conventions and refuses the authoritarian single-mindedness typical of such forms (see Chapter Two). Her two earlier essays discussed here operate a democratic principle of participation in bringing about change. Her ideas and theories about modern fiction continued to evolve in response to the influence of, and rivalry with, her modernist contemporaries (such as James Joyce, T. S. Eliot, Katherine Mansfield and Dorothy Richardson) and through her active role in reviewing and publishing. Woolf was a prolific essayist and reviewer and critics have explored the productive interconnection between Woolf's essays and her creative work. As her career progressed, Woolf continued to explore new possibilities for fictional form and experimental techniques in her essays and reviews (and in her diary and letters). As with *Three Guineas* and *A Room of One's Own*, these two earlier essays also engage (though perhaps more indirectly) with gender issues as these impact on the writer's role and the perspectives offered. The realist conventions Woolf critiques operate a hierarchy of authority whereby the omniscient narrator's voice takes precedence – a power dynamic Woolf perceived as masculine and limited, particularly in connection with the domination of the literary sphere by male writers and critics. As Hermione Lee states, 'her essay-writing was at all points intimately bound up with her work as a novelist and her thinking about women, politics and society' (2000: 91).

Typical of the manifesto form, both essays evoke the present moment as one of imminent change and convey the excitement of being balanced on a threshold about to take the plunge into something new. Both have a prophetic quality, but also a sense of the unknown: they anticipate a different future but do not pin down an absolute definition of this. Both invite the participation of the reader in bringing about change and suggest that readers with a heightened critical awareness can create the context in which new forms of fiction can flourish. Woolf's essays encourage readers to refuse to be satisfied with the inadequacies of conventional forms and content. One of the key ideas that Woolf is keen to stress as she articulates her ideas about the development of new, 'modern' forms of fiction is that the prevalent literary convention of realism is ineffectual in representing the constant flux of experience, perception, emotion and thought typical of life in the modern world. For her, the literary 'tools' and techniques that realist writers use are cumbersome and produce only a deadening effect. In stark contrast, she considered it to be the modern writer's task to invent new methods and modes with which 'to convey this varying, this unknown and uncircumscribed spirit' of modern life (*E4* 160).

Realism and 'new realism'

Woolf strongly asserts her criticisms of realist literary conventions in a number of essays. Her focus on what she refers to as 'materialist' forms of fiction is perhaps unsurprising given the dominance of realist modes of writing since the novel's inception in Britain and Europe from the mid-eighteenth century onwards. The novel as a new form of narrative aimed to represent ordinary, plausible events and characters and as a genre it purports to offer an accurate imitation of the empirical world and a realistic depiction of lived experience, offering 'a slice of life' or 'a window on reality'. While some events that happen in realist novels may in fact be quite unrealistic – plots often rely on unlikely coincidences and result in neat pairings of characters and decisive conclusions – realist novels retain the quality of verisimilitude in their focus on material details and social issues. Woolf does include real (factual) details in her fiction (notably, the names of London streets) but the delineation of materialist fictional methods that Woolf presents in her critical essays is in many ways a simplified (and at times a caricatured) version of this literary method. However, this is effective in achieving her goal of creating a clear distinction between this literary tradition and her own experimental forms.

Fiction's relationship to life and the sense of reality it should depict was the focus of a debate that emerged in the late nineteenth century. These issues became increasingly contested in the early decades of the twentieth century and Woolf's essays contribute significantly to this discussion. The public disagreement between novelists H. G. Wells and Henry James illustrates the key elements of this debate. In 'The Contemporary Novel' (1912), H. G. Wells considered the novel to be a medium via which the problems of 'our contemporary social development' can be represented and social, political and economic reality debated along with the *'moral consequences'* of conduct in the modern world (8, 6). In contrast, for James the novel should be a work of art, evoking (and even enhancing) the rich complexity of human experience and sense of reality through a focus on impressions, imagination and artistic technique (rather than on plot and material detail). In his essay, 'The New Novel' (1914), James praised certain aspects of new fiction but also criticized a number of novelists, including Wells and Arnold Bennett, because of their focus on material details at the expense of artistic technique. Articulating his criticism via food metaphors, James's essay suggests that although the description of facts and details is 'delectably thick' so that the reader is left 'full-fed' (1914: 324, 326), this is at the expense of conveying an awareness of the richness of 'human complexity' which is reduced 'to comparative thinness' (324). He likens this technique to that of 'squeezing out to the utmost' the pulp of a 'plump and more or less juicy orange' (325).

Instead, James privileged the consciousness of his characters and developed a nuanced method of representing feelings, memories and a 'stream of thought', a method influenced by the work of his brother, William James (see Chapter Three). Woolf's own experiments with fictional form and the representation of reality are in tune with Jamesian ideas of the novel as an aesthetic form which can convey ordinary, everyday experience. A central motivation for her literary experiments is to find ways of representing the new experiences of modernity and of capturing the 'unlimited capacity and infinite variety' of any one, ordinary individual (*E3* 436). In place of an omniscient narrative voice articulating an objective, 'truthful' picture of reality, Woolf's fictions represent what can be called a 'new realism'. Her texts privilege subjective perspectives to represent a more realistic sense of the uncertainty, provisionality and relativity that constitutes modern experience. Just as Woolf refuses the authority of the literary conventions of the past, so her fiction refuses an authoritarian approach to the writing and reading of modern literature. Her 'modern fiction' displaces the usual notions of the author or narrator as source of authority and meaning, emphasizing instead multiple narrative perspectives that invite a more open response and interpretation. Her conception of an interactive relationship with her readers is of central importance to the success of her literary innovation. For Woolf, to read is to enter into a dialogue with a text and to take part in a process of interpretation and response which is on-going: meanings are not fixed but change with each reading and re-reading, and are specific to each reader. In this sense, Woolf envisages her ideal reader as a co-writer or co-creator, a role that demands far more of the reader than conventional literary forms.

Reading and readers, 'How Should One Read a Book?'

In her essay 'How Should One Read a Book?'[2], Woolf addresses a question that anyone approaching a literary text may ask (and particularly, perhaps, a reader new to reading Woolf). Woolf describes this topic to be 'a matter of dazzling importance and breathless excitement' in her letter to Vita Sackville-West (L3 220) and her essay explores the process of reading and interpretation as a collaborative relationship between writer and reader. Importantly, her ideal reader is an active participant and co-producer, a 'fellow-worker and accomplice', approaching books with an open mind as well as with 'imagination, insight, and judgement' to give life and meaning to the narratives and characters (E5 573, 581). She encourages her readers to cultivate discernment and taste, but not to simply acquiesce to the expert opinion of authorities (such as the authors themselves or professional readers, such as scholars and critics). Readers' 'independence' of judgement is of paramount importance and they are 'to take no advice, to follow [their] own instincts, to use [their] own reason, to come to [their] own conclusions' (E5 573). She also makes clear the impact that readers can have on writers: the judgements of 'people reading for the love of reading' with 'great sympathy and yet with great severity' offer a valuable counter to the judgement of the critics (*E5* 582).

Woolf's ideas of the reader here chime with her wider democratic ideal of the 'common reader' in which everyone has access to the rich cultural repository of literature and in which ordinary readers are able to engage fully with it. Much as we might consider Woolf to be an 'expert', she saw herself as a 'common reader' given that she had little formal education and no training as a critic. She published two collections of essays in her lifetime called *The Common Reader* (1925 and 1932, respectively) with the intention of fostering a critical and independent response to, and engagement with, literature in a diversity of readers. She borrows the term and notion of the 'common reader' from the influential eighteenth-century poet and critic, Dr Samuel Johnson, who similarly celebrated readers whose pleasure was not determined by academic or professional expertise. Although Woolf is often narrowly perceived as a highbrow and part of the privileged elite, she aimed to dismantle social and intellectual barriers and to encourage the ordinary reader in their appreciation of, and pleasure in, literature. Her celebration of the 'common reader's' intellectual and creative independence is connected to her wider political principles. Melba Cuddy-Keane argues that Woolf's 'essays... have a social project: she wrote about literature to inculcate good reading practices, and she did so because she believed that an educated public is crucial to the success of democratic society' (2003: 2).

'Modern Fiction'

'Modern Fiction' is one of the best known of Woolf's essays; it is the most anthologized and quoted and has assumed a central role in critical discussion of modernist literature and innovative literary practices.[3] In this essay, Woolf takes to task contemporary novelists who continued to write in the realist mode (whom she calls the 'Edwardians'), arguing that their literary method of representing 'reality' largely through reference to material, exterior details (describing furniture, the style of dress and so on) is inauthentic and unrealistic. She argues that writers such as H. G. Wells, John Galsworthy and especially Arnold Bennett focus on 'the body' (extrinsic details) rather than 'spirit' (interior processes) and so miss 'the essential thing' which is the evocation of 'life itself' (*E4* 158, 160, 161). Characters might be accurately 'dressed down to the last button of their coats in the fashion of the hour' (*E4* 160), but without a sense of the life of the mind this is increasingly unconvincing and disappointing.

In stark contrast to the 'materialist' novelists, Woolf praises the methods of other experimental writers (whom she refers to as the 'Georgians'), notably Joyce, whose fiction is more 'spiritual' in its 'attempt to come closer to life' (*E4* 161). His writing displaces what is usually thought of as the 'proper stuff of fiction' and instead records the 'flickerings of that innermost flame which flashes its messages through the brain' and attempts to capture the immediacy and simultaneity of experience, recording the 'atoms' of sensation and perception 'as they fall upon the mind' and make impressions on the consciousness (*E4* 161). However, Woolf acknowledges that these new methods might be problematic for the reader, disregarding as they do all novelistic conventions of form, structure and content. In her view, Joyce rejects 'probability, or coherence, or any other of these signposts which for generations have served to support the imagination of a reader when called upon to imagine what he can neither touch nor see' (*E4* 161). It also misses what Woolf considers essential to the creation of 'life itself' which are the more elusive aspects of experience, those which remain ambiguous and not fully knowable, aspects that she goes on to describe as 'the dark places of psychology' (*E4* 162). Joyce's work, she finds, exposes too much about a single mind, his method evoking the 'sense of being in a bright yet narrow room, confined and shut in, rather than enlarged and set free' (*E4* 162). She finds this method to be egotistical and solipsistic rather than illuminating and suggestive.

What is apparent is that Woolf steers a course between what she perceives as these two extremes: her modern fiction is aware of the importance and effects of material circumstances, *and also* of the fluctuations of consciousness and emotion. As she says in *A Room of One's Own*, 'fiction is like a spider's web…attached to grossly material things, like health and money and the houses we live in' (*AROO* 41) and our perception and experience of reality are shaped by our subjective engagement with, and perspective on, the world around us. What a 'new realism' in fiction should do is to represent 'an *ordinary* mind on an *ordinary* day' (my emphasis) which receives 'a myriad impressions…an incessant shower of innumerable atoms' (*E4* 160). We all register these sensations and impressions in different ways and it is this interaction between the material world and our interior life (not just how a button is sewn on to a coat) that creates our sense of reality. Our everyday experience is rich in such sensations and it is these that 'shape themselves into the life of Monday or Tuesday' (*E4* 160).

Woolf's essay also raises awareness of the pressures and expectations placed on writers to comply with the tacit agreement between reader, writer and publisher about what constitutes a narrative in terms of content and form. Woolf considers that writers (and to an extent, readers) are enslaved to such conventions which command obedience and constrain imaginative freedom at every level. In the grip of 'some powerful and unscrupulous tyrant who has him [the writer] in thrall' (*E4* 160), writers are compelled to conform to given conventions and the predictable plots of established genres such as comedy, tragedy and romance. Her own challenges to generic and formal conventions are an indication of her persistent testing of boundaries of definition and classification. Modern fiction should refuse the well-worn plots and in her own fiction Woolf displaces plot from the centre of the narrative. More specifically, she argues that the linear, chronological sequences of events around which most narratives are shaped is completely at odds with how we really experience life. Although the physical limitations of writing on a page mean that one word, sentence and paragraph follows another with an inevitable linearity, our real, lived experience is created from a simultaneity of perceptions, sensations, stimulations, responses and thoughts and Woolf adopts various fictional methods to convey this. Thought and emotion are 'layered' (palimpsestic) as we experience more than one thing simultaneously and as our past is always entwined with our present. Our experiences are not ordered into a neat series of discrete events which we encounter and then pass by: 'life', Woolf famously argues, 'is not a series of gig lamps symmetrically arranged; life is a luminous halo, a semi-transparent envelope surrounding us from the beginning of consciousness to the end' (*E4* 160).

Towards the end of her essay, Woolf looks beyond a British context and explains what she sees as the positive influence of modern Russian writers, particularly Anton Chekhov. She finds their writing to be inspiring for the ways in which it explores psychological depths and examines the everyday experience in a profound way, drawing powerful significance from the seemingly insignificant and privileging the indefinite and inconclusive. Her own essay is similarly inconclusive: it recognizes the necessity for destruction in order for new forms and modes of fiction to come into being, but her manifesto on modern fiction does not propose to simply replace the old conventions with a new set. Woolf deliberately seeks to avoid imposing the kinds of prescriptions that have constrained the development of fiction as she saw it. Instead, her essay promotes the idea that literature is organic in its development, undergoing constant renewal. In the final sentence of the essay, fiction is imagined as a woman 'come alive and standing in our midst', prepared to be broken and bullied, honoured and loved, 'for so her youth is renewed and her sovereignty assured' (*E*4 164).

'Mr Bennett and Mrs Brown'

Woolf developed several versions of this essay which can be read as an indication of the importance she attributed to the concerns she discusses and of her enthusiasm for setting out her manifesto for character in modern fiction.[4] This essay was, in part, written as a response to fellow writer Arnold Bennett's article, 'Is the Novel Decaying?' (1923), in which he asserted the over-riding importance of creating 'real', 'true', 'genuine' and convincing characters and his criticism of the younger generation of writers for failing to achieve this (Majumdar and McLaurin 1975: 112, 113). Woolf's novel, *Jacob's Room*, had been particularly singled out as being 'packed and bursting with originality, and…exquisitely written' at the expense of the creation of memorable and 'fully true' characters (Majumdar and McLaurin 1975: 113). Although both writers clearly agree that character is of central importance, their differing approaches demonstrate a fundamental disagreement about what 'character' entails. Woolf's essay is about the aesthetic choices that writers make as they create their fictions, but this, for Woolf, is inseparable from the historical, cultural, political and philosophical changes that shape modern experience. Gender issues are not explicitly foregrounded in this essay – indeed, in the final version of her essay, Woolf only draws attention to the work of her male contemporaries to the exclusion of women writers such as Dorothy Richardson and Katherine Mansfield. However, Woolf's response to Bennett's ideas seems also informed by her feminist anger about his discussion in an earlier book, *Our Women: Chapters on the Sex-Discord* (1920), in which he queried the ability of women writers to produce great fiction. Her focus on the ways in which Bennett may (inadequately) construct a female character seems to comment critically not only on his adherence to outmoded literary methods, but also on his reliance on outmoded and limited notions of female identity. By contrast, her choice of a working-class female character, a cook, to signal a new era of 'sunshine and fresh air' for women offers a pointed corrective to Bennett's views.

As Woolf's alternative title for her essay, 'Character in Fiction', indicates, her focus is on the creation of fictional characters as a novelist's most central, yet most frustrating, pursuit. She sets out to demonstrate the difficulties of this task for a younger generation of writers more attuned than Bennett and other older novelists to the complexities of modern experience, a fundamental aspect of which is the problematic notion of 'reality'. For the older generation of writers, reality is something evident, material and empirically proven, whereas for the younger writer aware of the subjectivity of experience, 'reality' is something more ambiguous, provisional, varied and indeterminate. Woolf's essay, therefore, addresses three interconnected central points: what is meant by 'character' in fiction, what is meant by 'reality' and the difficult task the young writer must negotiate which is how to represent a modern perspective on both concepts. Far from accepting Bennett's criticism of her own generation of writers as contributing to the 'decay' of the novel, Woolf redirects Bennett's criticism back at him: it is *his* generation of writers and their literary methods of creating character that are a source of the novel's atrophy. She points out that each reader will judge and assess fictional characters differently (just as we engage 'in the art of reading character' as we encounter others in our own lives) so that a character that seems realistic to one reader maybe 'quite unreal' to another (*E3* 426). The idea of 'reality' is also difficult to delineate given the many and varied cultural influences that impact on personal experience, perspective and relations with others. She famously cites December 1910 as the (seemingly arbitrary) date on which 'human character changed' (*E3* 421) and critics have noted a number of shifts in social hierarchies and power relations (particularly gender roles and class structures) to which Woolf's date may be indirectly making reference (see Introduction).

She sweepingly declares, 'All human relations have shifted – those between masters and servants, husbands and wives, parents and children', shifts that necessitate new paradigms for articulating individual characters and social relations in life as well as fiction (*E*3 422).

To illustrate her arguments, she includes in her essay an anecdote in the form of 'a simple story' of a train journey. In fact, this story closely resembles her short story (or 'sketch' as Woolf called it) titled 'An Unwritten Novel' (1920). Her earlier short story recounts her narrator's train journey and her conversation with a fellow woman traveller, Minnie Marsh, and is told using the fluid, 'free indirect discourse' technique that Woolf adopts and refines throughout her career (see Chapter Three). The narrator imagines a life story for Minnie (echoed in the later construction of Mrs Brown), speculating that she is a spinster, bullied by her sister-in-law (Hilda), and has possibly committed a petty crime. Although this version of Minnie is derailed by her being met at the station by her son, the narrator is filled with new curiosity and so the process of fiction-making goes on beyond the end of the story. This story self-consciously reveals the mechanisms of fiction writing itself, laying bare the creative process of creating scenes, characters and building emotional tension. Woolf makes obvious the decisions and indecisions, the different 'trains' of thought, and the process of selecting narrative elements and determining how these should be represented. In this sense, we could consider Woolf's writing to be 'metafictional' – that is fiction that provides an insight into the process of fiction writing itself. Critic, Pamela L. Caughie, suggests that the title, 'An Unwritten Novel', refers to the process Woolf is undertaking in her creation of modernist fiction – she is 'unwriting it [conventional narrative], taking it apart to show how it could be put together' in new ways (1991: 93). A similar process is at work with Woolf's inclusion of a 'story' in 'Mr Bennett and Mrs Brown': as she comments as a critic on methods of characterization, she simultaneously reveals the potential for various techniques for the creation for character.

The story of a train journey also serves as a metaphor for the transition in literary conventions that Woolf perceives is in motion, from the material realism of writers such as Wells, Galsworthy and Bennett to the modern fictional forms of her contemporaries. To illustrate their approaches to fiction, she imagines their different perspectives on an imaginary fellow traveller, Mrs Brown; however, it is Bennett's approach that forms the focus of Woolf's critique. Taking his novel *Hilda Lessways* as an example, she notes his skill in building a meticulously detailed description of the houses characters occupy. Material details serve to convey the intricacies of social status and relations, but any sense of the *life* of the character herself is missing. Similarly, Bennett's literary 'tools' put to work in imagining Mrs Brown would also result in his missing what is vital and human about her – her spirit. Writers such as Bennett 'have laid an enormous stress upon the fabric of things' rather than the 'human beings' with which fiction should be primarily concerned (*E3* 432). These literary conventions she likens to social conventions, to social manners, and recognizes their important function as 'bridging the gulf between...the writer and his unknown reader' in order to proceed two more interesting and intimate matters (*E3* 431). But, although readers have come to expect and even rely on such fictional convention, this 'becomes...an obstacle and an impediment' for the modern reader for whom there is a discrepancy between the 'reality' represented by the Edwardian novels and the rich interchange of ideas, sensations and emotions contemporary readers experience (*E3* 434). As Woolf points out, 'In one day thousands of ideas have coursed through your brains; thousands of emotions have met, collided, and disappeared in astonishing disorder' (*E3* 436). Echoing her ideal of the reader-accomplice, she also points out the readers' responsibility in bringing about necessary change. Readers are 'partners in this business of writing books, as companions in the railway carriage, as fellow travellers with Mrs Brown' (*E3* 435-6). Readers must 'insist' that writers create more realistic characters to reflect a modern awareness of the indeterminate nature of identity, and the 'infinite variety' of experience (*E3* 436). Finally, she appeals to her reader, stressing that this is very much a transitional phase: 'we are trembling on the verge of one of the great ages of English literature' and modern writers may indeed be seen to fail in their production of fiction and characters which may seem 'spasmodic...obscure...fragmentary' (*E3* 436). As she says towards the end of her essay, 'The Narrow Bridge of Art', literature needs to 'learn a new step' and this will take time (*E3* 439). Woolf's story, 'The Lady in the Looking-Glass: A Reflection', can be seen to illustrate this process of transition.

'The Lady in the Looking-Glass: A Reflection'

The story is ostensibly concerned with the problem of trying to represent a character called Isabella Tyson largely through the narrator's observation of her. Repeatedly, the narrator is frustrated to find that the information available about Isabella's appearance and her possessions is insufficient to reach a satisfactory understanding of her. Written around the time of Woolf's experiments with biographical form in *Orlando: A Biography* and her early work on *The Waves* (see Chapters Two and Four), this story wrestles with similar preoccupations. Most significant is the need to discover or devise literary techniques and formal methods with which to represent the life of an individual and to capture the complexities of their lived experience in writing. In her diary, Woolf records one stimulus for her story as being a visit to her friend Ethyl Sands and her observation that her friend did not open her letters (*D3* 157), but this story can also read as a metafictional text and it seems to be a story that comments on and makes obvious the processes of writing a story. More specifically, we can read this story as a fictional realization of the ideas Woolf articulates in her literary manifestos, most obviously the inadequacy and inauthenticity of realist literary conventions for representing experience. By contrast, her story demonstrates the effectiveness of more modernist narrative techniques and, in-keeping with Woolf's sense of the reader's role and responsibility in the co-creation of modern fiction, self-consciously draws attention to the processes of reading and interpretation. There is an emphasis on a subjective perspective and on the ways that a particular point of view can shape or even determine a specific understanding of reality. As we see in 'Modern Fiction' and 'Mr Bennett and Mrs Brown', the expectations of the narrator-as-reader in this story need to move away from a focus on material details if a fuller, more realistic a sense of character is to be conveyed.

From its title onwards, the story makes self-conscious reference to a mimetic mode of writing. The 'looking-glass' seems to function as a metaphor for a realist approach to literary representation which focusses attention only onto external details – on how things appear and appear to be – and which claims to simply and unproblematically *reflect* reality. However, the narrator, who is also in the position of a reader trying to make sense of the scene and character and to reach a satisfactory interpretation, is repeatedly frustrated by this fictional approach. S/he can see *both* the static 'realist' reflection of the world in the mirror, and can also glimpse the more mobile and intriguing space that lies beyond the mirror's frame. His/her attention is continually drawn to the unknown but imaginatively stimulating outside, but the familiarity of realist conventions for delineating character (descriptions of furniture, Isabella's social status and gendered expectations) repeatedly draws the narrator back. In this, Woolf's story acknowledges the 'security' that realist details offer in contrast to the difficulty and challenge of interpreting more ambiguous, fluid, uncertain, differently organized narrative elements. In *A Room of One's Own*, Woolf compares the experience of reading modernist experimental fiction to a somewhat startling journey on a 'switchback railway' or 'out at sea in an open boat' (*AROO* 78, 77). Her manifesto-essays and this story also recognize that literary innovation and the seeking of new forms for representing life and experience involve a transition for writers and readers alike. This said, 'The Lady in the Looking-Glass: A Reflection' scathingly exposes the power of realist conventions as the narrator recognizes the control that the mirror exerts over *what* can be seen and *how* it can be seen. The mirror excludes 'the unessential and superficial' (*CSF* 225), delimiting what can be contained within its frame, ordering and arranging the different elements and determining the perspective we are given. The circular structure of the story itself compounds Woolf's critique: the story ends where it begins – with the same imperative: 'People should not leave looking-glasses hanging in their rooms' (*CSF* 221, 225). Like the mirror itself, the story of Isabella itself is framed and limited, and, like realist conventions as Woolf saw them, unable to (make) progress.

The first sentence confirms the illusion that a realist mode creates – that all can be revealed about a character through a focus on certain details, such as having access to Isabella's financial status (via her cheque book) and, related to this, her social status. The speculation about the letters on her table being confessions of a crime invite a judgement in relation to established ideas of acceptable behaviour and moral codes. However, it quickly becomes apparent that such a mode of writing is severely limited: the partial view the narrator has from the reflection in the mirror is synonymous with the partial understanding that realist modes (as Woolf defines them) can convey. The violence with which this effect is described compounds the criticism of such forms and conventions. Although the 'Italian glass' seems to offer a refined, artistic and sophisticated reflection, the full view of Isabella's garden (and Isabella herself, located as she is in her garden at this point) is shockingly restricted, 'slicing off an angle, the gold rim [of the mirror] cut it [the view outside] off' (CSF 221). The recurrence throughout the story of this violent image of the mirror's edge slicing and cutting off a fuller view reinforces Woolf's point about the failure of realism as a mode for conveying the complexity or fullness of experience.

The final image describing the effects of the mirror on Isabella extends this criticism to raise an ethical concern about realist fiction in which a character is rendered a mere spectacle to enthral the reader rather an imaginary being created to explore the complexity of lived experience: 'At once the looking-glass began to pour over her a light that seemed to fix her; that seemed like some acid to bite off the unessential and superficial and to leave only the truth. It was an enthralling spectacle' (CSF 225). Earlier the narrator had considered the importance of empathy – the virtue of being able to imagine the experience of another. But the metaphor commonly used to describe an empathetic response – to stand in the shoes of another – results in the narrator being distracted by the style and quality of Isabella's shoes and the ethical gesture towards empathy is deflected by the materialist detail.

This failure to move beyond external description is a recurrent disappointment in this story and we see how the tentatively suggested possibility of richness and complexity implied by the metaphor of Isabella's mind being, like her room, 'suffused' with life and possibility, is shockingly reduced. This simile likening Isabella's mind and being to her room recalls Woolf's point about the innovative qualities of Chekhov's work in 'Modern Fiction' and her story points to the potential that literary forms have (as with the stories of Chekhov) 'to compose something new' by allowing 'the shapes of things in a room' to be subtly discerned, our eyes adjusting to a new light and to a new, 'unexpected' literary emphasis (E4 163, 162). As Isabella approaches the mirror, there is a sense of mounting anticipation: she should get closer and clearer and the 'denouement' in a realist text would be a full knowledge of Isabella and the secrets her letters contain. However, this familiar plot pattern is confounded and the bright and 'pitiless light' cast by the mirror only reveals Isabella to be 'perfectly empty' (*CSF* 225). With a profound sense of deflation and disappointment, the realist mode strips her of all that is sensual, vital, ambiguous and individual about her and only 'the hard wall' of the basic external facts about her (her aged appearance and mundanity of life – her 'letters' were only 'bills') is seen (*CSF* 225). As Woolf claims in 'Modern Fiction', realism 'more often misses than secures the thing we seek... life or spirit, truth or reality... the essential thing[,] has moved off, or on, and refuses to be contained any longer' (*E4* 160).

The structure of this story serves to emphasize (and exaggerate) the contrast between the realist and modernist modes. Throughout we have sections that seem to be 'typically' realist – externally narrated, building an accumulation of detail and privileging metonymic codes – and these are interspersed with more richly metaphorical and suggestive sections which invest even the 'solid' material world with life and vitality. The second paragraph of the story illustrates this well. Instead of the room being simply a static scene with its contents solid and fixed, as an empty room in a realist novel might be described, a modernist mode of representation brings it to life. With a more imaginative, metaphorical and associative approach, new things seem to 'happen' and the room is imbued with vitality, with colour and movement (*CSF* 221). Observing and representing things differently, shifting the focus (as Woolf suggests modern fiction does) from what is 'commonly thought big' to what is 'commonly thought small' has a profound effect (*E4* 161). The solid the objects in the room – the 'rugs and stone chimney-pieces, [the] sunken book-cases and red and gold lacquer cabinets' (*CSF* 221) – would, in a realist narrative, carry narrative weight as they function as metonymic codes for social facts (wealth and intellectual interests). But these are displaced by the effects of what is less 'solid' and barely registered at all in conventional fiction, the 'lights and shadows, curtains blowing, petals falling' (*CSF* 221). Here the narrator-reader is overtaken by a different sense of reality as s/he becomes attuned to the non-empirical qualities of the room – its fluctuating mood and rapidly shifting atmosphere which seems to breathe and sigh. If we look beyond what we expect to see and read in fiction, Woolf seems to say, we, like the narrator-reader, can open our minds to a bombardment of 'atoms' of sensation and can participate in the ballet of movement and colour that a more metaphorical, ambiguous, speculative and imaginative mode opens up for us. Reality is not neatly ordered, fixed and stable but is provisional and indeterminate, dynamic and in continual flux, as the movement of the metaphorical creatures Woolf imagines to convey the qualities of the room suggests: 'They came pirouetting across the floor, stepping delicately…and pecking allusive beaks' (*CSF* 221).

'But', begins the next paragraph, and the return to the realist mode – where scenes and objects are described 'so accurately and so fixedly' – is one of containment and stasis. Objects in this mode of writing 'seemed held there in their reality unescapably' (*CSF* 221). As Woolf's narrator comments, 'It was a strange contrast – all changing here, all stillness there. One could not help looking from one to the other' (*CSF* 221). As in her manifesto-essays, Woolf invites her readers to see a stark contrast between a realist mode (which cuts off and deadens experience) and a modernist mode which brings things and experience to life. Her story invites us to recognize the latter as one more capable of conveying a modern sensibility in tune with the interior world of thought, sensation and emotion. This idea is consolidated when attention shifts from the room to Isabella herself. Responding to an impression Isabella has evoked, the narrator begins to speculate on the kinds of flowers it might be 'natural' to assume Isabella is picking in her garden: 'something light and fantastic and leafy and trailing, traveller's joy, or one of those elegant sprays of convolvulus that twine round ugly walls and burst here and there into white and violet blossoms' (*CSF* 222). However, this imaginative response to an intangible feeling or idea about Isabella is quickly quashed by 'the truth', by facts that can be empirically proven. Here, Woolf's story points out another danger of realist conventions which is that they are closely bound up with social conventions that also severely limit our knowledge and understanding of others. Isabella has lived an unconventional life: she is 'rich' and an intrepid traveller, taking risks to build up her collection of rare and exotic objects; she has many friends and, it is assumed, has had many involved and even passionate relationships. Yet, the fact that she has remained a spinster at odds with gender conventions (which deem marriage the only worthy achievement in a woman's life), means that her adventures and relationships 'had led to nothing – that is, she had never married' (*CSF* 222). Although a more intuitive, speculative and imaginative representation of Isabella might allow the 'more shadowy and symbolic' aspects of Isabella's experience to be appreciated, the realist mode with its focus on absolute and proven (real) 'facts', drains away this hidden richness. The more of these hard and fast facts are revealed to us, the more elusive our understanding of Isabella becomes. The dramatically related arrival of the post a confirms this: the letters that arrive could be revelatory, prophetic, like biblical tablets of stone, 'all dripping with light and colour ... crude and unabsorbed', but this narrative event and the objects in question are soon 'drawn in and arranged and composed and made part of the picture' (*CSF* 223). The letters, rich in potential for new, significant and vital human communication, are merely 'granted that stillness and immortality which the looking-glass conferred' (*CSF* 223).

However, Woolf's story also identifies the danger in some modernist literary approaches as well. In 'Modern Fiction', she praises some aspects of Joyce's literary experiment: he focusses on the 'spiritual' qualities rather than the material and seeks to reveal the fluctuations of human consciousness, regardless of 'probability, or coherence' or the other 'signposts' other writers use to make fiction accessible to the reader (*E4* 161). Woolf's narrator, frustrated by what cannot be revealed about Isabella using a materialist approach, resorts to a plan to 'prize her [Isabella] open with the first tool that came to hand – the imagination' (*CSF* 223). However, just as Joyce's method proves too exposing and solipsistic – his modernist approach creates a fictional space that is too brightly lit, 'shut in' and inward-looking – Woolf's narrator's quest to 'fix one's mind upon her [Isabella] at that very moment' and to 'fasten her down there' (*CSF* 223) to expose 'her profounder state of being' (*CSF* 224) is also problematic. Realizing that what is vital and captivating about Isabella's mind is that it is, like her room, elusive and indefinite, the narrator's desire to expose Isabella's mind to severe scrutiny and to 'penetrate a little farther into her being' is 'impious and absurd' (*CSF* 224, 225).

Woolf's story, like her manifesto-essays, seems to suggest that what is needed for a convincing representation of reality and experience is a sense of both material and spiritual existence. Modern fiction must be prosaic and poetic, must capture the lived experience of the everyday in ways that convey the complexities of our multi-layered, simultaneous consciousness of experience.

The onus that the story puts on looking and interpretation also stresses the importance of the role of the modern reader as both everyday literary critic and a participant in the creative process. Like the modern writer, the modern reader must also take the risk of stepping beyond the familiar narrative modes and conventions to explore a more unknown and uncertain literary territory.

CHAPTER TWO

Formal Innovation

Formal innovation is at the heart of Woolf's literary experiments and she worked with determination to challenge and revise the conventional forms of the novel, short story and essay that she inherited from her Victorian predecessors. For her, the prevalent conventions of 'literary realism' were no longer adequate to represent a modern awareness and experience of reality. In her fiction and non-fiction, she worked to create new forms and structures that could open up textual spaces in which the multiplicity of modern experience and the diversity of influences could be represented. Her experiments with form are far from simply technical exercises and, as various critical approaches indicate, Woolf's formal developments can be seen to engage with political concerns (feminist, pacifist and anti-imperialist), with new ideas about human consciousness and 'the self', and with new technologies and scientific ideas.

Although 'form' and 'content' seem to be two separate aspects of writing, what quickly becomes apparent as we analyse further is that form and content are interconnected. Form is not simply a 'container' for the content but is intricately involved in shaping the content, adding significance in certain ways and impacting on the interpretation we may give to a piece of writing. We can say that form *in*forms all aspects of writing and the meanings we attribute to it. This chapter will explore the importance of form for Woolf's modernist vision of how fiction and non-fiction could be written as well considering the challenges that Woolf's formal experiments present for the reader in texts such as 'The Mark on the Wall' (1917), *Jacob's Room* (1922), 'In the Orchard' (1923), *Orlando: A Biography* (1928) and *The Waves* (1931). It will also explore Woolf's extended essays, *A Room of One's Own* (1929) and *Three Guineas* (1938).

Ezra Pound's rallying call for modernist writers and artists to 'make it new' – to cast off the constraints of existing literary conventions and to challenge readers' expectations – is felt strongly when encountering Woolf's writing, particularly for the first time. She deliberately pursued the goal of testing and transgressing the boundaries which mark off one 'form' (or genre) of writing from another – the novel from the essay, biography from fiction, prose from poetry – and she set herself the task of stretching and revising generic boundaries with each new publication. In 'Modern Fiction', she considers that what *can* constitute the 'proper stuff of fiction' exceeds what conventional genres and narrative structures are able to articulate. Woolf adopts established generic forms, but reframes them to explore aspects of experience that conventional forms omit or fail to consider. She reconceptualizes the *Bildungsroman* in *Jacob's Room*, parodies biography in *Orlando* and writes *The Waves* as 'a playpoem' (*D3* 203). These novels are discussed below.

In literary terms, 'form' also refers to the patterns or structures of a text – to plot structures or thematic or linguistic patternings – and innovations in relation to these aspects of writing are also central to Woolf's literary experiments. Key to Woolf's literary innovation is a stripping down of the complexity of plot, rendering this aspect of her fiction minimal and displacing it as a central narrative concern. Whereas the narratives of realist novels derive shape, pace, coherence and pattern from a strong plotline, in Woolf's writing the emphasis is on language, imagery, linguistic patterns, associations, allusions and repetitions and it is these elements which create coherence and shape. Her prose is often lyrical, poetic, condensed and highly metaphorical and this has the effect of disrupting the boundaries assumed to exist between prose and poetic form. Like other modernist writers, Woolf was conscious of her writing as a deliberately created piece of art and sought to draw attention to this. Whereas realism seeks to create a sense of narrative form as somehow 'natural' and works to distract attention from its artifice, modernist literature draws attention to the 'material' from which it is constructed by emphasizing the artistic medium – language – out of which it is made. The proliferation of figurative uses of language, such as simile, metaphor and personification, create a self-consciousness about the form of Woolf's writing, drawing attention the creative process via the deliberate manipulation of language.

Time and narrative form

The form of fiction is also intricately connected to time. A narrative is a sequence of events unfolding in time and conventionally this is given a linear structure so that events occur in a forward moving, chronological order. However, for Woolf such linearity was unrealistic because this is not how we really experience life: our experiences are not ordered into a neat a series of discrete events, the 'series of gig lamps symmetrically arranged' that Woolf discusses in 'Modern Fiction' (*E4* 160). The new forms of fiction Woolf devised attempted to represent experience and the sense of self in a more complex way as she tried to capture the sense of multiple and simultaneous experience. She argues that we are bombarded by 'myriad impressions' (*E4* 160) every second of every day and our experience of thought and emotion is 'layered' (palimpsestic) as we experience more than one thing at the same time. Our consciousness is also complicated further by time: our past is always entwined with our present experience and, as Henri Bergson's theories suggest, we experience two levels of time simultaneously – clock time and subjective time (see Introduction). In Woolf's fiction there is a sense of the forward movement of narrative time, but also of a more personal, subjective experience of time as the narrative focus shifts between different characters' centres of consciousness to explore their memories and the emotions and flow of thoughts set in motion by recalling the past. Woolf's narrative technique and use of free indirect discourse disrupts the narrative linearity found in realist fiction (see Chapters Three and Four).

Woolf's experiment with literary form to capture the sense of subjective time and to represent a multi-dimensional and fluid sense of human consciousness can be seen in two of Woolf's short fictions, 'The Mark on the Wall' and 'In the Orchard'.

Innovation and experiment – shorter fictions

It was in her shorter fiction that Woolf initially began her more radical experiments with form and genre, these fictions acting as a kind of testing ground for her innovations. Her first published short story, 'The Mark on the Wall' (1917), signalled this new departure from the forms of prose fiction in her first two novels, *The Voyage Out* (1915) and *Night and Day* (1919). In a letter, she describes the excitement and exuberance of making her creative technical breakthrough, it happened 'all in a flash, as if flying' (*L4* 231). The short story is often seen as the quintessential modernist form and this is, in part, because its typical generic features lend themselves well to the expression of what we might call a modernist sensibility (an awareness of the uncertainty and ambiguity of modern life) as well as to a deliberate self-conscious about the constructedness of the text. Building on late nineteenth-century forms (the prose poem and the psychological sketch), modernist short stories often revolve around a moment of intense awareness or insight, what James Joyce terms an 'epiphany'. There is a focus on subjective impressions and psychological processes, but also on the fleeting nature of experience. Atmosphere and mood, sensory impressions and responses, emotional intensity and psychological exploration are of central significance. These experiences or realizations are not directly stated, however, and the reader has to work hard to interpret modernist stories, looking to imagery, metaphor, symbol, as well as to form and experiments with form, to understand the significance of what has taken place.

Woolf wrote a large number of short fictions that vary in length and focus. Some are 'traditional' in the sense of having a clear plot and characters, whereas others are more abstract and speculative. All are concerned in different ways with the everyday and draw attention not only to what is seen but also *how* it is seen and experienced, with some stories radically disrupting expected perspectives by focalizing through non-human creatures (notably giving us a 'snail's eye' view in 'Kew Gardens' and a heron's in 'Monday or Tuesday').[1] Woolf admired the work of contemporary Russian writers, particularly Anton Chekhov and her experimental forms seem to have been influenced by what Woolf recognized as his literary innovations. In 'Modern Fiction', she praises his ability to lay 'emphasis ... upon ... unexpected places' to reveal unanticipated and profound significance 'compos[ing] something new' (*E4* 162, 163). Woolf's own method of taking an ordinary, everyday experience and exploring its deeper significance yet refusing to conclusively define it seems influenced by Chekhov's approach in his short fiction. Woolf's experiments with form in one genre also spill over into her innovations in other genres so that there is a creative continuum between stories and novels, and fictions and essays, that challenges ideas of clear-cut generic boundaries. In her diary, she speculates that 'one thing should open out of another' (*D2* 13). She saw three of her earliest short stories – 'The Mark on the Wall', 'Kew Gardens' (1919) and 'An Unwritten Novel' (1920) – as 'dancing in unity' and helping to shape her 'idea of a new form for a new novel' which would become *Jacob's Room* (*D2* 14, 13).

'The Mark on the Wall'

In 'The Mark on the Wall', we see 'an ordinary mind on an ordinary day' (*E4* 160) at work: the narrator notices a mark on the wall (a seemingly trivial detail) and contemplates what could have made it. We soon realize that, despite the title, the literal mark on the wall is not really what the story is about. What is most important is the series of reveries that are prompted by the narrator's shifting perception of what the mark could be: a hole left by a nail, a stain left by a rose petal, 'the head of a gigantic old nail' or 'a crack in the wood' (*CSF* 83, 84, 87, 88). It is the working of the narrator's (and the reader's) mind and imagination ('How readily our thoughts swarm upon a new object, lifting it a little way, as ants carry a blade of straw so feverishly, and then leave it' *CSF* 83), and what is revealed about the inner processes of cognitive and emotional response that are the focus of the story. This, Woolf insists, is how we experience reality and she pursues her quest to create a new form with which to express this.

Woolf's construction of a fragmented narrative comprised of reveries draws attention to the fluidity of mental processes: the narrative focus slips easily from one to another just as the mind experiences a flux of ideas and subjective impressions. These range widely (and with seriousness as well as humour)

over the contemplation of ordinary as well as philosophical
ideas, speculations, perceptions and imaginative possibilities.
The narrator contemplates the previous owners of the house and
the transitoriness of acquaintance, and offers a meditation on
existential experience and the temporary and 'haphazard' nature
of modern life, comically illustrated by the variety of possessions
lost and the sense of discombobulation resulting from a ride on
the Tube (*CSF* 84). S/he expresses a longing for the pleasure of a
contemplative state in which thoughts can range freely and an ideal
self can be imagined. S/he also ponders the nature of historical fact,
questioning the male authorities and experts who assert a certain
kind of knowledge as objective and absolute, implying a connection
between hierarchical order of society as laid out in the peerage and
war. Finally, the narrator puts forward a meditation on wood, its
natural growth and uses in the human world.

As this summary suggests, the structure of the story is markedly
different from realist conventions which would build up a sense
of experience from material details and plot these developments
in a linear, chronological form. In fact, on first reading, we might
question whether 'The Mark on the Wall' is a story at all: it has no
plot or character development and offers only a very inconclusive
ending. One critic expresses doubts since 'it is as much an essay
on the nature of reality' and the capacities of the imagination as
a piece of fiction (Whitworth 2005: 119). Although the narrator
makes an attempt at providing typically realist details – the story
begins by pinning down the time of year and providing material
'evidence' to prove this and then later reveals this to be war time –
the importance of this story lies in exploring the inner workings of
the mind and consciousness, in 'record[ing] the atoms as they fall
upon the mind' (*E4* 161). Indeed, it is the non-linear form of the
story that creates a narrative space for this exploration of subjective
experience. Thinking simply about time in the story also makes
apparent Woolf's opening up of textual spaces: the actual ('clock')
time that passes can only be a minute or two, but the subjective time
experienced expands beyond this.

The literal mark on the wall not only acts as a visual prompt
for a number of imaginative flights of fancy and for subjective
meditations, but also acts as an important formal structuring
device. The repeated return to the mark – 'the mark on the wall',
'as for that mark', 'yet the mark on the wall', 'in certain lights that

mark on the wall', 'that mark on the wall is really – what shall I say? – the head of a gigantic old nail' (*CSF* 83, 84, 86, 87) – acts as a kind of narrative punctuation that returns us to the question posed at the start of the story and which marks a starting point for each new train of thought. It works as a formal centre from which the story spirals out and then returns. We could also say that the story takes the conventional form of a puzzle: a question is posed and then answered; the puzzle is solved and this brings about the story's closure. However, in keeping with the strategy seen throughout Woolf's work (and discussed in relation to the *Bildungsroman* and biography below), this established form is used as a structuring device but is simultaneously radically revised or even undermined. What is most valued in the puzzle form – solving the puzzle – is here not important: that the mark on the wall is revealed by another person in the room to be a snail is an anti-climax after the many intriguing digressions. In the final words of the story, material 'reality' replaces reverie – the war, newspapers and the snail are proven, 'solid' facts – but this definitive and conventional conclusion seems too simplistic and reductive. It is also a paradox – the story has structural closure but the many issues and themes raised are still on-going and open for discussion. This ending parodies the convention of narrative closure and far from 'hitting the nail on the head', as it were, it uses a conventional form (emphasized in the ending of the story) to self-consciously highlight the artifice and constructedness of itself *as* a story.

For Woolf, form is important – it should work not to contain and constrain meaning but to enable new ideas and trains of thought to flow. The transformation of the mark from a linear nail, which functions 'to pin things down', to define and hold them in place, to a snail seems a significant metaphor for the experimental form of this story. Like the snail's shell, the story is ultimately self-contained with its a definite ending bringing a conclusion to all the speculations. However, inside this formal 'container', the story is, like the snail itself, more fluid in form and trailing off in different, unpredictable directions. It is this narration of the inner life of fluid mental processes and sensory perceptions, the workings of the imagination, and the complex and multi-layered states of consciousness and self-awareness that Woolf sees as important for the future of fiction. Her story has already made this clear: if only the exterior 'shell of a person' is known, the world would be 'airless, shallow, bald...A world not to be lived in' (*CSF* 85). Rather it is the psychological depths that modern writers recognize as important and seek to explore. This idea of the self as having an exterior/interior duality resonates with Bergson's ideas where he conceptualized the self as having two different but complementary mental states – one more superficial and attuned to negotiating the material world (the 'intellect') and one more introspective and diffuse ('intuition'). While Bergson viewed intuition and the interior life as the most meaningful, the former is necessary for survival. Drawing an analogy with Woolf's story, we can see the importance of the intellect at work – the snail is the object of intellectual scrutiny and solving the puzzle it presents is the goal of the story. However, that it is (illogically) out of place on the wall means that it sets in motion a wide range of subjective and imaginative speculations, revealing the interior life as meaningful. The story suggests a sense of being as 'in process', of the self as incomplete and evolving and the narrative 'gaps' denoted by ellipses create a sense of indefinite and indeterminate experience. Yet form and content, the shell and the snail, also complement each other: the material presence of the snail prompts a repeated return to the contemplation of the 'mark' it makes. This functions structurally to repeatedly introduce new fragments of the story and simultaneously adds new layers of thought and ideas. This suggests that the mind, like the structure of this story, is stratified and palimpsestic, with thought processes and subjective experience in a state of flux.

Jacob's Room

This was the third novel that Woolf published and her first overtly experimental novel. It was the first novel she published with her own Hogarth Press and her diary records the sense of creative freedom the Press accorded her, 'I'm the only woman in England free to write what I like' (*D3* 43). The structure of this novel experiments with text and typographical form as it is organized into fourteen chapters comprised of varying numbers of sections which are unnumbered so that only the space on the page marks a break between them. Overall, the form is episodic and is composed of a series of short 'scenes' or vignettes with a movement back and forth in time that disrupts a strict linear chronology so that consecutive scenes sometimes seem to be disconnected. None of these scenes or characters' points of view are prioritized or given a special significance and so the onus is on the reader to prioritize what is important. For readers accustomed to heightened attention being given to certain events or moments this is frustrating, as some early reviews make clear. In an unsigned review called 'Dissolving Views', the *Yorkshire Post* offered a damning assessment: the novel has 'no narrative, no design, above all, no perspective' and with a 'method [that] is snapshot photography' the 'result is a crowded little album of pictures', yet it ends with praise for Woolf as 'a genuine artist' (Majumdar and McLaurin 1975: 107, 108). This does, however, get to the heart of Woolf's experiment in which her fiction makes a sharp movement away from a realist literary mode with its linear chronology and detailed description and discussion of the plot events. Other earlier critics perceived the influence of cinema with Woolf employing 'the cinematograph technique' (Holtby 1978: 117); some saw it as 'a portfolio' 'connected closely with the pictorial arts', as well as drawing parallels with the 'syncopated' rhythms of Jazz music (Majumdar and McLaurin 1975: 101, 105). As Alex Zwerdling notes, however, even more recent critics find this to be a challenging novel: it was certainly 'Woolf's first consciously experimental novel, and it has remained her most baffling one' with its 'rapidly shifting tone, now somber, now mocking' (1986: 62).

The novel relates the life of Jacob Flanders from a point in early childhood, through his adolescence and young manhood, and ultimately to his death in the First World War. This kind of narrative which traces the development, maturity and education of the central character is most often associated with the *Bildungsroman* form and follows the protagonist, traditionally a boy, through a sequence of events and 'rite of passage' experiences, 'usually including a contrasting pair of love affairs' (as Case and Shaw note, 2008: 75) and a phase of rebellion against social expectations. Typically, at the celebratory end of such narratives the protagonist (fully mature and developed) returns home and completes a process of social integration in conforming to the values of his society in terms of gender identity and role. This was a very popular form in a number of nineteenth-century novels, such as Charlotte Bronte's *Jane Eyre* (1847), Charles Dickens' *Great Expectations* (1862), George Eliot's *The Mill on the Floss* (1860), to name but a few. We can see that in some ways Jacob's narrative conforms to the narrative pattern of the *Bildungsroman*: we are aware of his early childish preoccupations (with crabs and skulls) and perceptions (his shock at seeing the couple lying on the beach, for example), and the narrative maps his formal education, his friendships, his taking up of a profession and his sexual awakening. Like many other middle-class young men, he travels to the great cities of Europe (Paris, Italy, Athens and Istanbul) to widen his horizons and follow his intellectual pursuits, and it is here that he falls in love. However, Woolf experiments with this form and in effect subverts what would be the usual narrative focus, which is to reveal the details of the central protagonist's path to maturity so that the reader has a fuller knowledge and understanding of him. Instead, Jacob is displaced from the centre of this narrative and the reader is continually kept at a distance: we only ever catch glimpses of Jacob, hear snippets of his conversations, and have the vaguest insight into what motivates him. We are offered only varied and superficial snapshots of moments of his life from other characters. Not only do such external views fail to capture a full sense of Jacob, but also the *Bildungsroman* form is significantly derailed by what we infer to be Jacob's death. In conventional narratives, the death of the hero would be a momentous event for the plot and character, yet in Woolf's novel it is not narrated. Although Jacob's mortal end coincides with the narrative end and seems to draw form and content neatly together, the final words of the novel do not bring closure but rather leave a question hanging in the air – what is Jacob's mother to do with his old shoes?

The title itself also gives a clue to Woolf's method of parodying this particular form of realist narrative – it is Jacob's *room* that is the subject of this novel and, although she paints a vivid picture of this room, complete with the accumulation of detail usually found in realist fiction, the room is repeatedly described as 'empty' and 'listless' (*JR* 31, 155). It would seem that the inanimate objects – the creaking 'wicker armchair' and the curtain 'swelling' in the breeze – have more life than Jacob narrated as he is always from an external perspective. As Woolf argued in 'Modern Fiction', realist writers can create immaculately constructed fictional worlds, rich in abundant detail, but such forms cannot effectively represent a sense of 'life!'. That Jacob's room is again described as 'empty' and 'listless' as his mother, Betty Flanders, and his friend, Richard Bonamy, clear it following Jacob's death as is very poignant. Many

critics have identified the elegiac qualities of this novel, reading
it as mourning the generation of men lost in the war as well as
Woolf's more personal mourning for her brother, Thoby (for
example, Zwerdling 1986; Clewell 2009). Woolf's experiments
with form also have a political significance and her adoption and
simultaneous subversion of the *Bildungsroman* form can be seen
to take on a political impetus when combined with the idea of an
elegy. Jacob's compliance with the values of his society results not in
his social integration and future role in his society, but in his death
(see also Chapter Four). Woolf's experimental reconception of this
kind of narrative as elegy derails the established narrative form and
conveys a powerful pacifist criticism of the cultural and gender-
specific roles men are expected to assume. The novel acknowledges
the tremendous national loss of a whole generation of young men,
but also points to the cultural codes and expectations that led to
such pointless loss of life.

Orlando: A Biography

Just as she revised the conventional form of the *Bildungsroman* in
Jacob's Room, Woolf also radically revised the other form of writing
most closely associated with the telling of the story of a person's life
and experience – the biography. Drawing on some of the details
of the life of Woolf's lover and friend, Vita Sackville-West (and on
Sackville-West's own history of her ancestral home, *Knole and the
Sackvilles*), this novel is presented as a fictionalized biography and,
as such, it tests generic boundaries of various kinds. This generic
ambiguity is reflected in the fact that when it was first published
booksellers shelved it in the biography section of their shops rather
than with other fiction. Like conventional biographies it includes
images of its subject and others related to the subject, as well as an
index and a wittily ironic preface which acknowledges other authors
and friends who have helped in different ways in the production of
this text. That Sackville-West, whom we might consider had helped
the most, is not included suggests that this book is untrustworthy
as fact from the beginning. With its time span of over three hundred
years and with a central character that changes sex from male to
female, Woolf's 'biography' clearly plays with the conventions of
this form in creating the fantastical tale of Orlando's life. Although

Woolf describes her novel as having begun as a 'joke' she also records her sense of exuberance, and the feeling that the energy of her experiment 'could revolutionise biography in a night' (*L3* 429). At this time, biographies were usually written following the death of the subject and had a commemorative function, typically recording the life of the subject from birth to death. Woolf's subject, however, is still very much alive at the end of the novel, racing home through the streets of London in her car.

It is assumed that biography is based on fact and has a truth-telling function, whereas fiction is the opposite – imagined, made-up, and so 'untrue'. However, Woolf recognized that these two seemingly disparate forms are closely connected: both forms relate the life stories of individuals and their textual construction involves the selection and representation of details from a particular perspective. The images included in biographies are seen to add a greater sense of authenticity, with photographs in particular assumed to be a source of objective, realistic and reliable 'evidence'. The images included in the early editions of *Orlando* (photographs of Vita Sackville-West but also of Woolf's niece in historical costume and paintings belonging to Sackville-West's family) mock this assumption as the photographs and paintings are deliberately falsely labelled. As Helen Wussow states, '[Woolf] undermines the supposed faithfulness of a biography toward its subject by presenting false photographic evidence' (1994: 2). This also draws attention to issues of representation more generally, raising the point that even the most apparently realistic forms of representation are not neutral or objective but can be manipulated and shaped by a particular perspective and personal or political purpose. In 1920s and 1930s, there was a surge of interest in biography and in the changing form of this genre as 'new' biographies became more streamlined and more psychological in approach. In her essay, 'The New Biography' (1927), Woolf contributes to this discussion and questions whether biographical form, with its focus on the facts of a person's life, can also convey the truth of personality. For her, these are diametrically opposed: truth has 'granite-like solidity' whereas personality has a 'rainbow-like intangibility' (*E4* 473). She considers that although the meticulously researched biographies in vogue in the late nineteenth-century amalgamated details and documents to confirm the 'truth' of their subject, they failed to evoke the personality. Woolf notes that the 'new phase of the biographer's art' (*E4* 476) attempts to synthesize fact and fiction, with fictional devices and techniques employed to more subtly evoke a sense of the life of the biographical subject. These shorter and more selective biographies also acknowledge the impact of the biographer in the construction of the narrative, again confirming the impossibility of objectivity in any form of representation.

The biographer-narrator in *Orlando* attempts to reveal the 'granite-like solidity' of the facts of his subject's life but stumbles with what we might assume is an incontrovertible fact – Orlando's sex: 'He – for there could be no doubt of his sex, though the fashion of the time did something to disguise it' (*O* 9). This teasing first sentence immediately raises questions about which facts we can trust and about how we come to see and know these facts, especially as cultural conventions (such as dress codes) change over time and even work to obfuscate the truth – as here, 'disguise it'. Orlando's change of sex later recalls this uncertainty: although the biographer-narrator emphatically states this is the 'Truth!' (*O* 86), he can do nothing more than record this 'simple fact', impatiently refusing to engage in any explanation: 'we quit such odious subjects as soon as we can' (*O* 87). Other 'facts' also prove elusive and as the narrator biographer aims to fulfil his traditional function to tell the truth, he is forced to admit that the unreliability of his sources necessitates the use of speculation and imagination on his part. His impatience and frustration are also evident when the factual record is incomplete: the documents and other evidence typically relied upon to produce a sense of authenticity and integrity are damaged and of dubious provenance. Having 'reached a moment of great significance in his [Orlando's] career' – his attainment of a Dukedom, an achievement both 'famous' and 'much disputed' – the narrator narrator evokes a strong sense of the scene but is unable to verify the details. With comic self-consciousness the narrator reveals that corroborative documents had been damaged: 'the fire had its way with all such records, and has left only tantalizing fragments' (*O* 79). Quotations from eyewitness accounts in the form of the diary of a naval officer, John Fenner Brigge, and a letter written by the daughter of a general present are included with ellipsis used to represent illegible sections and the holes burned through the paper. This use of punctuation textually marks the 'gaps' in the record which are impossible to ignore. In any case, this evidence is also highly subjective and biased as the two views of the same scene are coloured by the preoccupations and desires of the witnesses.

Woolf's revision of biographical form can also be seen to have a personal and political dimension. Her father, Leslie Stephen, was the first editor of the prestigious and influential *Dictionary of National Biography* which firmly established a biographical tradition that focussed primarily on male figures. In this light, Woolf's 'biography' of Orlando can be seen as a feminist parody of a male-dominated tradition as it traces the life of a woman writer over the course of several centuries noting the prejudices and hindrances she faces. In *Jacob's Room*, Jacob asks, '"Does History consist of the Biographies of Great Men?"' (*JR* 31), a question Woolf seems respond to with her 'revolutionising' of biographical form in *Orlando*. Her new form of fictional biography makes textual space for women in what would otherwise be male-dominated traditions of history and biography.

The Waves

The Waves is often seen as Woolf's most challenging novel with its highly poetic and at times abstract use of language, alongside the 'big' philosophical questions it seems to raise about human identity and the place of humanity in a random universe. It also seems to offer a complex (and contradictory) critique of the violence of imperialism. Woolf's seventh novel is also perhaps the most challenging in terms of form: she intended to create 'an entirely new kind of book' (*L4* 35) and describes it as 'prose yet poetry; a novel & a play' (*D3* 128). In her diary, she confirmed her intention to move away from novelistic conventions, 'I am not trying to tell a story' and 'I shall do away with exact place & time' (*D3* 229, 230), and more so than with any other of her works, she traced her own creative process, recording her struggles and progress with this new innovative form. The challenges that this novel presented are evident in the many drafts and reworkings Woolf undertook. The idea for the novel occurred to Woolf in 1926 as she finished *To the Lighthouse* and she wrote two complete drafts of *The Waves* in the three years in which she worked on it most intensively. Woolf's own assessment that this is 'the most complex, & difficult of all [her] books' (*D3* 298) is a view with which many of her readers agree. Its complexity has led to a wide variety of critical responses, from readings focussed on gender and empire, to those focussed on ecology and post-humanism, as well as the visual arts, music and new physics (see Jane Marcus 1992; Jane Goldman 1998; Michael Whitworth 2001; Elicia Clements 2005; Christina Alt 2010; Derek Ryan 2014).

The Waves is composed of ten italicized 'interludes' charting the diurnal movement of the sun across the sky from dawn until dusk, alternating with nine 'episodes' recording the voices of six characters (three male and three female) as they develop from childhood to middle age. Percival is a seventh character who plays a central part in the lives of the others but who has no voice in the novel and who dies young. The interludes describe changes in the natural world (and particularly the sea) over the course of a day. In contrast, the episodes are comprised of the dramatic soliloquies of the six characters and create a sense of their relationships with each other, with the final soliloquy spoken by one character, Bernard (an aspiring writer), as he attempts to sum up all of their lives. The two elements of this text are in many ways quite distinct and in tension – the natural world versus human experience, the seamless movement of the sun across the sky versus the (sometimes) dislocated sequence of speeches, the single 'body' of water (the sea) versus the individuality of the multiple characters. Yet there is a mirroring relationship and a sense of interconnection as well. For example, the sun's progress through the day is echoed in the progress of the characters through their lives, with sunrise and the start of the day finding a parallel in the start of the lives of the characters in childhood and so on. Within the episodes there is also a sense of fragmentation or disconnection – as they speak, the individuals seem to 'perform' their words as if they are lines in a drama and there is no sense of direct interaction between them as we might expect in a conversation or dialogue. Yet, like 'a mosaic' as Woolf terms it (*D3* 298), the separate 'pieces' are held together and given a coherence through the similar imagery the monologues share and through the similar memories and concerns expressed.

Woolf refers to *The Waves* as 'an abstract mystical eyeless book' (*D3* 203) and, with no single line of narrative development or obvious central focus, it might be called an anti-novel. However, Woolf also wanted to imbue her novel with life – to 'run all the scenes together...so as to make the blood run like a torrent from end to end' (*D3* 343). In the final chapter of a novel, we might expect there to be a sense of 'closure' and of narrative threads being woven together. Instead, we find a repeated reference to the *idea* of reaching an ending, of achieving completion, but such wholeness, in life or in a narrative, is just an illusion. As Bernard makes clear, 'a plain and logical story' which proceeds 'in an orderly manner' from one experience to the next is simply 'a lie' (*TW* 198, 201). Bernard begins this section by offering 'to sum up...the meaning of [his] life' (which encompasses the lives of all of the characters) and his final words acknowledge his own mortality and the end of life, 'O Death', but also refuse to conclude the life story he is telling (*TW* 187, 234).

The highly poetic qualities of this novel also raise questions about its form and genre. Confirming Woolf's vision of her novel as 'poetry', one of her friends and early readers, Goldsworthy Lowes Dickinson, wrote to her that 'Your book is a poem' (Majumdar and McLaurin 1975: 271). As she wrote drafts of her novel, Woolf read them out loud 'like poetry' (*D3* 298) and felt that she was 'writing to a rhythm and not to a plot' (*L4* 204). This rhythm is felt strongly in the novel most obviously because of the formal structure created by the recurrent 'interludes', but also because these interludes foreground the powerful presence of the sea and other natural rhythms. Woolf intended this formal innovation to be intrinsically connected to content – the interludes are 'to bridge & also give a background – the sea' (*D3* 285). In keeping with her goal of fusing poetry, drama and prose she envisaged the form of her novel as 'a gigantic conversation' (*D3* 285), 'a tremendous discussion' (*D3* 298) and finally as 'a series of dramatic soliloquies' (*D3* 312), and this too must flow rhythmically – she aimed 'to keep them [the soliloquies] running homogenously in & out, in the rhythm of the waves' (*D3* 312).

Essays

Although Woolf's experiments with fictional form were effective and brought her a good deal of success, these did not always go to quite to plan. Her ambitious idea for a new combination of novel and political essay, expressed in her plan to 'remodel[led] [her] Essay' into 'an Essay-Novel, called the Pargiters' (*D4* 129), was abandoned. The two texts growing out of this project are the relatively conventional novel called *The Years* (1937) which became a bestseller, and a long polemical essay called *Three Guineas* (1938) in which Woolf not only criticizes the drive towards war, but also draws connections between fascism and patriarchal social and cultural institutions at home.

As with the short story form, Woolf wrote a vast number of essays in a variety of styles and for different audiences but these, like her shorter fictions, have until recently been seen as subsidiary to her 'main' work – her novels. However, in her experiments with the essay form, she blurs generic boundaries to create a more hybrid mode of writing. We might expect an essay to take an enquiring approach, to focus on a specific issue or topic and to build up a logical, watertight argument with which to persuade the reader, finally reaching a clear and definite conclusion. Woolf's essays differ from this: instead of presenting an exposition and demonstrating a certain 'truth', her essays blur fact and fiction, so that gaining knowledge and understanding of the topic being discussed is inseparable from the aesthetic and imaginative experience of reading about it. The *process* of engaging with the topic and exploring possible ways of understanding it are *as* important, if not more important, than simply reaching a secure conclusion.

Three Guineas

This essay puts forward an argument for ways to prevent war from a feminist perspective based on the need for women to have equal opportunity, financial independence and liberty to participate fully in intellectual, political and professional life. It takes a challenging and radical stance in its assertion of close parallels between patriarchy and fascism as it vehemently criticizes the ways in which men's experience of education, the professions and economic aspiration, and their status as the head of the family fuels their appetite for war. Over the course of the essay, the speaker announces her intention to give three guineas to the causes she feels will help to prevent war – to a fund supporting a women's college, to a society supporting women's advancement in the professions, and to a society for the prevention of war.

Described by Woolf as an 'Anti fascist Pamphlet' (D4 282), *Three Guineas* is a highly politicized and polemical essay, meticulously researched and conforming to certain characteristics typical of the essay form. It has an academic framework and is structured into three chapters, with scholarly footnotes which expand arguments and references which support details. Each chapter focusses on a specific topic and builds towards an overarching logical argument. The first chapter argues that women's participation in the social and political world via their equal education would help to prevent war; the second argues that women's economic independence and equal access to the professions (though problematic) is necessary; and the third points out that although women are asked to support activities to preserve 'culture and intellectual liberty' (*TG* 98), they are disempowered in significant ways. It includes reference to current debates in the public domain, as reported in the newspapers, and also includes material evidence in the form of photographs of men dressed in the elaborate clothes of their official office from the realms of the military, education, law and religion.

Yet it also diverges significantly from the conventional essay form and is hybrid in its combination of historical facts and a variety of documents, including biographies, photographs, literary allusion and imaginary letters, are responded to or quoted from. Commenting on Woolf's formal strategy, Pamela L. Caughie explains that 'Woolf refuses to play the game of assertion and denial, or accusation and defense' but rather 'her essay chatters, repeats, digresses, and disperses its argument over three letters, numerous notes, and endless evidence' (1991: 118). These strategies refuse the linear organization and logic more typically used to build a persuasive argument. Woolf's argument moves forwards by looking back, by recalling earlier points, and this creates a sense of indirection at odds with generic expectations of a teleological drive and a logical line of reasoning. *Three Guineas* is, in fact, very difficult to categorize generically given its seemingly multiple functions as feminist polemic, pacifist propaganda and a political manifesto. Laura Winkiel argues that Woolf appropriates some aspects of the manifesto form as she simultaneously critiques and undermines 'the masculinity of the genre', the aggressiveness and the 'empty rhetoric' of the many manifestos in circulation at the time (2008: 198, 199). *Three Guineas*, she suggests, 'refashions the manifesto into a fluid, critical, and imaginative work in progress, one with an open-ended future that allows for unforeseen creative and critical engagement on the part of its audience' (2008: 206).

Most notably, *Three Guineas* diverges from the conventional generic form of the essay in its use of an overarching fictional frame.

The whole essay is set up as a response to a barrister who, working for a society to prevent war, has written to the narrator of Woolf's essay asking how war may be prevented. This fictional frame is extended further to also include reference to the narrator's responses to other imaginary letters received, also requesting support for worthy causes. In this way it creates a polyvocal context in which a palimpsest of voices and views can be expressed, rather than a single authoritarian voice articulating a single line of argument more typically found in politically focussed essays such as this. The essay is innovative in its use of the epistolary framework and this works as an effective rhetorical device aimed to persuade the reader to the narrator's point of view, emphasizing the importance of how ideas are received and responded to. But Woolf also extends the convention of using rhetorical strategies further: before the speaker can begin her response, she must first create an imaginary picture of her addressee since 'Without someone warm and breathing on the other side of the page, letters are worthless' (*TG* 5). This highlights the importance of dialogue and the active involvement of the listener – Woolf's essay has a powerful case to make but avoids imposing a single view and purpose, just as she veers away from the dictatorial authority in patriarchal and fascist contexts. Unlike other polemical and propagandist works, especially manifestos, *Three Guineas* adapts the essay and other generic forms to create a conversation, an ethical and human engagement with the issues so threatening to human society at the time. These formal innovations reinforce the main points of argument which stress the vital importance of communication, an understanding of difference and a willingness to work to find a common ground. These elements are both important to the new essay form Woolf devises here and to its political import.

A Room of One's Own

The discursive approach and privileging of a sense of dialogue and shared exploration of ideas also shapes the form of Woolf's polemical feminist essay, *A Room of One's Own*. As the narrator self-consciously announces at the beginning, she will not be able to reach a single conclusion about the complex topic of women and fiction, nor will she simply provide her audience with 'a nugget of

pure truth' to take away (*AROO* 5). Rather she will 'mak[e] use
of all the liberties and licences of the novelist to tell ... the story' of
how she arrived at her opinion (*AROO* 6). This essay grew out of
two lectures Woolf gave at Cambridge University in 1928 and her
essay retains a conversational quality. Instead of opening with a
clear explanation of the topic to be discussed, it begins *in medias res*
with 'But', as if interrupting a discussion already taking place before
the essay begins and introducing an alternative line of discussion.
The essay also actually begins with the narrator's conclusion on
the topic, which is that women need financial independence and a
private room if they are to write. This structural reversal means that
the reader's experience is not focussed on reaching the conclusion
but on enjoying and actively engaging in the process of exploring
the issues. Woolf's narrator adopts a playful and teasing address to
her readers and the inclusion of stories expands the scope of the
conventional essay form. Whereas the assertive stance and rhetorical
strategies typical of the conventional essay would lead the reader
to expect an authoritative exposition and an 'expert' knowledge,
the uncharacteristic formal features of Woolf's essay mean that the
reader is invited into a dialogue about the topics in question and
must work out the significance for her/himself.

A *Room of One's Own* blurs the generic boundaries between essay
and fiction by the inclusion of a fictional narrator called Mary whose
status as the voice of 'authority' on this topic is further complicated
and put into question not only by a sense of ambiguity and plurality
concerning her identity – 'call me Mary Beton, Mary Seton, Mary
Carmichael or by any name you please' (*AROO* 6) – but also by her
connection to other fictional sources since these names are drawn
from the Scottish ballad, 'The Four Marys'. Fictional sections are also
deliberately included to convey points of argument. For example,
Woolf invents a sister for Shakespeare called Judith and creates a
story which highlights her very different experiences as a talented
female dramatist. She also creates an imaginary contemporary
novelist called Mary Carmichael whose novel, *Life's Adventure*, is
described as experimental in ways that seem similar to Woolf's own
literary innovations. This approach to writing is metacritical in that
it uses fiction to comment critically on fiction.

In style, too, this essay is far from conventional. It is highly allusive
and makes reference to a wide range of other texts and writers,
for example, Shakespeare, Milton and Woolf's contemporary,

Radclyffe Hall. It also contains some striking (and unconventional) rhetorical features and sustained metaphorical sections, for example in describing the emergence of women as writers as an organic, plant-like growth and emphasizing the changes women writers need to make to the male-dominated literary tradition in terms of sartorial metaphors. There are also some apparent contradictions and inconsistencies in the arguments put forward – not least the argument about women's difference in view and experience which seems undone by the celebration of androgynous vision and creative energy in a later section. These elements, coupled with a sometimes teasing, sometimes satirical and ironical approach, means that, as with Woolf's fiction, we must read carefully and 'between the lines', not taking every statement at face value. As is discussed in more detail in Chapter Five, these experiments with form and the feminist perspective offered are interconnected, and Woolf's formal innovations here, as elsewhere, can be seen as politically motivated.

CHAPTER THREE

Narrative Technique

Woolf's use of certain narrative techniques is inextricably bound up
with other aspects of her writing, such as form and characterization,
as well as with political concerns and with the more profound
philosophical issues Woolf pondered in all of her work, such as
the nature of our subjective perception and experience of ourselves,
others and 'reality'. This basis in subjective experience and
perspective means that there is no one version of events, no single
truth and no one reality to which we all have access in the same
way. Many of the techniques she uses are not new and innovative
in and of themselves, but Woolf employs them in new ways to
achieve the aim she outlines in 'Modern Fiction' and 'Mr Bennett
and Mrs Brown', namely to represent the experience of modern life
in all its complexity, multiplicity and discontinuity as it is felt and
perceived by her characters from within. Her writing explores ways
of representing human consciousness in words and images to try
to convey its multiple states and infinitesimal shifts and changes.
The ways in which she uses and develops narrative techniques can
be seen to be influenced by the philosophical, psychological and
scientific ideas of her time, such as those put forward by William
James, Henri Bergson, Sigmund Freud, Ernest Rutherford and
Albert Einstein. Her techniques were also inspired by the energizing
artistic experiments taking place in music, the visual arts, ballet and
cinema.

The key techniques to be considered here are free indirect
discourse, allusion, metaphorical patterning, verbal networks,
repetition, associative uses of language and attenuated sentence

structures. These will be explored in relation to *Jacob's Room* (1922), *Mrs Dalloway* (1925) and *Between the Acts* (1941).

Narrators and narration

One of the most striking things about reading Woolf is the way in which she uses the narrative voice. As is typical in many realist narratives, Woolf employs an external third person narrator that exists separately from the lives of the characters, however, her narrators contrast sharply with the omniscient and authoritative narrator found in much realist fiction. As we see with *Orlando* and *Jacob's Room*, Woolf's narrators refuse the omniscient authority we might expect given the generic conventions these novels (in part) adopt (see Chapter Two). It is assumed that a biographer-narrator would be an authority on every aspect of the subject's life and yet Orlando's biographer cannot tell us all and confesses to gaps in his biographical account. The narrator of a *Bildungsroman* typically conveys insights into every aspect of the protagonist's character and development, yet the narrator of *Jacob's Room* puts herself at a distance – she insists on not knowing everything about Jacob due to her difference in age and gender (she explains that she is an older woman, *JR* 81). Similarly, her view from outside the men's college (from which she is presumably denied access as a woman) is only partial and full of supposition and speculation. This adoption of conventional narrative forms accompanied by a radical departure from typical narrative techniques associated with them works to emphasize Woolf's experimental approach. What is also very apparent in most of Woolf's writing is what we might call the 'slipperiness' of the narrative voice as it moves between different points of view. In contrast to the clear division between the omniscient narrator and characters found in realist fiction, the process of narration in Woolf's fiction is *shared* with the characters to create a fluid and shifting form. Characters' different perspectives and perceptions are interwoven into the third person narrative and the narrative is often focalized through different characters. This 'immersion' into a character's consciousness often begins immediately as we are plunged into the characters' lives, their actions, thoughts and feelings from the opening lines.

Jacob's Room

This is the case in the opening of *Jacob's Room* where the reader is plunged *in medias res* into the narrative, in fact into a letter, via the particular perspective of one of the characters, Betty Flanders. At the beginning of Woolf's first experimental novel, she makes it obvious that she will employ a third person narrative technique differently, so as to capture the character's immediate experience at times unmediated by an external voice. The view that Betty sees is described by the third person narrator but the perspective is Betty's, a point made obvious by the effect that her tear-filled eyes have on how the bay is perceived: 'The entire bay quivered; the lighthouse wobbled; and she had the illusion that the mast of Mr. Connor's little yacht was bending like a wax candle in the sun.' She blinks away her tears and 'The mast was straight; the waves were regular; the lighthouse was upright' (*JR* 3). That she is also writing a letter recounting her recent experience draws attention to the process of narrating personal experience and telling the story of someone's life. That Betty's tears also make the full-stop she has put on the page blot and dissolve also hints at the fluidity of narration since, as we read her letter with her, '"… nothing for it but to leave," she read', her full-stop has transformed into a comma (*JR* 3). This change in punctuation suggests not only that Betty's story and upset are on going, but also indicates the shared nature of narration. Here we see how Betty's emotional state is conveyed in and actually shapes the sentence structure itself and we become aware of the ways in which Woolf's subtle narrative techniques can affect the way we read this novel.

However, this 'scene' of Betty and her children on the beach is also being observed and represented through the eyes of the artist, Charles Steele. He has incorporated a representation of Betty into his picture because she is part of the scene he sees before him, but Woolf makes clear that this is not an objective view. As with Betty's subjective experience of external reality, Charles Steele's perception is shaped by his internal concerns and preoccupations. He considers how his work will be judged by others and represents Betty's black clothes (she is a widow) with 'a hasty violet-black dab' which will counter the critics's view of his work as being 'too pale' (*JR* 4). His artistic concerns also have a bearing on *how* he sees and represents *what* he sees: the 'effect' of the black is pleasing because it 'brought the rest together' (*JR* 4). At the beginning of this novel, then, we are made very aware of the importance of subjective experience and the ways in which emotions, one's frame of mind and personal preoccupations have an impact on perception and, importantly, on the representation of 'reality'.

Free indirect discourse

The narrative technique that Woolf employs in this novel and in much of her fiction is called 'free indirect discourse'. This is a narrative technique that moves between the voice of the third person narrator and the thoughts, feelings and perceptions (the consciousness) of the characters, shifting from exterior to interior so as to narrate the characters' views of others and themselves. It combines and intertwines an external narrative voice with the subjective experience of the characters so that the characters' perceptions, responses and concerns supplement, complement and, sometimes, replace the voice of the narrator. As Gerald Prince defines it,

> Free indirect discourse...is usually taken to contain mixed within it markers of two discourse events (a narrator's and a character's), two styles, two languages, two voices, two semantic...systems...[it] is sometimes extended to include discourse representing a character's nonverbalized perceptions as they occur in his or her consciousness. (1987: 35)

With this technique, the external narrator is not a source of authority or control but has more of an orchestrating function.

The movement in and out of the character's point of view and consciousness is sometimes obvious but is often quite subtle and we need to be alert to the indicators that mark the transition. These can include a shift in the style or tone of speech or thought that we associate with a particular character, incorporating their individual way of expressing things or their idiomatic uses of words or phrases. It can be indicated by the inclusion of sections of text that read like direct or reported speech but without the punctuation marks to distinguish these from the main narrative or to overtly attribute them to a character. It can also be detected by the way a character's emotions influence the way the narrative is written. This gives the narrative a sense of fluidity as it shifts between external narration and different centres of consciousness. The thoughts and perceptions of the characters are also often represented as free flowing or disjointed, moving between different, seemingly unconnected ideas. This has sometimes led to Woolf's narrative technique being defined as 'stream of consciousness', a metaphorical term deriving from the philosophical and psychological work of William James (brother of novelist, Henry James). He used this phrase to describe his conception of thought, consciousness and subjective life as continuous and flowing like a river rather than as being like segments connected together. As Stephen Kern explains, 'Each mental event is linked with those before and after, near and remote, which act like a surrounding "halo" or "fringe"' and our 'mental life' proceeds at an irregular pace (2003: 24).

Stream of consciousness

While this fluid sense of cognition, emotion and perception does capture some of what Woolf aspired to create in terms of her representation of subjective experience, the narrative technique Woolf employs differs from the literary technique of 'stream of consciousness'. Woolf's technique incorporates what is going on in her characters' consciousness (the thoughts, memories and feelings that they are able to consciously access) through the presence of a third person narrator. In contrast, the 'stream of consciousness' mode can incorporate different levels of a character's awareness (consciousness *and* unconscious) and this is narrated entirely without external commentary or mediation through a narrator. Novelist and critic, May Sinclair, is said to be the first to use the term 'stream of consciousness' in relation to literature in her review of Dorothy Richardson's experimental, multi-volume novel, *Pilgrimage* in *The Egoist*, April 1918. Her description of Richardson's narrative indicates how Woolf's narrative technique differs from stream of consciousness. Sinclair notes that only what is immediately present or passing through the character Miriam's mind (as in interior monologue) is included in Richardson's narrative: 'In this series there is no drama, no situation, no set scene. Nothing happens. It is just life going on and on. It is Miriam Henderson's stream of consciousness going on and on. And in neither is there any grossly discernable beginning or middle or end' (in Scott 1990: 444).

While Woolf's fictions also tend to begin *in medias res* and resist closure, her use of third person narration gives shape to the flow of thoughts and emotions. Woolf admired Richardson's creation of a form of narration and narrative style that captured the female point of view (see below), but she and other writers, such as Katherine Mansfield, criticized this technique because it produced what they saw as an abstract, egotistical, superficial sense of character. Richardson represents Miriam's immediate sensations, impressions and responses but Woolf found this excessive reference to the interior life in Richardson (and in Joyce) to be damaging to their literary experiment. In her diary, she refers to the 'the damned egotistical self' she perceives as dominating their narratives which has the effect of 'narrowing & restricting' (*D2* 14) (see Chapter One). In contrast, Woolf's use of free indirect discourse enables her to evoke the subjective experience of her characters and to create a shifting and mobile point of view, while simultaneously providing a narrative 'scaffolding' in the form of an external narrator that remains consistent. In anchoring the narrative in this way, she can open up textual spaces in which different (and sometimes contradictory) understandings of reality can be articulated and multi-layered conceptions of the self can be given expression. In *To the Lighthouse*, the artist Lily Briscoe describes the intention behind her modernist experiments with painting in a way that resonates with Woolf's own narrative technique: 'Beautiful and bright it should be on the surface, feathery and evanescent, one colour melting into another like the colours on a butterfly's wing; but beneath the fabric must be clamped together with bolts of iron' (*TTL* 163).

This effect is also made possible by other aspects of Woolf's narrative technique that provide a sense of shape, pattern and coherence as they simultaneously open up a variety of possible connections, associations and a fluidity of meaning. These techniques and devices include repetition, allusion, metaphorical patterns, parallel scenes and temporal markers. They encourage readers to be active participants (as 'accomplices') as we make associative connections, relying on our memory of narrative elements, earlier scenes or image patterns to create links within the narrative. She also uses language to evoke metaphorical, suggestive and symbolic meanings: words in Woolf's writing do not simply denote meaning but work metaphorically and figuratively to connote multiple possibilities for meaning. As she claims in her essay, 'Craftsmanship' (first broadcast on BBC radio in April 1937), 'it is the nature of words to mean many things' so that to reduce the making of meaning to a system such as a monetary system – 'to the size of a six penny bit' – where value can be easily calculated or accounted for is inadequate (*E6* 94, 93). We soon become aware as we read Woolf that, for her, language is not a reliable 'currency' with which to try to accurately or definitively 'transact' meaning: words have many values and meanings of words alter in different contexts. That Woolf's texts are rich in intertextual reference and allusion to other literary works and philosophical ideas (especially Shakespeare, Milton, the Romantic poets, Ancient Greek philosophers and dramatists, Plato, Virgil and Catallus) enhances this fluidity of meaning, unlocking associations and evocations of feeling and imagination for those who recognize the various points of reference.

Looking at *Mrs Dalloway*, we can see how Woolf puts these various narrative techniques and approaches to language into effect. This novel is concerned with time and the impact of the past on the present, including the traumatic legacy of the First World War. It is also concerned with the nature of psychological processes, including ideas of sanity and insanity. Adopting a fluid narrative technique and foregrounding metaphorical connections and associative uses of language enables Woolf to vary the pace of her narrative so as to articulate these complex issues effectively and to stress the importance of bonds between characters.

Mrs Dalloway

Mrs Dalloway said she would buy the flowers herself.

For Lucy had her work cut out for her. The doors would be taken off their hinges; Rumplemayer's men were coming. And then, thought Clarissa Dalloway, what a morning – fresh as if issued to children on a beach. (*MD 5*)

As with *Jacob's Room*, we are immediately plunged into the life of a character – this time the central protagonist Clarissa Dalloway – on one particular day in June 1923, when she is to host a party to be attended by the Prime Minister. Although not foregrounded as we might find in a realist novel, its setting in time and place is made apparent incrementally. In fact, the geographical and temporal context for this narrative corresponds to material reality. Using reference to real details, critics have mapped Clarissa's and other characters' walks around the London streets and have pin-pointed the actual date in June from information mentioned in the novel. But still, the reader is presented with a perplexing beginning as the opening pages shift fluidly between narrator's voice and the thoughts, feelings and opinions of the characters, notably Clarissa but also her neighbour, Scrope Purvis, who offers his view of her in passing. The novel begins with a statement reporting Mrs Dalloway's decision that 'she would buy the flowers herself' – though whether this is the narrator's voice or that of Lucy (Clarissa's servant) we cannot be sure. The naming of Clarissa as 'Mrs Dalloway' could indicate that this is Lucy's report given her deferential relationship to her employer. The narrative then immediately slips into what *seems* to be Clarissa's immediate thought, 'For Lucy had her work cut out for her' (*MD* 5), the familiar use of the servant's name and the colloquial phrase, 'her work cut out for her' seeming to suggest this is Clarissa's thought. However, it is not until we are informed in the following sentence that we are being told what Clarissa 'thought' and that this is a continuation of what has gone before, 'And then', that we can be certain of this transition to Clarissa's consciousness.

The slipperiness of the free indirect discourse technique continues as Clarissa's thoughts briefly displace the narrator's voice with her idiomatic phrases, 'What a lark! What a plunge!', and her emotions inflect the language of the narrative, energizing it as Clarissa recalls her eighteen-year old self (she is in her early fifties in the present time of the novel), invigorated by the sensory pleasures of the early morning at her home in Bourton: 'she had *burst* open the French windows and *plunged* at Bourton into the open air', the 'air…like the *flap* of a wave; the *kiss* of a wave' (my emphasis, *MD* 5). This description of Clarissa's memories is related by the external narrator, but the feeling of immersion into this experience is created by the intertwining of Clarissa's sensations, perceptions and experience into the narrative. It also includes words and phrases that Clarissa might use and these work as linguistic markers distinguishing the narrator's voice from that of Clarissa. In the description of the air at Bourton, for example – 'How fresh, how calm, stiller than this of course' – the 'of course' seems to be Clarissa's phrase based as this assertion is on *her* intimate and bodily experience of this sensation and her ability to compare this experience at Bourton with that of London in her present moment. It is also Clarissa's words and thoughts that return the focus to Clarissa's present moment as her questions concerning her memory of things that Peter has said in the past are incorporated into the narrative: 'was that it?', she asks, and reflects that '[h]e would be back from India one of these days, June or July, she forgot which, for his letters were awfully dull' (*MD* 5). The class-specific, idiomatic phrase 'awfully dull' indicates that these words belong to Clarissa. This flitting between Clarissa's different thoughts and sensory memory produces a fragmented narrative, a stream of thought and evokes an emotional response.

Time, mobile and spatialized

The linguistic markers distinguishing the voices of the narrator and Clarissa here are also temporal markers and we see that the mobile point of view is complicated by the shifting between past and present. This sense of time as fluid is sharply contrasted with the more overt and deliberate marking of time in the novel with the striking of Big Ben and other clocks. This reference to clock time serves as a reminder of the passing of this particular day and creates a narrative patterning that connects the disparate actions of the different groups of characters and moves the narrative on. These conceptions of time can be seen to coincide with Bergson's ideas about the duality of our experience at the levels of intellect and intuition and the way our experience of time registers this, distinguishing an awareness of clock time (which he calls *temps*) and psychological time (*durée*) (see Introduction). This interweaving of past and present is not only crucial to our understanding of Clarissa as a character, but also reminds us of the subtlety and complexity of this multivalent narrative technique. Looking again at the opening of the novel we can see that the shift in temporal direction – from moving forward in time as preparations for the party continue to a shift back to the time of Clarissa's youth – is entirely determined by Clarrisa's inner life. The sound of the hinges as the doors are removed prompts her involuntary memory of the sound of hinges at her family home (what we might call a Proustian moment, see Chapter

Four) and her past experience in the countryside overlays and shapes her experience of the city in her present moment. Woolf described her experiments with the representation of time in this novel as her 'tunnelling process, by which [she] tell[s] the past by instalments, as [she has] need of it' (D2 272), explaining that she excavates what is needed from her characters' pasts and brings this to light in the present: 'I dig out beautiful caves behind my characters…the caves shall connect, & each comes to daylight at the present moment' (D2 263). The fluidity of her narrative technique allows these pockets of memory and moments of intense sensation and self-awareness (what Woolf called 'moments of being') to be interwoven into the narrative. This draws attention to the significance of subjective experience as it is shaped by the interconnections of past and present.

As the novel progresses, the narrative quickly shifts to the consciousness of Scrope Purvis, a minor character who does not reappear but whose presence reveals much about the subtlety of Woolf's narrative technique. His impression of Clarissa as '[a] charming woman' may seem to be class-marked, clichéd and superficial, and his description of Clarissa as having 'a touch of the bird about her, of the jay, blue-green, light, vivacious' (MD 6) may seem simply a conventional way to describe a woman (conforming to a long literary tradition of drawing analogies between women and birds). However, this seemingly trivial moment at the beginning of the novel repays further attention, not only for what it adds to our sense of Clarissa as a character, but also because it sets in motion some key aspects of Woolf's narrative technique. These include the creation of a 'verbal network' whereby repetition of phrases and figurative description, allusion associated with specific characters and moods, and parallel scenes or events work to create a sense of metaphorical connection between characters, experiences and times. Accompanied by Woolf's careful manipulation of time in the novel, this network effectively creates the sense of a simultaneity of experience which serves to suggest unexpected connections and associations between characters, as it also makes clear the subjectivity of all experience.

A verbal network

Scrope Purvis's description of Clarissa as a bird introduces one of the important metaphorical threads of connection between Clarissa,

Septimus Smith and his wife, Rezia. Septimus is a psychologically traumatized war veteran whom Clarissa never meets, yet Woolf's experiments with narrative technique create verbal, metaphorical connections between these two very different characters so that Septimus functions as Clarissa's 'double' (a strategy, Woolf explains in her introduction to her novel, E4 549). Bird imagery echoes throughout the narrative, evoking a sense of the vulnerability, anxiety and fear that these characters experience. As she and Septimus await their appointment with the powerful nerve specialist, Sir William Bradshaw, Rezia is likened to a vulnerable bird: 'She was like a bird sheltering under the thin hollow of a leaf' (*MD* 73). Later, hearing of Septimus's death at her party, Clarissa feels similarly exposed and at risk, 'she could crouch like a bird' (*MD* 204) in the shelter of her marriage to Richard. Even just a few pages after Scrope Purvis's positive association of Clarissa and birds, Clarissa considers her inadequacies in terms of what she sees as her 'ridiculous little face, beaked like a bird's' (*MD* 13). Septimus is similarly described as 'pale-faced, beak-nosed' (*MD* 17) and, Rezia also has pointed features. But bird imagery also evokes a sense of pleasure and peace. In the moments of happiness before Septimus's death, Rezia recalls her sense of him as 'a young hawk' and Septimus likens Rezia to a bird at times of joy, as he watches her creatively dressing a hat for Mrs Peters. Even in his state of mental disturbance, 'the voices of birds' herald a turn towards life and away from horror (*MD* 77). For Clarissa, the blowing out of her curtain decorated 'with its flight of birds of Paradise' signals the success of her party which brings relief and pleasure (*MD* 188).

Parallel scenes

Throughout the novel there emerges a more complex and richly metaphorical pattern involving allusion to Shakespeare's play, *Cymbeline*, and to waves and barking dogs. This has a strong associative effect and works to connect Clarissa and Septimus. The creation of parallel scenes involving these elements, as well as reference to sewing as a means of repair and creation, powerfully connects Clarissa and Septimus. One scene describes Clarissa in a moment of tranquillity sitting on her sofa repairing her dress in preparation for her party, the motion of her needle like the motion of waves. Her recalling of lines from *Cymbeline*, 'Fear no more, says the heart', is woven into the narrative, and she hears sounds of a 'dog barking, far away barking and barking' (*MD* 45) before she is interrupted by Peter's unexpected visit. Later Septimus is also described as sitting on a sofa in a state of calm as Rezia sews the decorations for a hat. He imagines 'the sound of water...in the room, and through the waves came the voices of birds singing...while far away...he heard dogs barking and barking far away' (*MD* 154). The allusion to *Cymbeline* 'Fear no more, says the heart in the body; fear no more' (*MD* 154) seems also to be his thought. These two scenes echo one another in terms of imagery and allusion, though they differ crucially in outcome: Peter's interruption leads to his invitation to Clarissa's party, whereas Dr Holmes's intrusion on Septimus's moment of peace causes Septimus to kill himself. The final iteration of 'Fear no more the heat of the sun' comes as Clarissa reflects on her response to the news of Septimus's death – 'She felt somehow very like him' (*MD* 206).

Critics have speculated on the different ways in which Clarissa can be seen to be 'like' Septimus and one strong thread of connection is the distress they both experience, one source of which seems to be their repression of their culturally taboo homoerotic desires. Clarissa still recalls Sally Seton's kiss as 'the most exquisite moment of her whole life' (*MD* 40) more than thirty years afterwards and experiences this as a loss bound up with her decision to conform to social norms in her marriage to Richard. Septimus, on the other hand, suffers profound grief at the loss of his fellow officer, Evans, killed in the war. His shell-shock or post-traumatic stress disorder is inseparable from the loss of this love and central relationship. He and Evans 'had to be together', their relationship is likened to 'two dogs playing on a hearthrug', but when Evans is killed, Septimus is emotionally numbed and is terrified to realize that 'he could not feel' (*MD* 96). Both Clarissa and Septimus experience loss and it would seem that their accompanying grief provokes different degrees of mental instability. Septimus's 'madness' is foregrounded in the novel through the specialist medical treatment he receives and though his nightmarish visions and thoughts. Less obvious is the way that, at times, Clarissa's thoughts and words are equally 'deranged'. Without obvious reason, she is suspicious and fearful of Sir William Bradshaw, even though he is a guest at her party, and her feelings about Doris Kilman, her daughter's tutor, are extreme, irrational and disturbed. Her feelings for Doris are entirely ambivalent – she loves and hates her, pities and resents her – and she describes her hatred as monstrous and as a physical pain – 'this brutal monster!' which 'had power to make her feel scraped, hurt in her spine' and destroyed all her everyday 'pleasure[s]' (*MD* 15). In this and other ways, the novel suggests that psychological processes are complex, fluid and shifting but also that the line between sanity and insanity is sometimes quite precarious. As Woolf says of her plans for her novel, 'I adumbrate here a study of insanity & suicide: the world seen by the sane & the insane side by side' (*D2* 207).

Woolf's narrative method suggestively connects these two contrasting characters at a deep level, regardless of the 'real' social distance between them, and also makes apparent Woolf's philosophy of self and identity. She considers that, although we are individuals and have a sense of our identity as separate from others, we are also in many ways part of one another. Our lives are enmeshed with others since our sense of ourselves is shaped by the views, perceptions and responses of those around us. Woolf's techniques create a sense of narrative fluidity allowing for an ease of movement between characters' consciousnesses and producing the effect of multiple focalization. This technique also reveals that different as we may appear to be in our 'public' selves, there is 'the unseen part of us, which spreads wide', connecting us to others and to certain places, even after death (*MD* 169). Clarissa has 'Odd affinities... with people she had never spoken to... even trees, or barns' and feels herself to be somehow part of others like a 'mist' and, as noted above, 'very like' Septimus though markedly different in class, gender and experience (*MD* 169, 12). As Woolf explained, 'Septimus and Mrs Dalloway should be entirely dependent upon each other' (*L3* 189), a point that raises aesthetic and philosophical questions, as well as political issues about class and war.

Simultaneity

The moment in which Scrope Purvis sees Clarissa is the first of many moments in the novel where Woolf attempts to create a sense of the simultaneity of experience. In the brief period of time in which Scrope Purvis observes Clarissa waiting to cross the street and contemplates his vision of her, she is seemingly already on the move, 'crossing Victoria Street' and, in contrast to the way he perceives her stillness and solemnity, she is enthusiastically contemplating her love of life in London (*MD* 6). Woolf's narrative technique in producing this sense of a simultaneity of experience enables her to fluidly shift the focus of the narrative and to change the narrative direction, as it also creates connections between characters who share experience.

The shifts in narrative focus and the disrupted chronology give the novel an episodic feel, but the potential sense of fragmentation this might produce is countered by the insistence on connection produced by the shared experience of the characters. They coexist in the same city and their paths cross and crisscross although they never actually meet. Many experience the same events – the car tyre bursting and the aeroplane advertising toffee. The striking of Big Ben and other clocks throughout the novel is a repeated reminder of the diurnal passage of time as measured by mechanical means and this repeated temporal marker provides an aspect of patterning, helping to create an impression of simultaneity as we see what the different characters are doing at the same points in the day. Combined with Woolf's fluid narrative technique and the creation of a verbal network of images that connect characters, the simultaneity of experience works to create a sense of the complexity and mobility of modern life. It emphases unexpected points of connection, as well as differences in perception and different responses to the experience of modernity.

One of these central shared experiences is the sight of the official car halted by a burst tyre outside the florists where Clarissa buys her flowers, an event drawing the attention of a large range of characters in the street and, once the car moves off towards Buckingham Palace, the crowds of poor people waiting there. The car prompts widespread speculation about who might be inside. The vast majority of characters feel the enthralling effect of 'greatness...passing' and respond bodily by standing, 'even straighter' and 'very upright', these repeated phrases signalling a sense of loyalty to the crown and respect for authority (*MD* 21, 23). However, the free indirect narrative technique employed ensures that there is no single, authoritative view presented, but rather a number of contrasting opinions. The narrative incorporates the questions the public typically ask, as well as the conflicting views of what kind of 'greatness' is inside, and even the 'tut-tut' (*MD* 23) of the disapproval Mr Bowley feels about the war. It is at this point that Septimus is introduced into the narrative, his presence signaling a more severe criticism of the war.

Like 'Everyone', Septimus and Clarissa 'looked at the motor car' (*MD* 18) and at this point, the narrative shifts focus towards Septimus. His thoughts and verbal responses are woven into the narration and are mostly indicated as belonging to him by phrases such as, 'Septimus thought' and 'he thought'. However what constitutes his 'thought' is not rational or thoughtful but is rather a visceral, irrational 'horror' that 'had almost come to the surface and was about to burst into flames' and which 'terrified him' (*MD* 18). His sensation of heat produced by his nightmarish perception of the scene seems also to infiltrate the third person narrative in the odd (irrational) causal link between the sun and the car: 'The sun became extraordinarily hot because the motor car had stopped outside Mulberry's shop window' (*MD* 17). Again we see the subtlety of Woolf's free indirect narrative technique whereby not only the thoughts, words and emotions of the characters inflect the third person narrative, but also their mental states and psychosomatic experience. Septimus's extreme response is displaced by his wife Rezia's contrasting self-consciousness about his odd behaviour, 'People must notice; people must see', thus shifting the narrative focus back to more rational ground (*MD* 18).

Here it seems that Woolf's narrative technique has an important political function which is to undermine the systems of authority the novel overtly represents, many of which we see here: the state and monarchy, empire, religion, class, money and the power this confers. Her use of free indirect discourse interweaves and gives equal weight to a variety of ordinary characters who assume the role of 'authorities' on this display of power and the systems it represents. This shared experience is followed immediately by the aeroplane display which displaces attention from the car and ideas of established greatness towards one of the new experiences of modernity and commodity culture. Although for some the plane is associated with the dangers experienced during wartime, here it is performing an advertizing function, though what is being inscribed in the air is open to debate. At one point the plane seems to write 'a K, and E, a Y perhaps?' (*MD* 24) and Woolf's narrative technique here at once offers a tantalizing (single, authoritative) 'key' to understanding, even as it puts that very notion of certainty into question with the use of a characteristically Woolfian word, 'perhaps'. The 'readers' of the sky writing cannot agree and even as they work to make sense of it, the words vanish into air, so that speculative interpretations are given space and the ambiguity of meaning keeps possibilities in play.

The language of narrative

This moment in the novel eloquently highlights another central feature of Woolf's narrative technique which is her use of language, not simply as a referential tool for communication, but as an artistic medium for evoking different and sometimes contradictory meanings. Likening the aeroplane's movement (it moves 'swiftly, freely') to that of 'a skater ... or a dancer' enhances the sense of its fluidity and poise and simultaneously refuses to pin down a specific meaning (*MD* 24). Woolf's narrative method suggests other artistic influences on her writing, such as the Russian Ballet and the newly developing technology of cinema. Cinema also uses new methods for creating narrative – camera movements (such as panning and close up) and techniques such as cutting and montage – and we can see how Woolf adopts and adapts these techniques for her own literary innovation. The speed and scope of the plane's movement seems to represent in literary form the continuous movement of a camera panning quickly over a landscape. In her essay, 'The Cinema', published shortly after *Mrs Dalloway* in 1926, Woolf anticipates cinema's capabilities: 'The most fantastic contrasts could be flashed before us with a speed which the writer can only toil after in vain' (*E4* 352). Her narration of the plane's rapid and fluid shift in location seems to suggest how she has realized this effect in her novel. In one extended sentence, the plane moves from Regent's Park, shoots out from central London to the 'fields spread out and dark brown woods' beyond the city, a movement that offers a rapidly changing the perspective, shifting from an aerial view to that of 'adventurous thrushes' on the wood floor smashing snails against a rock (*MD* 32). Her essay also recognizes the capacity cinema has for representing unconscious thought, unacknowledged and ambiguous emotions and psychic processes without recourse to the usual literary techniques: 'the cinema has within its grasp innumerable symbols for emotions that have so far failed to find expression' (*E4* 350). Woolf recognizes the ways in which new visual technologies impact on how people see and know the world, providing a new vocabulary with which to reconfigure reality and experience. The viewer's apprehension of 'reality' is complicated by cinematic 'reality': the images on the screen are 'real [but] with a different reality from that which we perceive in daily life'; they do not physically (materially) involve the viewer and the events represented happened in the past (*E4* 349). 'Reality' is revealed to be a complex negotiation of the past in the present, presence and absence, distance and a feeling of immersion in experience – all of which Woolf's narrative techniques strive to represent as she explores the multiple states of consciousness.

Sentences, feminine and otherwise

Woolf's creation of a continuous, fluid movement shifting seamlessly between places, characters and different centres of consciousness is achieved through her narrative technique at the level of the sentence. She often aligned her writing with music and uses musical terms to describe her literary 'compositions'. Critics have detected musical influences and have drawn musical analogies to describe her creation of a polyphonic literary texture and the effects on the process of reading. The length of Woolf's sentences varies but what is most distinctive is her construction of long sentences composed of phrases and clauses that can extend for a page or more held together by semi-colons. This syntactical framework creates a flexibility and an openness, so that sentences seem porous and able to encompass the unchecked flow of thought, emotion and impression so central to Woolf's engagement with character and event. The composition of such sentences creates a palimpsestic effect, as phrases extend and qualify units of meaning but also create a sense of layering and simultaneity. Sentences expand to encompass multiple thoughts, feelings, perspectives and emotions happening simultaneously. Just as she departed from narrative linearity in relation to the overall structures of her novels, so Woolf also deliberately rejected what she described as 'a formal railway line of sentence', with thoughts and ideas moving in a linear fashion, as unrealistic: 'people don't ... feel or think or dream for a second in that way' (*L3* 135, 136). Instead, Woolf's sentence structures open up to create the impression of multiple, simultaneous lines of thought, feeling and voice. The opening of *Mrs Dalloway* demonstrates this fluidity of sentence composition where Clarissa's involuntary sensory memory and the shift back to her present moment are conveyed in a long sentence, layered with clauses and held loosely together with a series of commas, semi-colons, dashes, question marks and parentheses.

Woolf's use of contrasting sentence structures also at times helps to indicate a sense of public and private self, the self presented to the world and the more nebulous self-in-process. We see this as Woolf narrates Clarissa's sense of her dual self as she gazes into her mirror and contemplates the demands and expectations of her public role as Mrs Richard Dalloway which are in stark contrast with her inner sense of the more uncertain, unfocussed and fragmented aspects of self. The metaphor of herself as a diamond is appropriate for conveying both a sense of her public self as 'one centre' from which radiates what others need from her, as well as the multifaceted sense she has of herself, the 'different ... incompatible' parts of her identity which she struggles to assemble (*MD* 42). The sentences describing her public persona, 'pointed; dart-like; definite' and concerning her dress (her outward appearance as Mrs Dalloway), are short and compact (*MD* 42), whereas those describing her inner life are long, fluid, encompassing ideas of the self as plural, layered and indefinite so that the sentence structure itself expands to include the stream of her thoughts, doubts and questions. Although Woolf uses this fluid sentence structure in relation to male characters as well, it is far more frequently associated with her female characters as Woolf explores the deep-seated tensions women experience: the social compulsion to conform to gender norms and accommodate the needs of others, alongside a sense of the self as disparate and contradictory and with ambitions at odds with the circumscribed roles conventionally available for women in a patriarchal society. There are many other instances of this technique (for example, Mrs Ramsay's reverie about her life and identity in *To the Lighthouse*, see Chapter Five).

In her 1923 review of *Revolving Lights*, Woolf praised Richardson's invention of what Woolf termed 'the psychological sentence of the feminine gender', a sentence structure 'of a more elastic fibre than the old, capable of stretching to the extreme, of suspending the frailest particles, of enveloping the vaguest shapes' (*E3* 367). Woolf criticized what she saw as the severely limited subject matter of Richardson's writing, namely its exclusive preoccupation with the self. However, her description of Richardson's style and creation of 'a woman's sentence' used to explore 'a woman's mind' by a writer unafraid of 'the psychology of her sex' could equally apply to the sentence constructions Woolf employs (*E3* 367). As Anna Snaith states, 'no form [of writing] is implicitly feminist: innovation can only be feminist within a specific historical and literary context' (2000: 4). Woolf deliberately sets her own more fluid sentence structures at odds with the 'man's sentence' (*AROO* 73) that dominates the literary tradition, so that the techniques she uses to create her more fluid style can be read as part of her feminist stance (see Chapter Five). She shapes her own extended sentences by employing unusual syntax, ellipses and punctuation so as to break with conventions ingrained in a male-dominated literary tradition and to undermine assumed hierarchies of value that we might term 'masculine', such as the privileging of the narrator's voice over that of the characters.

Between the Acts

Woolf's last novel was published posthumously and offers further insight into her narrative technique as it seems to magnify and make apparent certain aspects that were more subtly employed in her earlier novels. This includes use of free indirect discourse, allusion, self-conscious attention to language and image, the 'framing' of points of view and insights into the inner lives of characters. In her diary, she planned that this novel would somehow combine aspects of two very different novels, the more conventional *Night and Day* and her highly experimental novel, *The Waves* (*D4* 151–2). Woolf was writing this novel just as Britain entered the war with Nazi Germany and it is set in June 1939, just weeks before the outbreak of war. It revolves around the staging of an annual village pageant which presents a satirical retelling of the history of England in highly stylized playlets. These indirectly refer to the coming war as they lay bare the belligerence deeply embedded in the British and European psyche. The novel includes real factual details that her contemporary readers would have recognized (such as newspaper reports, reference to the decisions of the French Prime Minister and gossip about royalty). As a pacifist Woolf felt increasingly politically isolated from friends and family in this period, but she was also extremely anxious about her writing and indeed about the ability of art and literature in general to survive in the face of the powerful discourses of war and fascism. Woolf's narrative technique seems to resonate with what for her was a concern to preserve a record of English literary and cultural history. In this novel, we see what is possibly Woolf's most complex and intense use of allusion with (often fragmented) references ranging widely from the English literary tradition, to ancient Greek drama, Shakespeare, popular culture, music hall tunes, nursery rhymes, geological history and the sounds of nature, all of which seems aimed to demonstrate the fecundity and diversity of the literary art form. This technique also self-consciously draws attention to language itself, to words and images, in a way that is marked and insistent.

In 'Craftsmanship', Woolf states, 'Words, English words, are full of echoes, of memories, of associations – naturally. They have been out and about, on people's lips, in their houses, in the streets, in the fields, for so many centuries' (*E6* 95) and this multivalency is made evident in the sometimes excessive play on and with words in *Between the Acts*. It is evident in the figurative uses of language, the inclusion of cliché, puns and repetition and in the play with the auditory qualities of language, such as rhyme, alliteration, assonance and onomatopoeia, often to startling or comic effect. For example, as the audience impatiently await the final part of the play about 'Ourselves' they comment with irritation on the change in music: 'What a cackle, a cacophony! Nothing ended. So abrupt. And corrupt. Such an outrage; such an insult. And not plain. Very up to date, all the same. What is her game? To disrupt? Jog and trot? Jerk and smirk? Put the finger to the nose? Squint and pry? Peek and spy?' (*BTA* 109). Here the banal rhyme and wordplay create a sing-song effect and the rhetorical questions set many ideas in motion. The self-conscious use of sentence structures also draws attention to the writing itself creating a sense of tension between meaning and syntax. The sentence 'Nothing ended' is contradicted by the shortness of the sentence itself, and the next sentence seems to comically confirm this: 'So abrupt' (*BTA* 109).

Woolf also draws words from a wide repertoire of discourses: historical, evolutionary, political, mythic, commercial and monetary, as well as from discourses associated with nature, war and violence. The narrative technique could be described as polyphonic as disparate words butt up against one another with comic effect, seeming to jostle with each other, just as the different voices of the characters are juxtaposed and sometimes clashing, both in their dialogue as well as in their inner thoughts. One example is the word play around fish, faith, evolution and social and sexual entanglements. This begins as Isa, a poet composing a poem in secret about human destiny, struggles to find a word but is then interrupted by the telephone and the need to order fish. The word 'Sole' resonates with its homophone, soul, and as a Christian symbol evokes references to spirituality and Christianity (*BTA* 12). A play on these ideas juxtaposes the serious and more banal throughout the novel. For example, when the fish arrives it is taken to the ironically described 'semi-ecclesiastical apartment', the larder, which in earlier days had been a chapel (*BTA* 22). This network of ideas and word play surfaces later in the collage of voices expressing disparate views on the play as the audience disperses, with comments about the Greek oracles being a 'foretaste' of Christianity, leading to other issues: 'Which is what? ... Crepe soles? That's so sensible ... They last much longer and protect the feet ... But I was saying; can the Christian faith adapt itself?' (*BTA* 118). These final group conversations are composed of multiple scraps of phrases, with characters cutting across each other's dialogue, sentences and ideas, creating a palimpsest that overrides any sense of authority or definitive meaning. A clashing of views and a jumble of reference points and ideas are interspersed with phatic elements.

The shifting between different characters or centres of consciousness that we see in earlier novels, such as *Mrs Dalloway* and *To the Lighthouse*, is more marked, sometimes creating a comic effect. We see this when Lucy Swithin 'helps' Mrs Sands to make the sandwiches for the pageant. The sentence construction suggests an initial balance and harmony: 'Mrs. Sands fetched bread; Mrs. Swithin fetched ham. One cut the bread; the other the ham. It was soothing, it was consolidating, this handwork together' (*BTA* 23). That this last statement belongs to Lucy is made clear however by what follows – her digressive musing which takes her from bread to Bacchus and wine. Meanwhile, 'Sands heard the clock tick ... noted a fly buzz; and registered, as her lips showed, a grudge she mustn't speak against people making work in the kitchen' (*BTA* 23). The comic effect is created by their different preoccupations and levels of concentration and by the word play on the servant's name and what they are making – Sand/wiches. Equally, this shifting between characters' views can create a sense of dislocation and disjunction. For example, as Mrs Lynn Jones contemplates ideas of home, she is sharply cut off by Etty Springett's snappily delivered comment, '"Cheap and nasty, I call it"' (*BTA* 103). Characters are also more self-conscious about their streams of thought – 'Dear how my mind wanders, she [Mrs Jones] checked herself' (*BTA* 103).

The play within the novel also introduces another level of self-referentiality, drawing attention to narrative framing and to the process of creation and writing itself. Woolf's preoccupation with identity is more self-consciously represented through the process of performance. The characters in the novel have a double identity as themselves and as performers in the pageant. However, this dual idea of identity is complicated by the 'slippage' between the characters' performed and 'real' selves. For example, as Eliza Clark, 'licensed to sell tobacco', enacts Miss La Trobe's fictional version of Queen Elizabeth I (whose conquest of South America first brought tobacco to Britain) there is literally a slippage of identity (*BTA* 52). Even in costume, Eliza is easily recognizable as herself but soon her 'Elizabethan' 'ruff had become unpinned and the great Eliza had forgotten her lines' (*BTA* 53), provoking hilarity in the audience yet somehow enhancing this representation of the Elizabethan age. More overtly and comically than in other of her fictions, here Woolf again puts notions of identity into question, destabilizing any idea of the self as a discrete and individual entity and revealing not only the communal production of our sense of self (as we rely on others for their views of us) but also the historical, national and social production of this sense of self. The section of the pageant called 'Ourselves' entails the actors holding pieces of broken mirrors to reflect the audience in order to represent the present day. This shows, as Woolf has suggests in many ways throughout her fiction, that identity is plural, fragmented not whole and consistent. We each see ourselves and others in different ways and art (pageants and novels) can open up complex and possibly uncomfortable explorations that trouble ideas of identity and our conception of reality. The final ambiguity and blurring of reality and art comes in the last words of the novel when it seems that the narrative we have just read is what has taken place in the interval between two acts: 'Then the curtain rose. They [Giles and Isa] spoke' (*BTA* 130). The 'ending' of Woolf's novel, it seems, is just the beginning of the next act about to resume.

CHAPTER FOUR

Characterization

As is clear from the heated debate between Woolf and fellow writer, Arnold Bennett, the issue of 'character in fiction' is of central importance to her as she works to find effective ways to represent modern experience (see Chapter One). She identified 1910 as the year in which she detected a social and political shift in '[a]ll human relations' which heralded in wider cultural change in systems of belief, behaviour and in the aesthetic realm – 'a change in religion, conduct, politics and literature' (*E3* 422). In successive novels, shorter fictions and other writings, Woolf sought to register these changes through her experiments with literary form and structure, and through her attempts to bring character to 'life'. This chapter will consider Woolf's own complex philosophy of the self as this seems to be informed by contemporary ideas about identity and human consciousness explored in the fields of philosophy and psychology. It will also consider some of the literary influences that seem to be significant for the way Woolf radically revises familiar paradigms for creating character, inviting us to also move beyond our understanding of character as simply mimetic. Discussion will focus particularly on *Jacob's Room* (1922), 'In the Orchard' (1923), *Mrs Dalloway* (1925) and *The Waves* (1931).

The 'modern mind'

In her essay 'Mr Bennett and Mrs Brown' (also published with the title, 'Character in Fiction'), Woolf makes two key points in relation to characterization. These are that the creation of fictional characters is a novelist's most central, yet most frustrating, pursuit, and also that, for the new generation of writers, this task is compounded by the complexities of modern experience and the necessity of finding ways to represent what she calls 'the modern mind' (*E4* 433). This term refers to the ways in which the mind is impacted upon by the phenomena of modernity, including an increased pace of life and new technologies which alter sense perceptions, modes of communication and interaction. This term also seems to reference the paradigm shift in the fields of physics and philosophy as new theories radically altered the ways in which the physical world ('reality') and our cognitive and affective processes could be understood. Woolf argues that for the older generation of writers, like Bennett, reality is something that is self-evident, material and can be empirically proven, and that their representations of character work from this assumption. The characters created in such 'realist' fictions are seemingly 'solid', 'fully rounded' and 'knowable' through their engagement with the material world and its social relations, and they are brought to life through the voice and authority of the omniscient narrator. By contrast, the modern writer seeks to convey a more complex sense of reality, one that, as modern physics demonstrates, is less self-evident, ordered and solid: in the popular imagination, all is in motion and time and space are relative. While Woolf is keen to register the importance of the material aspects of existence ('like health and money and the houses we live in' *AROO* 41), she is also keen to stress that there is no *one* objective 'reality' that we all experience in the same way. Rather, the ways in which we each perceive, respond to and make sense of the world around us are entirely subjective: we are continually bombarded by a 'myriad impressions', a continuous flow of stimuli, and our consciousness and sense of reality are shaped by our cognitive, sensory, emotional and imaginative responses to this flow. She considers it to be the writer's responsibility to create characters that are more 'realistic' and 'life-like' according to this new sense of 'reality' so as to encapsulate the experience of modern life and identity.

Woolf remarks in her diary that the modern sense of self is more dynamic and disparate than previously assumed: 'we're splinters & mosaics; not, as they used to hold, immaculate, monolithic, consistent wholes' (*D2* 314). To represent this multi-dimensional, fragmented and provisional 'composition' of self, she sought to represent character from 'a different angle' (*E4* 435). Her fiction focusses not simply on external description and social relations, but on the interior life, on the varied and indeterminate internal processes of thought, cognition, memory and response to stimuli (sensory, emotional and intellectual). She sought to capture the shifting complexity of lived experience, to articulate the inner life of characters, their emotions and responses towards ordinary everyday things and others, as well as to convey the solitary and personal experience that is not shared with others – 'imagination…dreams…the closeness and complexity of life' (*E4* 436). In 'Modern Fiction', she discusses the attempt of the modern writer to 'record the atoms as they fall upon the mind' (*E4* 161) and in her own fictions, experience is represented as mosaic-like, including joy and pleasure, as well as discomfort and hostility, ambiguity and uncertainty. She sought to devise methods of characterization that evoke a sense of identity as fluid, indeterminate and of an infinite variety: for her 'every feeling, every thought; every quality of brain and spirit is drawn upon; no perception comes amiss' (*E4* 164).

This is not to say that Woolf's characters exist in a world oblivious to social context and cultural expectation – far from it. Her characters are part of a social fabric and a rich interchange of experience which connects them in sometimes unexpected ways with others. Indeed, a key element in Woolf's method of characterization is this interconnection with others: our understanding of characters and their sense of understanding of themselves is in part a result of the ways in which they are perceived and received by other characters. Her characters register the pressure to conform to powerful ideological structures, values and expectations which impact upon their lived experience in a male-dominated and class-stratified society and culture: they are shaped by these wider forces, but also resist them. Her methods of characterization record the tensions, ambiguities and complicated negotiation of the difference facets of experience acting upon us and pulling us in different directions.

Cultural scripts

One way to think about these ideological forces at work is to consider the 'cultural scripts' Woolf's characters are expected to follow. These can be thought of as patterns of experience and behaviour deemed appropriate for our gendered, sexed and classed identities. They are reinforced in a variety of ways – through literal 'scripts' such as myths, fairy tales, literary texts and visual arts, as well as through less tangible scripts and assumptions made apparent at personal and familial levels. Such scripts are maintained by directly and indirectly prohibiting certain actions and decisions about what individuals can do and be and the kinds of roles and relationships they can pursue. Heterosexual romance narratives (courtship and marriage) are some of the most powerful in reinforcing ideological values and Woolf makes self-conscious reference to such scripts in her creation of character, simultaneously highlighting and subverting their effect.

From her first novel, *The Voyage Out*, we can see how Woolf's characters are shaped in relation to romance narratives. Rachel Vinrace and Terence Hewitt look set to follow the courtship plot: they meet and become engaged as the cultural script dictates. However, Woolf's critical questioning and challenging of such expectations and social imperatives is made evident as this 'voyage out' – a literal and metaphorical journey to the next predicted stage of life, marriage – is severely derailed when Rachel contracts a fever and dies. Other novels, such as *Mrs Dalloway* and *To the Lighthouse*, focus on the roles of wife and mother and both Clarissa and Mrs Ramsay consider the cultural compulsion they feel to be a particular kind of person, to fulfil the role expected of women to accommodate the needs of others. Mrs Ramsay is a committed advocate of the heterosexual romance script, asserting the imperative that everyone should marry and encouraging Minta Doyle and Paul Rayley in their courtship. Yet, in a state of reverie she contemplates her thwarted ambition, an ambition perceived to be at odds with the script mapped out for her as a middle-class woman, wife and mother. In contrast, the modern artist, Lily Briscoe, wrestles to resist the marriage script imposed on her and instead finally succeeds in fulfilling her artistic endeavour (see Chapter Five).

Clarissa Dalloway in many ways conforms to gender and class expectations: she is a privileged, upper middle-class hostess whose party will both display her status and enhance her husband's connections with the most powerful figures in their society. Yet, her own reverie and recollection of the past reveals a far more precarious sense of self than appearances would suggest. She feels her 'self' to be vulnerable, fragmented and dispersed, but feels compelled to 'assemble' the public self, 'Mrs Richard Dalloway', that others expect. Her desires for women and the palpable effect of her remembered homoerotic past with Sally Seton also radically disrupt what seems, on the surface, to be Clarissa's perfect performance of the heterosexual romance script. Woolf's characters' relation to the dictates of cultural scripts also invite us to reflect on our own sense of the 'real' self: we are all, Woolf seems to suggest, shaped by these expectations and the fictions via which they are transmitted. This is apparent in the ways in which some of Woolf's characters reflect self-consciously on the scripts imposed on them, also revealing their knowing manipulation of them. In his pursuit of an unknown woman through London streets, Peter Walsh, Clarissa's old friend and rejected suitor, knowingly enacts the role of 'romantic buccaneer', indulging his self-fantasy as a romantic hero for a sense of 'fun' (*MD* 60, 61). Although the romantic fantasy script fails and the woman eludes him, Peter acknowledges the importance of such fictions to the sense he has of himself. He considers that such imaginary selves and plots, 'making oneself up', constitute 'the better part of life' (*MD* 61). Such conventional cultural scripts may be 'smashed to atoms' (*MD* 61) and, like the literary conventions, 'comedy, tragedy, love interest' (*E4* 160), demolished by new aesthetic and critical perspectives. However, Woolf's writing also makes clear the persistence of such scripts in the ways in which we make sense of fictional characters and plots and, indeed, in the way we make sense of our own 'real' selves and life stories. As she suggests in 'Mr Bennett and Mrs Brown', there is a parallel between the ways we judge characters in fiction and our assessments of people in real life – 'every one … is a judge of character … Our marriages, our friendships depend on it' (*E3* 421) and it would seem that reading fiction not only offers us a representation of reality, but also informs our sense of reality.

Representing the subjective self – Proust, Bergson and Freud

As seen when examining Woolf's use of the narrative technique of free indirect discourse and of other literary devices (see Chapter Three), she aimed to represent her characters as 'centres of consciousness' and to convey a sense of the cognitive, psychological and emotional processes at work as her characters interact with the material and social world around them. Although Woolf claimed not to have read the work of French philosopher, Henri Bergson, nor that of Sigmund Freud until 1939 (*D5* 249), their new ideas and understandings of the mind were discussed by friends and family and Woolf would have been very aware of these developments (see Introduction). Indeed, her methods of characterization resonate strongly with these theories and explore similar psychological territory, particularly in the attempts to convey a sense of the multi-layered and simultaneous nature of experience, and the shifting and complex workings of conscious thought and unconscious processes.

One important aspect of Woolf's creation of character is the interweaving of different strands of experience so as to convey a sense of identity as multiple and always changing. This conception of the self anticipates later theoretical ideas of the self as always in the process of becoming (as demonstrated in the work of post-structuralist feminist theorists such as Julia Kristeva, for example[1]). Woolf sees identity as 'layered' or 'palimpsestic' as it is produced from multiple and simultaneous experience, as well as from the intertwining of past experience with the present. Memories, and particularly the experience of involuntary memory, play a key role in the representation of the subjective self and Woolf's writing demonstrates how the past can powerfully affect a character's response to the present moment, helping to shape our sense of their identity. Bergson's ideas about the centrality of voluntary and involuntary memory to the generation of the self can be seen echoed in Woolf's representation of her characters' external and internal 'selves'.[2] Woolf's admiration for the work of her contemporary, the French novelist Marcel Proust, can be seen to have influenced Woolf's creation of character, particularly the representation of her characters' sensory perception and response and the sense of an intensity of experience. His work seems also to have influenced her experiments with time, particularly the use of involuntary memory.

Proust's multi-volume novel (often translated, *In Search of Lost Time*, 1913–27) is preoccupied with remembering the personal and historical past, but also includes moments of involuntary memory triggered by a sensory stimulus (most famously, the smell of a madeleine cake). Unlike memories deliberately recalled, these involuntary memories open up pockets of time and moments of intense sensation and self-awareness that Woolf called 'moments of being'. We see this, for example, at the beginning of *Mrs Dalloway* when the squeak of the hinges triggers Clarissa's involuntary memory of a morning at her family home in Bourton and evokes an intense bodily response so that the air is experienced as 'like the flap of a wave; the kiss of a wave' (*MD* 5). Later, as Clarissa deliberately recalls her past 'the words meant absolutely nothing to her now'; yet as she begins to 't[ake] out her hairpins' this sensory and bodily stimulus triggers an involuntary memory – a return of 'the old feeling', her blissful excitement in 'coming down to dinner in a white frock to meet Sally Seton' and her feeling of 'being in love' (*MD* 39, 40). In both moments time is compressed, the thirty year gap collapses and Clarissa is simultaneously a woman in her early 50s and aged 18. Woolf's representation of character as palimpsestic with each 'layer' as interconnected and simultaneous, not distinct and chronological, is a method employed in a number of her other fictions.

This interconnection of past and present is made powerfully apparent in much of Woolf's fiction and is central to the representation of subjective experience. In this sense, Woolf's ideas about the self and representations of character also resonate with Henri Bergson's ideas about memory, intuition and our subjective experience of time. A central idea in Bergson's philosophy of the self is concerned with the experience of time: 'clock time' is the sense of time that is mechanized and spatialized into distinct periods – past, present and future; it is linear, logical, and moves forwards in incremental measurable units. On the other hand, subjective time (*durée*, translated as 'duration') is the sense of time as we *experience* it, palpably in the body and mind, and is bound up with the process of becoming so that being, doing, thinking, feeling and remembering are indistinguishable. Unlike the regulated movement of clock time, subjective time is flowing and comprised of indivisible moments, it is elastic and 'duration' can extend or contract to encompass our experience and the flux of our inner lives (see Introduction).

Freud's ideas of the self seem also to chime with Woolf's concepts and methods of characterization. In the 1920s, the popularization of Freudian ideas led to a kind of craze for psychoanalysis but even without this it would have been impossible for Woolf to have avoided discussion of Freud given that she was surrounded by friends and relatives who were both fascinated by Freudian theory and closely involved in its dissemination and popularization (see Introduction). However, Woolf, along with other writers, was disparaging of Freudian ideas. Katherine Mansfield criticized the fascination for Freudian theory and what she saw as the simplistic employment of Freudian ideas in literary writing. This chimed with Woolf's views too, as is evident in her review of J. D. Beresford's *An Imperfect Mother* called 'Freudian Fiction' (1920) where she criticizes the reductive effect of psychoanalytic ideas when crudely applied in fiction.

Woolf's dismissive attitude may be attributed to the associations Freud's writings made between the artist (and artistic production) and neurosis, ideas that led other of Woolf's friends, notably, Roger Fry and Clive Bell, to attack Freudian ideas in public and in private. Yet is clear that Woolf's writing and her methods of characterization explore similar territory to that in Freud's theories, particularly in relation to childhood psychosexual crises and their persistence into adulthood, so that some aspects of her fiction seem to invite a Freudian reading. In *To the Lighthouse*, for example, the child James's violent anger towards his father and his desire to kill him with 'an axe' or a phallic 'poker' (*TTL* 4) seems symptomatic of what Freud theorized as a child's Oedipal rage against his father as rival. Lily Briscoe's longing for Mrs Ramsay many years after her death seems also to suggest an Oedipal desire for the mother, finally made manifest in her life's work – a portrait of Mrs Ramsay as a Madonna figure. Woolf also discusses the process of writing this novel as a kind of catharsis, enabling her to let go of some of her intense feelings for her parents, and for her mother in particular: 'I suppose that I did for myself what psycho-analysts do for their patients. I expressed some very long felt and deeply felt emotion. And in expressing it I explained it and then laid it to rest' (*MOB* 90). In *The Waves*, Louis's childhood trauma at being kissed by Jinny, '"All is shattered"' (*TW* 11), persists into adulthood. In his recollection of this incident, Jinny has become metaphorically transformed into '"a cowled man with a red-hot iron"' (*TW* 77) who brands his neck, suggesting that the trauma has left an irrevocable psychic scar. In *The Voyage Out*, Rachel's disturbing dreams seem to bring the repressed fears she has about marriage and sexuality to the narrative surface. However, Freudian readings can only ever offer a partial understanding of these characters: Woolf's characters remain complex and indeterminate, eluding any ready definition.

In her story, 'A Lady in the Looking-Glass: A Reflection', Woolf demonstrates the inadequacies of realist literary conventions in the effective creation of character and also criticizes the expectations that such modes set up that characters can (and should) be fully revealed to the reader (see Chapter One). These criticisms also resonate with Woolf's objections to psychological approaches in the creation of plot, character and in interpretation. Her narrator's frustrations at the way Isabella seems to resist interpretation result in the desire to violently 'prize her open with the first tool that came to hand – the imagination' (CSF 223). Yet the ways this imaginative objective is expressed also resonates with the goals of a rational, scientific psychoanalytical interpretation. The narrator's quest to 'fix one's mind upon her [Isabella] at that very moment' and to 'fasten her down there' (CSF 223) to discover 'her profounder state of being', to expose Isabella's mind to light and to 'penetrate a little further into her being' (CSF 224) chimes with the kind of reductive goals she attributes to Freudian interpretation. As she explains in her essay, 'Freudian Fiction', 'the new key is a patent key that opens every door. It simplifies rather than complicates, detracts rather than enriches' (E3 197). This scientific examination of characters is a simplification that turns them in to 'cases' an approach that is, as her story claims, 'absurd'.

Many 'selves'

For Woolf, such approaches were too simplistic and her writing strives to explore ideas of the self, and therefore characterization, in more complex ways. Her creation of characters conveys her sense that we are not single entities but multi-dimensional selves composed of complexly layered, interfused experience, our past is always entwined with our present and continually in a state of flux. This idea of multiple selves finds expression in a number of different ways in Woolf's fiction, for example, in the '[f]ifty pairs of eyes', Lily feels she needs to fully see Mrs Ramsay (TTL 188), and in the creation of the six characters in The Waves who, Woolf suggests, could also be one character or indeed none. Towards the end of Orlando, the time-travelling, gender-swapping central character seems to have finally conformed to an appropriately gendered role as wife and mother, shopping in a department store for prosaic

household items. However, this stability of character is brief and
the scene quickly leads to a comical iteration of the philosophical
idea running throughout Woolf's fiction, which is that our identity
is not single and readily definable but is, in fact, composed of many
selves. The biographer-narrator somewhat randomly speculates
that the number of selves maybe 'two thousand and fifty-two'
and conveys this sense of multiplicity using the simile of selves
as being like 'plates...piled on a waiter's hand' (O 192). We are
repeatedly reminded that it is pointless and even unethical to try
to neatly define or sum up others, to 'say of anyone in the world
now that they were this or were that' (MD 10). Further, although
Woolf's characters experience 'moments of being' that are specific
to them, her philosophy of self holds that we are also inextricably
connected to others. As Clarissa Dalloway explains, she feels 'laid
out like a mist' across time and between self and others (MD 12),
and as North in *The Years* expresses it, he longs to 'be the bubble
and the stream, the stream and the bubble – myself and the world
together' (TY 359). While it is often only the reader (working as an
'accomplice') that can see the connections between the characters –
as suggested by verbal networks of imagery and repeated patterns
of experience – this idea of connection is a powerful one and an
important aspect in understanding Woolf's creation of character.

In her memoir, 'A Sketch of the Past' where Woolf discusses
her idea of 'moments of being', she also considers that it is the
experience of 'non-being' which forms the 'great[er] part of every
day' and which is 'not lived consciously' (MOB 79). Although this
experience of non-being is 'embedded in a kind of nondescript
cotton wool' (MOB 79), Woolf develops a 'philosophy' that 'behind
the cotton wool is hidden a pattern; that we – I mean all human
beings – are connected with this; that the whole world is a work of
art; that we are parts of the work of art' (MOB 81). It is the 'sudden
violent shock[s]' (MOB 79) experienced in a moment of being that
can reveal this pattern. As we see in a number of ways, Woolf's
characters have a sense of their existence in relation to others, as
connected to and in part defined by others. The self is in continual
fluctuation with the responses of others impacting on the sense of
self. At this point in her memoir, Woolf seems to refer to the power
of the collective imagination in the production of works of art, but
also in the creation of a sense of ourselves and each other. Peter
Walsh refers to the process of 'making oneself up' and Woolf asserts

her belief in the power of art – of words and music – to create as well as to articulate a collective sense of experience: 'we are the words; we are the music; we are the thing itself' (*MOB* 81).

'In the Orchard'

Woolf's overtly experimental short story, 'In the Orchard', published in the year after *Jacob's Room*, can be read as a metafictional story that self-consciously exaggerates the literary mechanisms for representing character. As we see elsewhere, Woolf's characters are non-mimetic and in some ways impersonal. This story self-consciously demonstrates the importance of narrative perspective to the impressions we have of character. Even more so than Jacob, Miranda remains enigmatic: she is the character most fully explored in the story, but is far from fully knowable or even fully a 'character' in the realist sense. The story is comprized of three sections which deal with the same events: Miranda is (possibly) asleep in the orchard, she has been reading a French novel and wakes with a start, anxious that she will be late for tea. This repetition across the tripartite structure creates the sense of identity as multiple and palimpsestic: each of the sections represents a different 'layer' of Miranda's experience articulated from a different perspective and drawing on different narrative techniques. As readers we become aware of the various aspects of self that are revealed (and concealed) depending on the narrative perspective. Countering the seemingly inevitable linear chronology of a written narrative where one thing (word, sentence or paragraph) must follow another, time seems to be on a loop and we are returned repeatedly to the beginning of the 'story' which ends with echoes of another story – that of Lewis Carroll's *Alice in Wonderland* – with the reference to being late for tea. The effect created is that each section is happening simultaneously in time.

With a focus on a female character, the story also self-consciously examines the social machinery and cultural scripts that impact on the formation of female identity, as well as on the ways in which readers interpret characters. Elsewhere, Woolf comments on her own middle-class experience as a woman and in particular on her 'tea-table training' in serving tea and maintaining polite conversation (*MOB* 164). The anxiety Miranda expresses about being late for tea suggests a similar training. We infer Miranda's privileged, middle-class status from other internal 'evidence': she wears an opal ring, can read French, and is at leisure to sleep ensconced behind the orchard walls, protected from the harsh life experience happening beyond. The setting of the story in an apple orchard also suggests the ideological forces and cultural pressures working to shape Miranda as a character. That the novel Miranda is reading is set in a different cultural context – the Basque country – where a group of girls spontaneously bursts into laughter recalls a point Woolf made in her essay, 'Mr Bennett and Mrs Brown', about how cultural differences lead novelists from different countries to create characters in different ways. In Woolf's story, the contrast between the girls' enjoyment and freedom and Miranda's experience serves to draw attention to her isolation and to the sense of cultural and narrative constraint. As we read on, we realize that the orchard walls do not really protect Miranda as the sounds associated with violence outside the orchard not only travel into the orchard, but also infiltrate Miranda's psyche, impacting on her unconsciousness and dreams. The walls also have an oppressive function as is made clear in the final section where each apple has an allotted space and place (as does Miranda): the walls are said to have 'compacted' everything inside the orchard, containing both the fruits and Miranda through a sense of (horti)cultural control (CSF 151).

For each section, Woolf self-consciously employs three different narrative approaches, each of which demonstrates their impact on our perception and understanding of character. These approaches also seem to be overtly informed by new techniques drawn from other art forms – the cinema and visual arts – as well as from scientific and philosophical ideas of the self. The first section deliberately plays with the idea of narrative omniscience as the narrative perspective draws higher and higher so as to finally offer a (literally) god-like view of Miranda who, '[m]iles below', seems to occupy 'a space as big as the eye of a needle' (CSF 150). The smooth movement upwards resembles a cinematic panning shot and sights and sounds create a sense of the 'realism' of this. This god-like perspective can also be seen to be a pointed parody of a realist narrative technique which claims to offer an omniscient understanding of characters but which, as Woolf makes clear numerous times, is for her inadequate for conveying the more complex experiences of 'life' (see Chapter One). In this section, Woolf plays with these realist conventions for conveying character to show us just how *little* is conveyed about Miranda using such techniques. We are made aware of the 'material' aspects of her existence (her social position and conformity to gender norms), but this technique can only grant access to external details, and this kind of scrutiny reduces the significance of Miranda as a character – a point reinforced by the aerial view of Miranda as minute.

By contrast, the second section offers an interior perspective as it relates Miranda's dreams and fantasies and seems to promise a fuller understanding. The sounds from outside the orchard infiltrate Miranda's psyche and impact on her dreams, transformed into elements that reflect her desires: 'the shout of the drunken man', for example, prompts her to 'dr[a]w breath with an extraordinary ecstasy' and seems synonymous with an erotic impulse towards 'life itself crying out from a rough tongue in a scarlet mouth' (*CSF* 150). However, this psychological approach is also revealed to be reductive and Miranda's inner self is merely solipsistic. This is suggested by the way Miranda sees the whole world as an extension of herself: she sinks onto the earth and it carries her 'on its back as if [she] were a leaf, or a queen' (*CSF* 150). Further, what could be a rich and complex revelation of her inner life is reduced to a very conventional 'pattern' of life 'flying round [Miranda], across her, towards her' (*CSF* 150) and Miranda's desires are entirely shaped by the limiting life choices for women – marriage and motherhood. The final section is much shorter and, like Miranda's options, compacted and curtailed. Miranda is radically displaced – she is represented as merely a 'purple streak' that 'slit[s]' the 'blue-green' of the orchard (*CSF* 151). The geometric precision of the pattern of apple planting creates a very visual impression, suggestively abstract, and seems to suggest a rigid system in which the apples grow and ripen. As we saw in the opening section, Miranda is objectified, but this is a far more extreme perspective: Miranda's presence is merely a shape in the picture presented. This scene dehumanizes her completely and signals Woolf's most vehement critique so far. This final section, 'compacted' and 'clamped together' (*CSF* 151), suggests that narrative approaches which prioritize literary conventions, 'patterns', and rigidly insist on logic, order and a fixed and controlling narrative perspective over anything else objectify characters and literally sap the life from them.

Jacob's Room

In this novel, Woolf worked to articulate more complex ideas of the self and identity through her creation of a central character deliberately at odds with the kinds of characters found in more the conventional realist fictions produced by her contemporaries. Although *Jacob's Room* can be read as a *Bildungsroman* in the way it purports to chart the development and increasing maturity of the central character, Jacob remains elusive and inscrutable (see Chapter Two). Even what should be an event full of significance for our understanding of Jacob – his death – happens 'off stage'. As we might expect in more conventional narrative forms, there seems to be a correspondence between the ending of Jacob's life and the ending of the narrative, but whereas this would typically lead to a fuller understanding of the character and narrative closure, Woolf ends her novel with a question – simple yet profound – what is Betty Flanders to do with her son's old shoes?

In many ways, Jacob seems displaced from the centre of this narrative and the reader is continually kept at a distance. From his first appearance in the novel as a child, he is 'lost' on the beach and continues to be associated with loss throughout the novel. In contrast to many of Woolf's later novels, where she makes extensive use of the technique of free indirect discourse to grant the reader access to the shifting thoughts and emotions of her characters, we are largely refused access to Jacob's inner life. His thoughts and feelings are only rarely made apparent and we have only the vaguest insight into what motivates him. Although we have some insight into the thoughts and feelings of some of the other characters, Jacob remains elusive to the reader and to other characters: he is an enigma and likened to '"one of those statues...in the British Museum"' (*JR* 67). In this, her first fully developed experiment with characterization, Woolf not only makes a break with the illusion of omniscience found in realist fiction, where the narrator speaks with authority about the characters and every aspect of their lives, but also self-consciously draws attention to the mechanisms through which characters are typically produced to reveal these processes at work. Woolf's novel also seems deliberately to mock realist methods of characterization where a sense of character grows by means of a steady accumulation of external detail, including information such as the material facts of the character's circumstances (class, gender, education and profession) and the life 'events' they experience. Her narrator self-consciously draws attention to the details and 'evidence' she is amassing: 'Then here is another scrap of conversation; the time about eleven in the morning; the scene a studio; and the day Sunday' (*JR* 111). Here she provides 'realist detail' but simultaneously undermines this method as being, like the evidence she accumulates, 'scrappy': realist methods only convey a superficial idea of character and cannot grant access to inner experience. The title of Woolf's novel itself can be read as a means of parodying realist fiction and seems to refer back to her criticism of Edwardian writers in 'Modern Fiction', particularly Arnold Bennett. In her essay, Woolf praises the skill with which Bennett constructs his fiction, likening it to a room with 'not so much as a draught between the frames of the windows, or a crack in the boards' (*E4* 158), but she makes the point that this accumulation of rich external detail does not evoke a sense of 'life' or spirit. Woolf paints a vivid picture of Jacob's room, complete with the accumulation of the kinds of detail offered in realist fiction, including objects that signal Jacob's eclectic intellectual interests and his family and social connections (*JR* 30–1), all of which *should* grant the reader access to him as a character. But the room is repeatedly described as 'empty' and 'listless', the involuntary sounds of the inanimate objects (the creak of the 'wicker armchair' and the curtain 'swelling' in the breeze) seeming to have more life than Jacob, narrated as he is from an external perspective (*JR* 31, 155).

In contrast to the kind of mimetic character found in realist fiction (one we read as 'human'), Jacob is a composite of what other characters see, think and desire him to be. The narrator admits to having only limited information about Jacob: the facts and events are merely sketched in and the perspectives of others are varied, unreliable and biased. Woolf's third person narrator denies having full knowledge of Jacob and can only speculate on Jacob's thoughts and feelings. She states, 'it is impossible to say' what Jacob is thinking as he looks out to Lands End, and maintains a sense of uncertainty about his reaction to seeing Florinda with another man: 'Whether we know what was in his mind is another question' (*JR* 40, 81). In terms of narrative events where we might expect to see him in action or in relation to others, we only ever catch fleeting glimpses of Jacob or hear snippets of his conversations and debates with friends. These snippets are often unreliably reported, for example, the cleaning woman's report of a half overheard intellectual debate is put increasingly into doubt by her mistakenly referring to Jacob as 'Mr. Sanders' (*JR* 87). Even the views of the vast number of characters named in the novel (critics estimate numbers from 120 and 160) cannot fully capture a sense of Jacob and our understanding of him is dispersed and unsettled by conflicting and contradictory assessments. As one early review sums up, 'Life is seen in flashes, and the reader has a good deal to do' ('The Unconventional Novel').

What this experiment with character suggests is that in many ways Jacob's importance lies in the effect he has on others rather than who or what he is as an individual. When we consider that Woolf also conceptualized her novel as an elegy, this suggests a wider political significance. One of Woolf's earliest biographers and critics, Winifred Holtby, referred to *Jacob's Room* as Woolf's 'war book' (1978: 116) and although there is no direct account of the war, nor is it even made clear that Jacob dies in the war, his name, Flanders, would have been overloaded with significance in 1922. It inevitably recalls 'Flanders Fields', the term used to describe a number of battlefields on the Western front made vivid in the popular imagination by John McCrae's poem, 'In Flanders Fields' (1915). Jacob's childhood home of Scarborough only adds to an over-determined sense of this character's fate since this was the one of the first places in Britain to experience German raids in December 1914 (Levenback 1999: 42), leading to a loss of civilian life, outrage at Germany and also criticism of the British Navy for their failure to prevent it. The temporal frame in which Woolf's character reaches maturity contributes further to this sense of a culturally predetermined fate, since 'His growth from adolescence to young manhood takes place against the relentless ticking of a time bomb' (Zwerdling 1986: 65). That the narrator's ironic detachment serves to maintain a sense of distance from Jacob as an individual also resists a sentimentalizing representation of the loss of one individual, but rather infers the loss of a generation of young men across the whole of the British population. As well as creating her character as a composite of the views, values and expectations of other characters in the novel, Woolf's naming of Jacob suggests that he is also a composite of a particular cultural context. He is shaped by patriarchal ideology, nationalist identity and economic forces driving Britain to war. In this, we see how Woolf's aesthetic experimentation with character can be seen to have a political impetus: that Jacob's character as elusive, inscrutable and an enigma enables him to function as an 'everyman' figure.

These techniques of characterization confirm the sense we have in all of Woolf's fiction that identity is complex and it is impossible and inhuman to try to fix and pin others down. As the narrator states, 'It seems that a profound, impartial, and absolutely just opinion of our fellow-creatures is utterly unknown' (*JR* 60). Each character perceives Jacob differently, each seeing different aspects and possibly only what they want to see. This is evident in Richard Bonamy's idea of Jacob: what Richard Bonamy sees in Jacob is 'Richard Bonamy' and in Bonamy's interaction with Jacob, Jacob is 'endow[ed] ... with all sorts of qualities he had not at all' (*JR* 61). This confirms a central, philosophical idea that develops in Woolf's fiction that '[n]obody sees any one as he is' (*JR* 23), as it also asserts a political critique of methods of identifying individuals and groups as 'this or that' in order to categorize and constrain potential. This point is made clearly in Jacob's first foray out into the wider world as an independent young man. He travels by train from his home to Cambridge, but instead of his perspective or feelings about this 'rite of passage' experience, we only have the view of the older woman, Mrs Norman, who is his travelling companion. She assesses him from external evidence – his appearance and attitude – finding, 'All was firm, yet youthful, indifferent, unconscious ... he didn't notice her' (*JR* 23). However, his unasked for assistance with her bag surprises her and underdoes her assumption of Jacob being oblivious to her. That the narrator is somewhat disparaging or sceptical about Mrs Norman's view ('One must do the best one can with her report' *JR* 24) reminds us again of Woolf's self-consciousness in revealing the processes of constructing character. Unlike our experience of 'getting to know' a character when reading a realist novel, when reading Woolf's fiction we need to remember that 'It is no use trying to sum people up. One must follow hints, not exactly what is said, nor yet entirely what is done' (*JR* 135).

Mrs Dalloway

Mrs Dalloway also explores the idea of the self as multiple and echoes the impossibility of any absolute definition of the self or others. Character is not fixed and stable, nor are characters fully 'knowable' or easily narratable. The multivalent and shifting narrative technique that Woolf employs (free indirect discourse) allows for the creation of characters that are complex and ambiguous. Characters are composed of exterior detail provided by a third person narrator, as well as through a sense of a character's inner life evoked directly through the inclusion of reverie and memories and more indirectly through images and verbal patternings.

From the beginning of the novel, we have a sense of Clarissa's identity as complex and palimpsestic: she is both solemn and vivacious, alive to her present moment in London in June yet immersed in the memories and past emotions that flood her conscious awareness. The shifting narrative perspective gives the reader access to Clarissa's intimate feelings, as well as to her neighbour Scrope Purvis's view of her. In the opening paragraphs, we see Clarissa respond with a sense of vitality to the fresh morning air but she is also serious, as she recalls a sense of her younger self, 'solemn...standing there at the open window' and 'feeling as she did...that something awful was about to happen' (MD 5). Seeing her poised on the curb of the pavement in the present time of the novel, Scrope Purvis recognizes her vitality and compares her to a bird, but he also has the impression of her as being 'a particular hush, or solemnity; an indescribable pause; a suspense' (MD 6). This sense of Clarissa's self as multi-dimensional and fluid is developed in the metaphor of the diamond used to describe her sense of herself as fragmented and multi-faceted (see also Chapter Three).

Our understanding of character is also enriched by the double narrative in this novel which recounts the experiences of two very different characters: the eponymous heroine, the wife of a politician and a society hostess, and a traumatized, shell-shocked, war veteran, Septimus Smith. In Woolf's original plan for the novel Clarissa was to die (E4 549), but her introduction of Septimus does more than merely offer a substitute victim for this fatal plot. Woolf creates two characters that never meet but who in many ways constitute each other and, in doing so, Woolf complicates the idea of the self as multiple and interconnected with others. It is primarily the reader who is able to see the various and subtle ways in which these characters are connected as suggested by the verbal networks, metaphorical patternings and parallel scenes (see Chapter Three). However, the fact that Clarissa intuits a connection and similarity between herself and Septimus on hearing about his death suggests a further possibility about the self that Woolf's methods of characterization imply. This is that the boundaries of identity are permeable and that we live in and through others and, indeed, this is a central aspect of Clarissa's philosophy of life. Clarissa feels herself to be at the heart of things but also 'out, out, far out to sea and alone'; she feels that she and Peter 'lived in each other, she being part... of the trees at home' (MD 11) and 'laid out like a mist between the people she knew best', 'her life, herself' 'spread ever so far' (MD 12). Clarissa's sense of self includes a negotiation of the contradictions of her public and private selves, as well as an acceptance of the '[o]dd affinities' she has with others and a sense of dispersal, feeling interconnected to others and simply part of the flow of time (MD 169). However, what also becomes apparent is that this sense of self as interconnected and metaphysical, as permeable and as constituted by others, can also be a fragmented and fragile sense of self. Alongside Woolf's engagement with new understandings of identity and her creation of characters more in tune with modern life, she also recognized the dangers that such ideas and experiences of can hold. Her representations of characters such as Septimus (and Rhoda in *The Waves*) demonstrate an experience of alienation from the modern world. Septimus has lost the sense of coherence that familiar class and gender roles can provide, as in his roles as shop clerk, student and soldier. In the present time of the novel, he is unable to negotiate the social, emotional and psychological contradictions he experiences and his sense of dispersal and fragmentation mean that he cannot survive.[3]

The structure of the novel itself emphasizes the sense of connection between individuals as it also reveals multiple, subjective perspectives. Although the wide variety of characters (from a female vagrant to the Prime Minister and possibly the Queen) largely remain strangers to one another, they share common experiences of a particular city on a particular day. This shared experience of 'real' historical time and 'material' events is stressed by the sounding of Big Ben and other clocks throughout the day, literally recording the passing of time and the simultaneity of experience. However, this mechanical time is depicted as violent and oppressive, '[s]hredding and slicing' its way through the day and artificially 'dividing and subdividing' the flow of experience (MD 113). Although most characters seem oblivious to these familiar city sounds, for the reader these temporal markers create a sense of characters' simultaneous experiences and their different subjective responses to shared or similar events. Time is also crucial to Woolf's creation of character in the ways in which a sense of self is created through the interweaving of past and present. As she worked on her novel, Woolf found that she had developed a new technique of characterization which she referred to as her 'tunnelling process, by which [she] tell[s] the past by instalments, as [she has] need of it' (D2 272). She explains this process as an excavation of what is needed from her characters' pasts that she brings into the narrative present. These pockets of memory – the 'beautiful caves' she 'dig[s] out ... behind [her] characters' and what she calls 'moments of being' (the fleeting experience of intense sensation and self-awareness) – are interwoven into the narrative (D2 263). The significance of subjective experience, as this is shaped by the interconnection of past and present, is made powerfully apparent.

In her essay 'Modern Fiction', Woolf articulated modern philosophical questions about self and identity which find expression in her methods of characterization. Her essays and novels suggest that we all see and experience the world subjectively, but also put forward a view that each individual is part of the social, material and natural world around us: her characters are individual selves (demarcated by class, gender, sexuality and race), but are somehow also permeable and part of others.

The Waves

The idea of character as multiple and identity created through connection with others across time and space offered Woolf rich scope for considering the complexity of the self further. In this 'mystical' novel, characters even more explicitly constitute each other, their boundaries of identity permeable, yet their response to this shared experience is varied. In this novel, character is both individual and collective: the novel records the voices of six characters (three male and three female) as they mature from childhood through a series of dramatic soliloquies. A seventh character, Percival, has no speaking part though he does play a central role in the lives of the others. Inscrutable like Jacob Flanders, he is a focus for their different desires which they project onto him. Each speaker relates their everyday experiences and their engagement with the material world; they speak of specific concerns, articulated using a number of key phrases we come to associate with them as individuals. Jinny talks about city life and is preoccupied with the body, Susan speaks of nature and life in the country and she becomes a mother, Rhoda articulates her sense of fragility and alienation and speaks of isolated landscapes, Louis speaks of money and power, Neville of scholarly concerns and his longing for Percival and Bernard of his engagement with writing. In her plans for her novel, Woolf imagined it to resemble 'a gigantic conversation' and 'a tremendous discussion' (D3 285, 298) but the characters are not in dialogue with each other in an obvious way. In this sense, it is as if each speaker speaks simultaneously, undermining the linear progression that a 'turn-taking' conversation would create. The use of the present tense throughout the novel seems also to confirm this sense of their existence in the present moment of being.

At the same time, the speakers are in many ways impersonal and collective: their soliloquies are similar in style and this works to blur the sense of them as individuals. Their speeches echo similar images and shared ideas, thoughts and conceptions and they incorporate elements of each other's life stories and memories into their own, suggesting continuities between them. As we might expect, they share similar experiences and preoccupations as they each mature but, even more so than in earlier novels such as *Mrs Dalloway*, their soliloquies suggest an intimate connection. Indeed, Woolf's conception of her novel is that the six speakers are to be facets of one character, though she also aimed to have no characters in any conventional sense. As she states, 'I did mean that in some vague way we are the same person, and not separate people. The six characters were supposed to be one' (L4 397). More so than in *Mrs Dalloway*, *The Waves* creates a powerful sense of the characters' connection to the natural, non-human world through figurative echoes in their speeches and in the poetic language of the interludes. Language is central to our creation of self but also confirms our connection, as Bernard's words suggest: 'we melt into each other with phrases. We are edged with mist. We make an unsubstantial territory' (*TW* 14).

Woolf's highly experimental methods of characterization in this novel can be seen to be informed by certain aspects of her personal experience, specifically of the solar eclipse in 1927, as well as by her fascination with astronomy and the mysteries of the universe in the early 1930s, particularly as popularized by James Jeans in his textbooks, lectures and radio broadcasts (see Henry 2003). The wider scientific developments in the field of subatomic physics and the theory of wave-particle duality in relation to light have also led critics to infer connections between Woolf's novel and the new physics. Woolf recounts her experience of the solar eclipse in her essay, 'The Sun and the Fish' (1928), and in particular describes the sense of a loss of individuality as the sun was eclipsed: 'we had put off the little badges and signs of individuality. We were strung out against the sky in outline and had the look of statues standing prominent on the ridge of the world' (*E4* 521). The profound effect of this experience seems to inform her ideas about identity and human existence, specifically her representation of human identity as fragile in the face of powerful natural forces in *The Waves*. This experience is also echoed in the ways in which her speakers conceptualize character and their own sense of self in her novel. A similar image of 'some group in outline against the sky' (*TW* 156) is the one that Neville uses to articulate the unforced and gradual emergence of character in narrative. He derides the urgency of conventional narratives (and conventional readers) with their insistence on 'plot' and 'reason', insisting instead that patience is needed 'to see the sentence lay its dab of clay precisely on the right place, making character' (*TW* 155–6). A sense of character is created as both distinct from its background yet connected to others and the space it occupies. A more obvious connection with Woolf's experience is seen towards the end of the novel where Bernard uses an image of solar eclipse to describe his own sense of a dramatic loss of identity and existential crisis – 'A man without a self' is 'A dead man' (*TW* 225) – and also to reflect on the inadequate means we have at our disposal for recording a life. He feels that all human activities are emptied of meaning and his 'own indefatigable busyness' and efforts to record his life and that of his friends result in nothing: 'the earth was a waste of shadow' and the lives he recorded was merely 'tak[ing] note of shadows' (*TW* 224, 225). Bernard describes the shift in his mood from despair to the return of optimism as a sense of wonder, as if the sun had returned 'Miraculously' and the world fills again with light and colour (*TW* 226). Like Clarissa Dalloway, he is able to overcome this sense of dispersal, drawing not only his own but all the other characters' stories together in his final soliloquy. Although Bernard takes on the role of narrator of their collective story, he is also aware of the impossibility of completion for his narrative or for their lives. Bernard is alert to the shared experience of everyday life but also to the sense of unlived possibilities. Not only are there the 'shadows of people one might have been; unborn selves' but finally Bernard defies death, feeling within himself an energy rising, a wave sending self and time back not forward to an end point: 'And in me too the wave rises. It swells; it arches its back' (*TW* 228, 234). His account of their stories is also complicated by his sense that he *is* all of them: 'There is no division between me and them. As I talked I felt, "I am you". This difference we make so much of, this identity we so feverishly cherish, was overcome' (*TW* 228).

Further, if we are to read the individuals as facets of a single character, this creates a sense of incompletion and tension. Two of the characters die in the novel and there are many discrepancies in experience not least in relation to differences in gender, such as the different kinds of education and opportunities open to the male and female characters and the behaviour expected of them. There are also sometimes fraught and even violent emotional tensions between them. In *Mrs Dalloway*, Peter Walsh suggests that 'to know ... anyone, one must seek out the people who completed them' (*MD* 169) and although this idea of any character being 'complete' is in question in this earlier novel, in *The Waves* any sense of the self as harmonious, whole and complete in any conventional sense seems to be an impossibility. When discussing the innovative form of Woolf's novel, her friend Goldsworthy Lowes Dickinson described it as 'science made alive' and we can consider the ways in which new scientific ideas can be seen to inform Woolf's writing in terms of form, technique and characterization. What would conventionally be perceived as contradictory tensions in the creation of character here can be read in relation to new scientific ideas, particularly ideas about light energy as being dually comprized of waves and particles. Critics have noted parallels between 'the double focus of [Woolf's] book' on 'a group of discrete individuals' as well as on 'the wave-like structure of the novel as a whole' (McGee 2009: 392), a duality echoed in 'the tropes of table [solid matter, empirically proven] and waves' of energy that Beer identifies as Woolf seeks to reinvent narrative form (Beer 1996: 118). The six individual characters are both discrete 'particles' and speak their own stories, but they also complement each other and are swept up in the 'wave' structure of the novel as a whole, an effect created by the pastoral interludes which act as a kind of temporal punctuation, registering the movement of the sun and the waves. Here new scientific understanding seems to play a role in articulating the philosophical and metaphysical concerns Woolf's work is concerned with as these relate to our understanding of human identity and experience. She considers that we have a sense of ourselves as individuals but that we are, at the same time, inextricably inter-related to others, fused with others and nature, and also that we are a product of our cultural and historical context.

As we saw in 'In the Orchard' and as is apparent in many of Woolf's fictions, her experiments with character were deliberate and self-conscious. Her experience of writing this highly experimental novel seems to be reflected in the novel itself, with the male characters aligning themselves in different ways to the great male writers of the past (Catallus, Plato, Virgil, Shakespeare, Byron and Shelley). The recurrent reference to the figure of a woman writer, 'the lady writing' at the window, draws attention to the process of writing itself. She is both a figure of authority but also of mystery. In the context of a novel rich in the male-dominated literary tradition, this figure could represent a counter to such a literary heritage, signalling a new, 'modern' fiction as being in the hands of writers able to conceptualize literature differently. Bernard finally assumes the role of the group's biographer, relating their collective story, but this does not offer a sense of closure and gaps, ambiguities and uncertainties remain – 'life' (and the narratives that represent it) is 'imperfect, an unfinishing phrase' (*TW* 223). The novel ends with a new dawn, a new beginning and the next phase of an unending natural cycle.

CHAPTER FIVE

Gender, Sexuality and Class

Woolf is now one of the best-known woman writers on a global scale. She is lauded as a feminist thinker, novelist and critic. In her ground breaking essay, *A Room of One's Own*, she (now) famously asserted the centrality of female forebears in the building of a female literary tradition, 'we think back through our mothers if we are women' (*AROO* 72–3). For many writers and political thinkers and activists, Woolf *is* this 'mother' figure who played such a pivotal role in asserting women's difference in view. The second wave of feminist activism in the 1970s and 1980s saw the development of a strong feminist literary criticism and brought Woolf's writing to prominence. Lesbian Feminist criticism and the emergence of Queer theory in the 1980s have also opened new ways of reading Woolf's writing and understanding her political stance through a focus on the homoeroticism in her work and through reference her own sexual relationships with women. Her nephew, Quentin Bell, referred to her as 'a sexless Sappho' (1996: 185), but critics now take on Woolf's own witty and partly self-mocking proclamation of herself as 'the mouthpiece of Sapphism' (*L3* 530) to explore the various ways in which sexual diversity and homoeroticism permeate and shape her writing at every level in its content, themes, form and aesthetics. Critics consider the ways in which these elements of Woolf's writing challenge heteronormative social and cultural structures and values. Woolf's life-long involvements with organizations focussed on social and political reform have also played a key role in reassessments of the contradictory and sometimes offensive representations of the working classes in her work. Critics draw on Woolf's vision of the 'common reader' and her democratic goal of making literature available to all, as well as on her role as a publisher in supporting working-class writing and political views, as they consider the complexity of Woolf's class politics.

Once perceived as a 'lady' novelist, elitist and distant from social and political realities, critics now recognize the feminist, socialist and pacifist perspectives in Woolf's writing, assessing her roles as a political activist, thinker and writer whose work engaged with the political movements of her time albeit in complex and sometimes highly problematic ways. This chapter will examine these issues in relation to *A Room of One's Own* (1929), *To the Lighthouse* (1927) and *Orlando: A Biography* (1928).

Gender and sexuality

As a middle-class woman writer working to build her professional identity in a male-dominated literary sphere, Woolf personally had to negotiate the social, political and cultural limitations imposed on women. From the outset of her career as a professional writer, she confronted a literary tradition in which women writers were largely absent or perceived as secondary and in which fictional representations of women simply confirmed gender inequalities. Unsurprisingly, then, concerns with gender and sexuality are in many ways at the heart of Woolf's work as she challenges male-dominated perspectives and prerogatives. These challenges to gender norms and conventions are articulated in various ways. Characterization and character interaction are an obvious focus, but narrative techniques and devices, imagery, symbolism and use of particular kinds of discourse, form and structure, as well as the articulation of polemical argument all play a role. Her writing also draws attention to the ways in which literary traditions and conventions privilege a masculine perspective and influence that obscures women's voices and views. Concerns with sexuality also inflect aspects of Woolf's experience as a writer and homoeroticism works to intensify the feminist perspectives and criticisms of male-dominated culture found in her work.

Woolf's ideas and thinking about the relation of women and literature are the focus of three key and interrelated essays, 'Women and Fiction' (1929), *A Room of One's Own* and 'Professions for

Women' (given as a lecture in 1931; published in 1942) and these have been extensively discussed by critics focussed on gender issues in her work. For discussion of *A Room of One's Own*, see Bowlby (1997), Fernald (1994), Showalter (1977) and Laura Marcus (2004).

A Room of One's Own

Developed from two lectures she gave to women students at Cambridge University in 1928, *A Room of One's Own* is now considered to be a pioneering study of women's relation to literature. This essay comprehensively addresses the inequalities in the literary tradition, highlighting the ways in which fictional representations of women compound these inequalities. More provocatively, it exposes the underlying factors resulting in the virtual absence of women writers from canons of 'great' writing. She puts forward explanations for the deep-seated and seemingly intransigent ideological obstacles to women's advancement and argues strongly that creative production is dependent upon material things: 'a woman must have money and a room of her own if she is to write fiction' (*AROO* 6).

From the outset it is clear, however, that Woolf is refusing to assume the authoritative 'masculine' perspective expected in this situation, and, in fact, she creates a narrator, Mary Beton, through whose point of view the arguments are presented. In contrast to the usual format of the lecture or essay, which pursues a clear and logical path towards an assertive conclusion, Woolf's essay digresses and circles back and also includes fictional elements to convey certain points. This more open and ambiguous form has been read as a defensive strategy aimed to deflect negative criticism from the challenging ideas the essay raises and in her diary Woolf records that she feared being 'attacked for a feminist & hinted at for a sapphist' (*D3* 262). However, this more indirect method seems also to be a deliberate strategy and this essay makes a strong case for writing that is less rigidly structured and more suggestive as being better suited to women writers. Her essay puts forward a clear and rationally argued analysis but is also playful and teasing, at times using satire, parody and ironic overstatement, so that we must read carefully and not automatically take every statement at face value. Indeed, the style, tone and apparent contradictions and inconsistencies here have led to a number of different (and sometimes conflicting) ways of understanding the feminist arguments put forward. It is also important to keep in mind that Woolf's suggested prerequisites for allowing women to write – financial independence and a space to work (summed up as £500 per year and room of one's own) — remain an aspiration for many women across the world and we can see that Woolf's feminist arguments continue to have relevance today.

Woolf's essay discusses the social, political, economic and ideological factors historically impeding women's equal participation in public life and their contributions to the cultural sphere. Social pressures on women to marry and reproduce, legal structures which prohibit women's participation in business and prevent women's ownership of property, alongside the effect of powerful cultural conceptions of women as 'the mental, moral and physical' inferior of men mean that women's views have largely been excluded from historical records (*AROO* 32). This situation has created an unquestioned predominance of male authority, perspectives and values. However, this assumption of male superiority relies on the continued ideological belief that men and women are polar opposites and that women are inferior. The feminist debates and suffrage campaigns of the time were having a serious impact on these established ideas and many of the arguments Woolf puts forward echo and confirm those already in circulation. This political context has the effect of intensifying the focus on gender and sexuality in her present time: 'No age can ever have been as stridently sex-conscious as our own' (*AROO* 94). Invited as she had been to address the topic of 'women and fiction' in her lectures, Woolf focusses her feminist arguments through an examination of factual and fictional literature.

Woolf's essay draws attention to the highly contradictory impression of women produced in writing drawn from a range of fields of study. In fiction, women are represented as a version of the feminine ideal, a paragon of beauty and virtue worthy of worship, but the historical record stresses women's powerlessness and insignificance, to the point that women have 'no existence in fact' (*AROO* 43). As Woolf's narrator contemplates the empty shelves where books written by women *could* have been, she considers women's absence in relation to the literary record as well. With the great exception of Aphra Behn, the first professional woman writer, the narrator can only speculate on women's creative potential in the past and the ways it was thwarted by the hostile ideological and material forces that prohibit women's success. Speculation on what would have been the tragic fate of a female equivalent to Shakespeare, his imaginary sister Judith, illustrates this point effectively. This lack of literary heritage has a serious consequence since, as for male authors, the work of predecessors is of vital importance in creating a solid cultural and literary ground on which subsequent women writers can build. As Woolf states, 'masterpieces are not single and solitary births; they are the outcome of many years of thinking in common, of thinking by the body of the people, so that the experience of the mass is behind the single voice' (*AROO* 63).

The nineteenth century saw a marked increase in women's contribution to the literary sphere which is important in building a female literary tradition. However, this greater prominence was accompanied by women's increased sex-consciousness and anxiety about how they and their work will be judged. This anxiety provokes two responses – either a sense of anger, or fear and deference to male authority – both of which distort women's artistic vision and compromise integrity. As Woolf's study approaches her own time, the feminist perspective and arguments about gender become more complex, contradictory and ambiguous, particularly in relation to the approach, style and form that women's writing should take. On the one hand, a *materialist* argument is proposed which suggests that women's contribution to the literary sphere and women's writing are directly affected by their social, economic and political situations. Women writers need money and what this can provide – access to education and a physical space for thought and creativity. On the other hand, it would seem that women's bodies hold the key to their creativity and that their style of writing should articulate their *essential* differences in experience and views: 'The book has somehow to be adapted to the body, and at a venture one would say that women's books should be shorter, more concentrated, than those of men', taking into account the different ways 'the nerves... feed the brain' in men and women (*AROO* 74).

The final section of the essay raises one of the most problematic and controversial ideas which is that a state of spiritual or psychic androgyny is the most favourable for creative inspiration. For some critics this seems to contradict the core elements of Woolf's feminist arguments which are intent on laying bare the cultural and economic consequences of gender *difference* and they view this part of Woolf's argument as a 'flight' from the realities of women's historical conditions (as Elaine Showalter has argued). Once the different threads of Woolf's arguments are unravelled, however, it is clear that the different and seemingly conflicting dimensions here are an indication of the difficult task that explaining women's relation to fiction presents. Woolf's essay attempts to untangle the complexities in two ways:

1. by challenging the dominant gender ideology which perpetuates ideas of women's inferiority and justifies their political and economic inequality and their exclusion from the literary sphere
2. by making central women's experience, and the difference in view this engenders at all levels of the text – its form, style and subject matter.

Woolf exemplifies these two key strands of argument in her discussion of the new forms of writing developed by her imaginary contemporary novelist, Mary Carmichael.

Mary Carmichael's *Life's Adventure*

To counter the detrimental effects of the male-dominated literary tradition, Mary Carmichael must revise and reshape the literary conventions she has inherited for representing female characters and experience, just as she might alter clothing designed for the other sex, to suit her different approach. These 'rough and ready-made clothes' must be made to 'fit … close to every hollow and angle' to represent 'women as they are' (*AROO* 84). This sartorial metaphor emphasizes the difference in women's approach to literature but also suggests a wider point. In drawing attention to one of the central cultural signifiers of gender identity and difference, this metaphor suggests that, like clothes, the cultural patterns of gender relations can be altered – recut to suit a modern context and refashioned to suit a woman's style.

Mary's imaginary novel, *Life's Adventure*, revises the subject matter and, in contrast the prevalent representation of women's lives in fiction, her characters, Chloe and Olivia, are scientists whose marital and domestic roles are of secondary importance. This modern novel introduces a new 'sequence' of narrative events, disrupting the way a novel usually unfolds as well as the 'usual' responses this arouses in the reader 'about love, about death' (*AROO* 87). It is also shaped differently at the level of 'the sentence' because the expression of such new ideas and literary material requires a new, subtle, nuanced and suggestive style, able 'to catch those unrecorded gestures, those unsaid or half-said words, which form themselves, no more palpably than the shadows of moths on the ceiling, when women are alone, unlit by the capricious and coloured light of the other sex' (*AROO* 81). This description of Mary's novel in many ways echoes Woolf's own experiments with gendered style and form (see Chapter Three). For the reader, engaging with such new forms of fiction can be a shocking and unnerving experience, likened to the motion of 'a switchback railway when the car, instead of sinking, as one has been led to expect, swerves up again' (*AROO* 78). Mary's more associative, suggestive and ambiguous form of writing places more demands on the reader who must be more actively engaged and who must also accept a greater openness in terms of plot and ending 'as if the important point were just a little further on' (*AROO* 87).

Woolf's essay also suggests that new woman-centred perspectives and a more fluid, associative style pose a radical challenge to patriarchal literary and social traditions. Mary's open and suggestive style can also articulate women's subversive sexual desire. This is hinted by the teasing address to the reader when the relationship of Chloe and Olivia is described, 'Do not start. Do not blush' (*AROO* 78), alongside reference to the presiding magistrate at the trial of Radclyffe Hall's overtly lesbian novel, Chartres Biron (see Introduction, Sexuality). This potential for subject matter that focusses on women's sexual autonomy and the development of a literary style with which to express it intensifies Woolf's feminist argument by suggesting that her feminist polemic is not only concerned with contesting the inequalities between the sexes, but also with undermining the heterosexual dynamic on which patriarchal society is founded.

This sense of a difference in vision and creative expression seems to suggest an essentialist view of sex and gender. Yet, Woolf is also aware that the way men and women are culturally positioned and perceived, and the opportunities for and expectations on them, provides them with different experiences that shape their outlook on the world. As Woolf states in *Orlando*, 'clothes...change our view of the world and the world's view of us' (*O* 117). The narrator suggests that Mary could make great strides in overcoming the material, social and ideological forces which work to inhibit women's freedom of expression while still prioritizing her specifically female perspective. But, as the narrator continues to point out in hyperbolic style, she will still be 'encumbered' with a sense of sexual transgression, the '"sin" which is the legacy of [women's] sexual barbarity', and will still be 'fetter[ed]' by a sense of being considered second class (*AROO* 84).

Man-womanly, woman-manly, androgynous minds and creativity

Woolf's notion that a more productive, creative state of mind would be androgynous is seen by many as radical, controversial and confusing and has provoked conflicting critical responses. Given that Woolf's argument to this point has indicated the ways in which any attention to sex or gender works to impede creative freedom, this idea of a neutralized state seems in some ways logical. A state of harmony between the masculine and feminine traits present in all of us could create a 'marriage of opposites' in which different qualities of thought, feeling and perception are united, 'consummated' (*AROO* 99). This 'intercourse' can produce a state of fusion in which 'the mind is fully fertilized and uses all it faculties' (*AROO* 94). However, this concept of androgyny, which Woolf attributes to the Romantic poet Samuel Taylor Coleridge, clashes with many of the fundamental points of the feminist argument articulated in this essay. Indeed, Woolf notes that Coleridge's notion that 'a great mind is androgynous' is not one that 'has any special sympathy with women' (*AROO* 94). The ambiguity of these ideas is also compounded by a contradiction between the goal of androgyny (achieving balance and harmony through the neutralization of polarized sex and gender positions) and the highly sexualized language used to describe this state.

What seems to be the crux of Woolf's argument is that for a writer to be 'woman-manly or man-womanly' does not deny or obscure the social realities of gender difference and inequalities, but it *does* challenge binary modes of thought and meaning. Such binary thinking encourages a view of the world as hierarchical and divided into two oppositional categories in which what is deemed 'masculine' is always identified as positive, privileged and superior. An androgynous psychic state allows the writer imaginative access to the full scope of experience, sensation and inspiration available and Woolf demonstrated this ideal of the androgynous mind and spirit in the creation of her fantastical character Orlando (see discussion below). This proposal of androgyny, as Caughie suggests, signals a 'refusal to choose' so that 'The androgynous vision...affirms a "fertile oscillation" between positions' (1991: 82). However, the fantastical qualities Woolf employs in her fictional representation of this ideal of androgynous creativity also indicate her awareness of how difficult this state would be to actually realize.

In *A Room of One's Own* and in *Orlando*, there is a sense of *transition*, of a movement away from Victorian gender ideals as well as from outmoded literary and artistic conventions. Woolf's fictional writers, Mary Carmichael and Orlando, explore new ways to represent experience but also encounter difficulties in their challenges to social and artistic traditions. In *To the Lighthouse*, Woolf creates another woman artist, the painter Lily Briscoe, who also struggles to find new modes of representation for her picture of Mrs Ramsay and James. The subject of her painting, mother and child, locates Lily's work in a long and established artistic tradition which resonates strongly with the religious ideas about the Madonna and Child, and which supports and perpetuates conventional gender ideals. Here too, there is a sense of an androgynous creative process at work as suggested by the ejaculatory metaphors used to represent Lily's inspiration (see discussion below).

Orlando, gender and sexuality

Published immediately before she gave the lectures which became *A Room of One's Own*, *Orlando: A Biography* is a fantastical mock biography of a man/woman-manly character who is also a poet. Orlando lives for four hundred years, and changes from a man to a woman about half way through his/her life. It was in part inspired by the life of Woolf's lover, the poet and novelist Vita Sackville-West, who, as a woman, was not able to inherit her family estate. Although a playful novel, it has a serious intent and engages more explicitly than other of Woolf's fictions with current debates about gender and the categorization of sexual identity. In creating a time-travelling, sex-changing central character, Woolf can expose the fact that the gender identities and sexual categories that we assume to be 'natural' are actually culturally constructed and learned. As Caughie suggests, 'By employing three metaphors for sexual identity in *Orlando* – androgyny, transvestism, and transsexualism – Woolf shows us that there are different ways of talking about identity' (1991: 81).

As Orlando moves through time, the signs and signifiers which designate and define gender and sexual identities (such as clothing) change. This sense of gender and sexuality as mutable rather than fixed and as culturally and historically specific rather than innate is more obviously demonstrated following Orlando's change of sex after which she must *learn* to become a woman. Orlando experiences her change of sex as natural: at first 'Orlando remained precisely as he had been' (*O* 87). However, she soon becomes aware of the necessity of altering her appearance, behaviour and gestures to comply with what patriarchal society expects of a woman. Her first lessons about how to be a lady occur aboard the boat, the *Enamoured Lady*, ironically drawing attention to certain stereotypes of women as overly romantic and, as suggested by the tradition of gendering of ships and cars, as tools for men to use. Orlando must also learn to accept a position of social, political and economic inferiority and dependence, as the powerful institutions of law, marriage and family dictate. What Orlando the man took for granted as his *human* right – namely his right to his inheritance, to freedom of movement and economic independence – are all stripped away once he has become a woman and she learns that these rights and privileges are only available to men. What is made clear is that gender is a fundamental part of identity and that it forms a large part of the role we adopt in a particular kind of society. In this way, Woolf's novel can be read as a scathing attack on the sexual inequalities enforced in the heterosexual and patriarchal society to which Orlando belongs, as these inequalities are reinforced and perpetuated by traditions and conventions, as well as by social institutions. Anticipating the feminist theorist, Simone de Beauvoir's famous statement, Orlando demonstrates that 'One is not born, but rather becomes, a woman' (1988: 295).

More challenging than this is, however, is what Orlando's change of sex also demonstrates about the *way* the categories of gender and sexuality are constructed as binary opposites. We are told that 'Different though the sexes are, they intermix. In every human being a vacillation from one sex to the other takes place' and that clothes (cultural signifiers of one gender or the other) may indicate one gender 'while underneath the sex is the very opposite of what it is above' (O 118). Orlando's change of sex reveals the ways in which ideas about anatomical sexual difference are exaggerated so as to create the impression of absolute distinctions between the sexes and to polarize gender identities. Cultural ideas about gendered identities, roles and behaviour, overlay and inflate biological differences, thus making the seemingly clear-cut binary distinctions between men and women, masculinity and femininity, appear to be 'natural'. It is these gender binaries that form the fundamental structure of heterosexual relations. The fact that Woolf's novel exposes these binaries as constructed not natural attacks not only gender inequalities, but also seriously undermines the status of heterosexuality as *the* natural sexuality against which any other desires are judged unnatural and on which patriarchal society is based. Woolf's representation of so-called 'deviant' desires, then, also plays a role in her feminist challenges to patriarchal social and cultural structures, premised as they are on gender binaries and heterosexual assumptions.

Orlando sends up commonplace ideas about gender, ridicules compulsory heterosexuality and undermines the grounds for homophobia. Insisting on a central character that transgresses conventional boundaries of sexed and gendered identities – Orlando can be described as transgendered, queer, lesbian and transvestite – this novel mocks any sense of a stable, 'natural' or scientifically-proven meaning for sexed bodies and sexual desire. It satirically dismisses binary thinking at every level and privileges ambiguities and contradictions: Orlando is male and female, masculine and feminine, gay and straight. With 'or' and 'and' as part of Orlando's name, Woolf seems to suggest a refusal of the binary choice of 'either/or' in favour of the inclusive, and in this case contradictory, 'and'. Woolf understood that human experience and subjectivity are complex and not easily defined and her writing resists and undermines the ideas of fixed distinctions and divisions.

To the Lighthouse, gender and sexuality

This novel is considered to be Woolf's most autobiographical novel
and the Ramsays can be seen, in part, to be fictionalized versions
of Woolf's parents, Leslie and Julia Stephen. The given setting
for the novel is the Isle of Skye but the novel seems to draw on
Woolf's familial experiences, particularly what for her were idyllic
summer holidays spent in St Ives in Cornwall. In many ways, Julia
Stephen seems to have taken on the role of 'the Angel in the House',
a phrase encapsulating the ideal Victorian wifely role and drawn
from Victorian poet, Coventry Patmore's poem of the same title,
celebrating married love.[1] Woolf's creation of Mrs Ramsay is in
part a memorial to her own mother whose death when Woolf was
only thirteen had such a profound effect on her (see Woolf's memoir
'A Sketch of the Past'). The novel satirically undermines Victorian
ideals of femininity and masculinity and the gender relations that
structured her parents' marriage and that Woolf sees as persisting
into the twentieth century. Beyond this personal context, the novel
can be read as a scathing attack on these outmoded ideas, though
it also recognizes the nostalgic emotional pull, particularly of 'the
Angel in the House'. The modernist artist Lily Briscoe's ambivalent
response to Mrs Ramsay exemplifies the complexities and
ambiguities of the exploration of gender issues in this novel: Lily
criticizes her but also loves her deeply and mourns her loss. Woolf's
writing engages with issues of gender in multiple ways – through
characterization, form and literary techniques. It also criticizes
ideas of 'masculinity' and 'femininity' as these operate as cultural
abstractions – as sets of ideas and characteristics that are applied to
things and areas of experience which are not associated with sexed,
biological bodies. In this novel, the gendered discourse of reason,
logic and truth is perceived as 'masculine' and this competes for
priority over the 'feminine' discourse of emotion and intuition. The
novel opens with a protracted discussion about the weather and
the possibility of a boat trip to the lighthouse and this illustrates
the contrasts between these gendered discourses: Mr Ramsay relies
on logic and voices his views with certainty ('it won't be fine'); Mrs
Ramsay, not wanting to crush her youngest son's desperate longing
to go to the lighthouse, is less definite but optimistically hopeful ('it
may be fine') (*TTL* 4).

This discussion also highlights the central preoccupation of the novel with making a journey, a literal movement from one place to another – the trip 'to the lighthouse' – which is also implicitly a metaphorical journey, a transition from one social and political context to another. In her notebook, Woolf described the structure of her novel as 'two blocks joined by a corridor' (Dick 1983: 44), a plan that also implies movement down a 'corridor' of time. The 'two blocks' are specific historical and cultural moments, 'The Window' set on a single day in 1909 and 'The Lighthouse' set on another day in 1919, with 'Time Passes' mapping the cataclysmic ten-year period of transition between the two. This temporal setting has great significance for considerations of class and gender issues in this novel. This period saw massive social, political and economic upheavals brought about by the impact of the Great War and shifts in the balance of power between the classes and genders were a consequence of this and the changing political landscape. With vast numbers of men fighting on the front, women took on 'men's' jobs as manual and clerical workers and as engineers. Feminist campaigns had laid the foundations for women's suffrage in the decades before the war and, in a recognition of women's war-time contributions, women over the age of thirty were granted the vote in the Representation of the People Act of 1918 (though it took until 1928 for the voting age for women to be lowered to twenty-one, on equal terms with men). Women were also allowed to enter all trades and professions with the Sex Disqualification (Removal) Act of 1919. However, while women were granted more equal rights in this way, in reality the post-war period brought a backlash against women's new freedoms and rights as (more) equal citizens. As Woolf's novel makes clear, as with the literal journey to the lighthouse, the social and political 'journey' was equally halting and blocked by many obstacles. This is also echoed in the slow and hesitant progress of the feminist artist Lily Briscoe as she makes her own transition to greater independence.

Woolf's organization of her novel in to two distinct eras enables contrasts to be drawn between the expectations on, and experiences of, her middle-class female characters in the different historical periods. This contrast is heightened by the focus on two very different types of woman in the two sections. In 'The Window', Mrs Ramsay is a paragon of domestic virtue and duty, 'the Angel in the House' and in 'The Lighthouse', Lily, the independent artist, is a 'New Woman' figure. The highly metaphorical 'Time Passes' section indirectly evokes the horrors of war through the loss of Andrew Ramsay in the trenches and the destruction and decay of the Ramsays' house. This period of transition also importantly highlights a shift in relation to roles for women and records the deaths of Mrs Ramsay and Prue, the daughter that most closely follows in her mother's footsteps and who dies in childbirth. At a metaphorical level, this suggests the need to destroy the traditional and outmoded ideals of middle-class femininity that these characters represent in order that new, modern roles for women can emerge. 'Time Passes' focusses on the roles and experiences of working-class women, Mrs McNab and Mrs Bast, and stresses the importance of their role in this process. However, this transition is far from smooth and the distinctions between the different roles for middle-class women in the two eras are not as clear-cut as they might seem. While the modern woman, Lily, seems to resist a traditional female role (refusing Mrs Ramsay's imperative to marry, for example), the emotional pull of the past is powerful and she struggles to come to terms with her feelings of loss and grief for Mrs Ramsay and all that she stood for. Having said that, the overarching organization of the novel works to criticize what Woolf saw as outmoded and damaging gender ideals for men as well as women. 'The Window' offers a scathing criticism of polarized gender roles and identities, particularly as these are reinforced and perpetuated in the social institution of marriage.

Mr Ramsay and the masculine ideal

Mr Ramsay is represented in many ways as an embodiment of patriarchal masculinity as drawn from Victorian gender ideals. He is rigid in his views, authoritarian in behaviour, self-centred and insensitive in his relations with others. From the outset, he assumes the superiority of his masculine values – his belief in logic, facts and reason – in his uncompromising assertion of the 'truth' about the weather forecast based on the evidence provided by the scientific instrument of the barometer. In this, he is not only diametrically opposed to his wife's unfounded optimism and sensitivity to the needs of others, but also seems to take pleasure in disillusioning his children. He is described as 'grinning sarcastically' and he takes pride in his own self-satisfied sense of being right, having 'some secret conceit at his own accuracy of judgement' (*TTL* 4). The brutality of this masculine role is also suggested by the description of him as 'lean as a knife, narrow as the blade of one' (*TTL* 4), his physical attributes seeming to compound the brutal sharpness of his character. The damage wrought by Mr Ramsay's adherence to this masculine ideal is seen in the negative effects on others: James is full of inconsolable rage and resentment at his father and others find him to be petulant, immature, selfish and childish – as Lily thinks, 'Never was anybody at once so ridiculous and so alarming' (*TTL* 16). Woolf shows that Mr Ramsay's fulfilment of gendered expectations has also had a negative impact on him as well, curtailing his potential for positive human interaction. In occasional moments of self-awareness, he recognizes how his behaviour and attitude affect others, his being 'touchy' and losing his temper 'made things worse for her [Mrs Ramsay]' (*TTL* 60). He also has the capacity to respond to art and is emotionally moved by certain pieces of literature. However, his engagement with Tennyson's poem, 'The Charge of the Light Brigade', reveals that he also draws on literature to shore up a sense of his masculinity. His vigorous recitation of this poem, which describes a tragic miscommunication between the commanding officers at the Battle of Balaclava (1854) that caused the unnecessary deaths of hundreds of soldiers, allows him a vicarious sense of belligerence and he also charges about the garden. The repetition of the line, ' "Someone had blundered" ' (*TTL* 28), criticizes male authority and masculine belligerence in the past but also in Woolf's contemporary time given the more recent tragic 'blunder' of the First World War.

In other ways, too, Mr Ramsay's masculine outlook and qualities are satirically undermined: he may exemplify worthy qualities, such as 'courage, truth, and the power to endure', but his rigid pose and visual focus are limited and limiting: 'Mr. Ramsay would straighten his back and *narrow* his *little* blue eyes upon the horizon' (*TTL* 4, emphasis added). His upright posture parallels his rigid adherence to accepted social ideals, moral codes and intellectual frameworks for understanding the world, but these, Woolf's description seems to suggest, are also 'narrow' and 'little', short-sighted and limited in their perspective and sense of possibilities (as here, for good weather and for a happy life for his children). That Mr Ramsay's pessimism and severity are in part a result of his bitter sense of disappointment with his own achievements and his feelings of inadequacy and failure create a certain level of sympathy for him. He charts his intellectual progress with reference to the linear order of the alphabet, but fears he can go no further, the capacity of his 'splendid mind' has been halted and 'he stuck at Q' (*TTL* 31, 32). The irony of not being able to reach 'R' and of not understanding the kind of intellectual ability this letter signifies in this scheme suggests that his adherence to this ideal of masculinity actually prevents his understanding of himself, Ramsay: 'the intensity of his gaze...obscured the letter R...he was a failure' (*TTL* 32). However, Woolf's satirical treatment of his response to his perceived failure counters this sense of sympathy. Reflecting on his intellectual hardships, he reconfigures them as tests of physical endurance and indulges in a self-aggrandizing fantasy of himself as a hero – as a soldier braving treacherous conditions or an explorer on a dangerous expedition. Through this evocation of other overtly masculine identities he insists on his masculine qualities of leadership, bravery and stoicism. This heroic posturing is ridiculed and deflated by his actual position, however, safely ensconced as he is in the domesticated garden created by Mrs Ramsay: 'Mr Ramsay squared his shoulders and stood very upright by the urn' (*TTL* 33). Contrary to the myth of masculine independence on which Mr Ramsay relies for his sense of self, it is clear that he is utterly dependent on his wife for her unfailing support of him. Her wifely role silently sustains this myth by freeing Mr Ramsay from all domestic responsibilities and by sustaining him emotionally. Woolf's novel offers a scathing indictment of masculine strength and authority in likening Mr Ramsay's self-centred dependence on Mrs Ramsay to 'a fractious child' seeking comfort and nurture from his nurse. Having received Mrs Ramsay's assurance of his abilities, like a baby full of its mother's milk, he is 'Filled with her words, like a child who drops off satisfied' and he feels 'restored, renewed' (*TTL* 35, 36).

Mrs Ramsay and the 'universal law' of marriage

Woolf's criticism of the institution of marriage and the gender roles for women it reinforces is made clear in the exhausting effect that fulfilling her duties as a wife and mother has on Mrs Ramsay, leading, the novel implies, to her early death. In contrast to Mr Ramsay who is replenished by his relationship with his wife, Mrs Ramsay is left utterly drained, 'Immediately, Mrs. Ramsay seemed to fold herself together, one petal closed in another, and the whole fabric fell in exhaustion upon itself' (*TTL* 36). While she experiences a sense of satisfaction in fulfilling her wifely role, and appreciates the 'harmony' that the complementary roles of husband and wife are meant to create – the 'solace which two different notes, one high, one low, struck together, seem to give each other as they combine' (*TTL* 36) – she also fees the 'burden' on her to maintain a sense of peace, security and domestic happiness (*TTL* 37).

This wifely role and feminine ideal is also obviously a constraint on her. Mrs Ramsay is an intelligent and energetic woman, resourceful and socially aware, yet her sphere of action is circumscribed and limited to the domestic realm. Her will and power are asserted within this sphere and she is accused of 'Wishing to dominate, wishing to interfere, making people do what she wished' (*TTL* 53). In private with other women she also mocks men for their foibles and preoccupations, comically 'enact[ing]', 'adroitly shap[ing]; even maliciously twist[ing]' their words and mannerisms (*TTL* 46). This action of twisting serves as a trope for Mrs Ramsay's barely contained irritation and anger, and seems to be an habitual gesture, as the twisted finger of her glove suggests and as we see in response to Mr Ramsay's insistence that the weather will not be fine when she impatiently gives her knitting a 'little twist' (*TTL* 4). In a telling moment of semi-conscious reverie, Mrs Ramsay's most deeply felt and unacknowledged wishes come to the surface of her awareness. She recognizes that, on the one hand, without her social role premised on benefiting others she would be merely 'a wedge-shaped core of darkness, something invisible to others' (*TTL* 58). On the other hand, this invisibility brings the freedom she secretly longs for, 'This core of darkness could go anywhere, for no one saw it. They could not stop it, she thought, exulting' (*TTL* 58). Escaping her socially endorsed and enforced role, even if only in her imagination, frees her desires and ambitions, 'Her horizon seemed to her limitless' (*TTL* 58). Elsewhere in the novel we are made aware of the frustration she feels in her conventional middle-class role. She is aware of social problems and the need to reform 'hospitals and drains and the dairy' all of which endanger health (*TTL* 53) but, although she harbours a secret ambition to take her philanthropy to a professional level, to be 'an investigator, elucidating the social problem', she is constrained by her position as 'a private woman' (*TTL* 8).

Nonetheless, she worships male-dominated institutions of politics, law, business and empire and feels that, in her role as guardian of the home, 'she had the whole of the other sex under her protection' (*TTL* 5). She sees marriage as the pinnacle of women's achievement and 'insist[s]' that all young women 'must marry' because 'here she saddened, darkened … there could be no disputing this: an unmarried woman … has missed the best of life' (*TTL* 46). Her change of mood when she discusses marriage suggests, perhaps, how seriously she reveres this institution. There is no disputing it because it is the relationship sanctioned, endorsed, and insisted upon in a patriarchal society, a relationship that is taken to be 'the universal law' (*TTL* 46). However, it also suggests her own admission that she too is bound by this law, despite her deep-seated sense of thwarted ambitions and the physical, emotional and mental exhaustion that marriage brings. We are told that Mrs Ramsay is myopic and Woolf's novel suggests that she is socially short-sighted too: she is aware of wider problems and the limitations of the feminine ideal, but cannot conceive of a role beyond the domestic sphere for herself or other women.

Woolf's novel exposes marriage as a symbiotic, co-dependent relationship and vehemently criticizes the insidiousness of this 'universal law' which strips individuals of their autonomy. In particular, this critique attacks the feminine ideals and roles marriage enforces and the severe demands it makes on women who are trained to see the world through male eyes, to accept values and beliefs about their roles in life which work to benefit men and a patriarchal society. Their learned self-sacrifice is oppressive, exhausting and destructive. Yet, Woolf is also aware of the powerful allure of such culturally endorsed ideals. As she recognizes in her own account of entering the literary profession and being able to speak her mind, the phantom of 'the Angel in the House' is hard to exorcize and continues to haunt her present day. As she states in 'Professions for Women', 'Killing the Angel in the House was part of the occupation of a woman writer', but this opens up questions about the kinds of identities for women that will emerge as a result. In her essay, Woolf asks, 'what is "herself"? I mean, what is a woman?' (*E6* 481).

Lily Briscoe – a new vision

Critics have often seen Lily as a kind of surrogate for Woolf: both are feminist artists working with new modernist modes of representation to offer alternative perspectives on the social and political landscape of the post-war period. Through different art forms, they both seek to re-present and redefine gendered identities and modes of interaction, both complete their work and have their 'vision' at the same moment in the final words of the novel. Yet, there is a profound ambiguity about what these new identities might be: where Lily places the final line of her painting is not specified, nor does Woolf herself delineate a new identity for women. Woolf's decision to write her novel as a form of 'Elegy' (*D3* 34) highlights a number of different kinds of loss, including the certainty that the gendered identities of the past provided. The absence of specific definitions of new roles and identities for women suggests both a refusal to pin down what a new idea of womanhood could be, but also indicates the cultural battles still to be fought by women pursuing a career other than that of wife and mother.

Lily struggles to extricate herself from the cultural expectations that she will fulfil a domestic role as she simultaneously contests views that aim to undermine women's success in any other sphere. These views are summed up succinctly in Charles Tansley's chauvinistic assertion that '"Women can't paint, women can't write"' (*TTL* 45). The difficulties Lily experiences in completing her painting can be seen to mirror her difficulty in carving out a new social space for herself as an independent, unmarried woman. She is in 'perpetual combat' with 'habitual currents' of opinion (*TTL* 151). The subject matter of her painting aligns it with a long tradition of iconographic representations of the Madonna and Child, images largely produced by male artists and which idealize this relationship as an 'object[s] of universal veneration' (as William Bankes considers it, *TTL* 49). The difficulties Lily encounters as she makes different attempts to position the masses of colour and lines correspond with the two-fold difficulty of her task: to reconfigure a sense of women's roles and relations to others, *and* to find new forms with which to represent this re-visionary view. In this, she counters a great weight of social and artistic tradition.

The 'triangular purple shape' that Lily creates to represent Mrs Ramsay and James in her earlier painting and the 'odd-shaped triangular shadow' which forms over the step as Lily begins her painting afresh in 'The Lighthouse' section (*TTL* 48, 191) have been interpreted in a number of ways. This exemplifies the complex and conflicting ways of understanding the representations of gender in this novel and of understanding Woolf's feminist politics more generally. Representing human forms with a geometric abstract shape signals a radical break with artistic conventions in line with post-impressionist and cubist artistic forms. The triangle shape also echoes Mrs Ramsay's own image of the 'wedge-shaped core of darkness' that she feels is the centre of her being so that Lily's painting can be seen to give expression to this unconventional and hidden aspect of Mrs Ramsay. Lily's purple triangle has also been seen to have political resonance in that a three-sided form disrupts the gender binaries and dichotomies on which patriarchal power hierarchies are based and, as Jane Goldman argues, Woolf employs 'feminist colour tropes' (the tricolour of the suffrage campaign) in this novel (1998: 168). As Woolf makes clear in *A Room of One's Own* and elsewhere, however, the past cannot be simply rejected and women must adapt the forms they inherit. As much as Lily's feminist and modernist vision seeks to find new models for representing women other than the idealized forms found in male-dominated artistic traditions, some critics interpret her painting as echoing the triangular outlines that shape the iconic images of the Madonna from Renaissance to Pre-Raphaelite art, as well as in photographic representations of mother and child the Victorian period, including photographs of Julia Stephen with her children (as Jane de Gay demonstrates).

In other ways, Lily's battles with the new formal and aesthetic qualities of her painting begin a transformation of this artistic tradition and the patriarchal ideals of womanhood it embodies. Lily resists Mrs Ramsay's insistence on marriage and transforms the intense emotions and erotic passions Mrs Ramsay has stirred in Lily into a source of inspiration. Her complex feelings for Mrs Ramsay are suggestively homoerotic as she takes pleasure from physical contact with Mrs Ramsay and also longs for greater intimacy: 'Sitting on the floor with her arms round Mrs. Ramsay's knees, close as she could get', she imagines the possibility of 'becoming... one with the object one adored'; in her love for Mrs Ramsay, Lily longs for a sense of unity beyond what is possible 'in any language known to men' (*TTL* 47). Lily's experience of Mrs Ramsay is also at odds with her image as the Victorian ideal of femininity: Lily, like other younger women, is privy to Mrs Ramsay's mockery of men, experiences her commanding behaviour and is made aware of her sexual as well as her emotional power. Woolf's richly metaphorical and suggestive style powerfully conveys these more subversive qualities in Mrs Ramsay, making apparent her powerful vitality and vigorous fertility which is articulated in sexualized language suggestive of orgasm and ejaculation. Mrs Ramsay could 'pour erect into the air a rain of energy, a column of spray, looking at the same time animated and alive as if all her energies were being fused into one force, burning and illuminating (quietly though she sat, taking up her stocking again)...this delicious fecundity, this fountain and spray of life' (*TTL* 34).

In the later section of the novel, Lily, in need of inspiration, remembers Mrs Ramsay sitting on the beach and simultaneously imagines herself sitting beside her, feeling this to be an 'extraordinarily fertile' connection between them (*TTL* 163). The metaphorical description of Lily's experience of inspiration echoes the sexualized expression of Mrs Ramsay's phallic energy:

> Then, as if some juice necessary for the lubrication of her faculties were spontaneously squirted, she began precariously dipping among the blues and umbers, moving her brush hither and thither, but it was now heavier and went slower, as if it had fallen in with some rhythm which was dictated to her...by what she saw, so that while her hand quivered with life, this rhythm was strong enough to bear her along with it on its current (*TTL* 152).

While Lily's painting represents newness and innovation, these qualities are inspired by a connection with the past as Lily seems to harness Mrs Ramsay's potentially subversive sexual power to fertilize her new vision. Lily's new configuration of womanhood and female sexuality suggested in the purple/shadow triangle shape in her painting undermines the polarized and oppositional gendered identities underlying the Ramsays' marriage by triangulating the rigid binary organization of that relationship. Further, that Lily channels the androgynous sexualized power of Mrs Ramsay herself (her generative and procreative energy which assumes a phallic and fertilizing power) could be seen to resonate with Woolf's concept of the androgynous mind as an ideal mental state for achieving creative potential. Woolf suggests that a mental balance of masculine and feminine qualities can neutralize what she saw as the distorting effect of heightened sex-consciousness, as Lily experiences repeatedly when contemplating her position as a woman artist. However, this final section of the novel is clearly preoccupied with Lily's creative process as a woman and with the necessary 'achieve[ment of] that razor edge of balance between two opposite forces: Mr. Ramsay and the picture' (*TTL* 184), between patriarchal prohibition of her artistic independence and finding a new form and aesthetic for her art.

Finally, perhaps momentarily freed from the self-consciousness about trespassing on male (sexual and artistic) territory, Lily has her vision and 'drew a line there, in the centre' (*TTL* 198). The profound uncertainty about the placing of the final line of Lily's painting, however, maintains an openness and lack of narrative closure which has given rise to a number of speculations about its metaphorical meaning. Critics debate whether this final line divides or connects the 'masses' of colour and consider what might be its significance for Woolf's feminist politics, aesthetics and vision. Woolf herself maintained that she did not intend the lighthouse to be read as a symbol, but included it because 'One has to have a central line down the middle of the book to hold the design together' (*L3* 385). Yet, Woolf's densely figurative and associative use of language and imagery resists this simple formalist explanation. Critics have seen Lily's line as a refiguration of the lighthouse itself, a phallic symbol with which Mrs Ramsay erotically identifies (*TTL* 60). It can be seen to take on a wider significance, uniting the 'masses' on the left and right of the political spectrum. It can stand for a memorializing of Mrs Ramsay, as well as a resistance to her authority and the Victorian feminine values she stands for. The fact that we are not given a clear description of Lily's painting means that the final vision that completes the novel remains profoundly ambiguous, 'with all its green and blues, its lines running up and across, its attempt at something' (*TTL* 198). That Lily envisages that her painting will be 'hung in the attics' (*TTL* 198) points possibly to her anxiety about the quality of her art. It also suggests that this work marks a stage of development rather than a piece of art ready for display. Both implications confirm the sense we have of transition in this novel: for

Lily as she moves into a male-dominated sphere in which women's work is judged as inferior, and for her work itself as it signals the emergence of new artistic forms with which to articulate a feminist perspective. Lily's painting represents a revisionary artistic practice which signals a transition between one stage and another, but does not provide hard and fast solutions to the complex issues of gender and sexuality.

To the Lighthouse and class issues

Woolf has been criticized for a lack of positive and fully developed working-class characters in her fiction and for her unsympathetic representations of the 'lower orders' who are accorded only marginal importance when compared to the middle-class protagonists. Servants facilitate the day-to-day ease of middle-class life and shore up class-specific values, but Woolf's representations also bring to the surface concerns and anxieties which threaten to destabilize the seeming security of middle-class life. In this sense, the novel can be read as a scathing criticism of the middle-class home as an institutional centre of power which perpetuates class and gender inequalities. It reveals the interconnectedness of gender and class relations in the domestic realm with networks of power and authority in the wider public sphere. The complexities of class politics in this novel can be explored through a focus on the women servants in 'The Window' and those in 'Time Passes', as well as on the lower-middle-class character of Charles Tansley.

Geographical and temporal setting

As Woolf's most autobiographical novel, its fictional seaside setting is assumed to be based on St Ives, the harbour town in Cornwall where Woolf's family spent their summer holidays. Woolf names the setting as the Isle of Skye and this geographical location seems to be significant for a consideration of the class politics of this novel given the wider concerns about the North/South political and economic divide discussed in a number of Hogarth Press publications at this time. Importantly, the novel maps a sense of transition in class relations, a shift emphasized by the temporal setting and the movement from a pre-war to a post-war time frame. The period covered by the novel (1909–19) saw a political sea change brought about by the reforms introduced by Liberal Governments and the rise of the Labour Party, as well as by the devastating impact of the war. This time frame also obviously includes December 1910, the date 'on or about' when 'human character' and all social relations 'changed' (*E3* 421–2). The post-war period saw a loss of faith in upper and middle-class authority and leadership and a sharper sense of class conflict with economic depression resulting in industrial strikes and class disruptions. The historical period covered in the 'Time Passes' section of the novel includes the Great War and its immediate aftermath, but also seems to resonate with the period in which Woolf was actually writing her novel – the mid-1920s – in which various industrial actions took place, culminating in the largest general strike Britain had known in May 1926. Reports in the press represented the General Strike in terms of class 'war' and the discussions it provoked raised issues about new social and economic relations, as well as about more fundamental issues concerning how certain kinds of labour define identity and a sense of the self. Woolf was in support of the strike and kept a careful record of its progress in her diary. The effect of this social and political disruption temporarily halted her writing of her novel (see Levenback 1999) and we might consider the traces of this event in her depiction of her working women in 'Time Passes'.

In 'The Window', the Ramsay family confidently takes for granted its class superiority and assumes that others would want to share their class comforts and interests. Towards the end of this section there is a sense of a political shift as the lower-middle-class Charles Tansley, an aspiring academic and acolyte of Mr Ramsay, asserts his political views. These views are informed by his working-class family origins as the descendant of fishermen and lighthouse keepers 'off the Scottish coast' (*TTL* 86). Michael Tratner argues that '[t]he novel is built around the relationship between two houses, one full of rich people and one full of workers' (1995: 56) and that the drive of the novel, to get middle-class people to the lighthouse, suggests that a connection between the classes represents progress. Tansley's class background along with his hard work and educational achievement suggest his potential to bridge the social gulf between the classes.

Tansley's presence in the Ramsay household (which can be read as a microcosm for society as a whole) presents a challenge to the social structures and values which allow middle-class experience to run smoothly. His explosive outburst at the dinner party transgresses middle-class etiquette (he can barely contain 'the gunpowder that was in him', *TTL* 85) and his arguments expose middle-class thinking about class issues as outmoded and limited. His views literally disrupt the flow of social conversation and lead to a discussion of the policy of the Labour Party. Throughout the novel, Mrs Ramsay does express some sympathy for Tansley's situation, though she is condescending towards him at the same time. However, on the whole, her treatment of him can be read metaphorically as an attempt to contain the threat he represents to middle-class life. Mrs Ramsay aligns Tansley with the servants and he, like Mildred, bears the brunt of her irritation when things do not go according to her plan. Mrs Ramsay denies him the privacy of a soundproof bedroom enjoyed by the family and guests, instead allocating him to an attic room next to the servants, where 'every footstep could be plainly heard' (*TTL* 7). She is troubled by the disruptive effect his literal movements might have on her household and this seems to be symbolic of her more deep-seated concern with the effect that his social mobility might have on her class position. She overtly draws a parallel between his physical clumsiness (which suggests he does not literally fit in to this middle-class home) and his social 'clumsiness' (his ill-mannered and uncouth behaviour at dinner, which also marks his difference from the other middle-class guests). She thinks, 'since he said things like that about the Lighthouse, it seemed to her likely that he would knock a pile of books over, just as they [her children, Cam and James] were going to sleep' (*TTL* 107). This can be seen to suggest a middle-class fear about the lower classes attaining middle-class status, in this case via education and reading 'a pile of books'. Mrs Ramsay seems anxious about the detrimental impact this might have on future generations, disturbing the peace and ease of the middle-class life her children should have ahead of them.

The novel itself also seems to contain Tansley in the way his story develops. His potential as a force for change is dissipated by his desire to belong to a social group that keeps class and gender hierarchies in place. Far from wanting to fundamentally disrupt the power dynamic of middle-class life, he simply wants to emulate the middle-class men around him. At the dinner party, his demands for reform are premised on his fierce assertion of his masculine superiority and exclusion of women. Like the other middle-class characters, he is oblivious to the work of the female servants who make the party possible (Tratner 1995: 53). At the end of the meal, as he and William Bankes go out onto the terrace to continue their discussion of the Labour Party, Tansley willingly takes the lead from Bankes' middle-class authority and his working-class political anger is recuperated into a middle-class perspective. In the post-war period, he achieves the kind of success he aimed for – 'He had got his fellowship. He had married; he lived at Golder's Green' (*TTL* 187) – but he is represented as an unattractive character, self-seeking, egotistical and narrow-minded. In this sense, he has limited political credibility, not because of his working-class origins or political views, but because of his acquiescence in middle-class values. Whether this suggests a prejudice against working-class social mobility or disappointment that working-class politics remain male dominated and so not radical enough is not clear. Lily reflects that her idea about Tansley has become distorted, 'grotesque', and that he had become for her 'a whipping-boy', a repository of negative feeling, on whom she could expel her 'temper' (*TTL* 187, 188). Perhaps this is a good description of Woolf's representation of this character from her own conflicted class perspective too.

Mildred, Marthe; Mrs McNab and Mrs Bast

Turning to the representations of working women in the novel, we can perhaps see a clearer sense of political progress – though this is also in many ways contradictory and problematic. Critical assessments of Woolf's attitude to the working classes often make reference to the introduction she was invited to contribute to a collection of writings produced by members of Women's Co-operative Guild, *Life as We Have Known It* (Hogarth Press, 1931). In this introduction, Woolf controversially explains that, although as an intellectual and feminist she understands working women's political demands and calls for reform, she cannot fully engage and sympathize with their experience because she herself has never undertaken repetitive manual work. Further, because she sees the imagination as in part related to physical experience, she claims that she is unable to fully represent a working woman's life in her fiction. For some, this introduction excuses the limitations of Woolf's representations of the working classes, but for others it fuels the accusation of class prejudice. As with other aspects of Woolf's thinking that seem shocking and prejudiced, her self-awareness in relation to her position on class adds greater complexity. Her introduction also demonstrates her awareness of the ways in which her middle-class experience impacts on her class-based views and assumptions, distorting her representations of the working classes, 'making the picture false' (Woolf 1977: xxiii).

As discussed above, this novel can be read as mapping a transition for middle-class women from the compulsory fulfilment of the role of 'Angel in the House' represented by Mrs Ramsay's experience, to a more liberated and independent role, represented by the artist, Lily Briscoe. Considering the class implications of this, what the novel stresses is how fundamentally middle-class women rely on working women to enable them to fulfil their roles. In both the pre- and post-war periods working women consistently support middle-class experience and values: without Mildred and Martha, Mrs Ramsay's role as a mother, wife and hostess would be impossible, and without the hard work and creative energy of Mrs McNab and Mrs Bast, Lily would not have been able to return to the house to have her 'vision' and complete her painting. While in the earlier part of the novel, the women servants (Mildred and Marthe) are silent and kept in their place, the women working to restore the house in 'Time Passes' (McNab and Mrs Bast) have a greater vitality and agency. Although Mildred and Marthe are given first names, we have no sense of their individuality and they are disempowered. Marthe cannot go home to see her dying father in Switzerland and, although Mildred perfectly prepares the complicated dish of Boeuf en Daube for the dinner party, Mrs Ramsay claims its success as her own given that it was made following 'a French recipe of [her] grandmother's' (*TTL* 93). She credits Mildred with the hard work needed to prepare the dish but she and her dinner guests are in no doubt that the real value lies in Mrs Ramsay's own upper middle-class heritage and 'taste'.

The character of Mrs McNab is the main focus for debates about class in this novel. For some critics, Woolf's representation of this character confirms an unsympathetic and prejudiced view (Caughie 1992; Emery 1992), but for others Woolf's class politics are more complicated and contradictory. For example, Zwerdling notes Woolf's 'volatile mixture of class feelings' (1986: 87) which here generates a paradoxical depiction of Maggie McNab as inane and uncouth as well as a powerful, vital force. In many ways, Woolf's representation of this character can be seen to accord with negative stereotypes of working-class women, seeming to confirm a sense of her middle-class prejudice. Described as lumbering, 'she lurched … and leered' (*TTL* 124), Mrs McNab is physically forceful as she battles to restore the house to a habitable state. In fact, she is represented as dehumanized and described as simply 'a force working; something not highly conscious' (*TTL* 132–3). Employed for the momentous task of restoring the house to a habitable condition and its pre-war state, Mrs McNab and Mrs Bast seem to be part of a conservative restoration of the status quo as far as class relations are concerned.

However, the 'Time Passes' section (covering the First World War and the years before and immediately after) creates a narrative space in which the labour of working women, their voices and views are represented. This seems in keeping with the social and political transition this historical period witnessed and represents the war-time roles that working women did play in the workforce, ensuring industries could function and working to restore Britain after the war. The representations of working women as a vital energetic force able to voice their own views also resonates with the period in which the novel was written (the mid-1920s) when the working classes were making their voices heard via industrial actions. Mrs McNab and Mrs Bast express their feelings about their work, the physical hardships of their roles as servants as well as the satisfactions, 'the magnificent conquest over taps and bath' (*TTL* 133). Woolf does not romanticize their work but stresses that manual work is not dignified, but is rather monotonously repetitive and mechanistic, causing the working women's bodies to 'groan[ed]' and 'creak[ed]' (*TTL* 133). Woolf's description makes clear the energy that this hard work requires: 'stooping, rising, groaning, singing, [Mrs McNab and Mrs Bast] slapped and slammed, upstairs now now down in the cellars. Oh, they said, the work!' (*TTL* 133). Described as a vigorous procreative labour, 'some rusty laborious birth' (*TTL* 133), this work of restoration takes on a symbolic significance in the novel. The middle-class home is made habitable again and Britain is restored after the devastation of war.

In terms of the structure of the narrative, this restoration is vital for the emergence of the independent woman artist and critics have perceived parallels between Maggie McNab and Lily. Mrs McNab's work in restoring the house is seen as a creative act and her vision of Mrs Ramsay is echoed in Lily's vision which inspires her completion of her painting. The phrase 'it was finished' to indicate the completion of the working women's labours is echoed at the end of the novel when Lily completes her painting, suggesting that their work anticipates the fulfilment of Lily's vision (*TTL* 134, 198). However, whether this signals a positive change for working-class women is not clear. Mrs McNab is described as a 'care-taking woman' (*TTL* 124), but the question of who benefits from this labour and care forms the crux of much debate about the class politics of this novel.

In many ways, the work of Mrs McNab and Mrs Bast can be seen to simply fulfil the expected role of servants in enabling middle-class ease and comfort. Even Mrs McNab's vision of Mrs Ramsay is seen to operate structurally to prepare for Lily's more epiphanic recollection of Mrs Ramsay and her more profound and meaningful creative act as she has her vision and completes her painting. The third person narrative voice presents only a negative stereotypical view of Mrs McNab, of her 'witlessness' and her lack of individuality, and seems to confirm a class-prejudiced representation. Woolf may in part agree with her narrator's class prejudice but she is also self-critically aware of the way this distorts her representation, the 'picture', of the working classes (as she recognizes in her Introduction to *Life as We Have Known It*) and her narrative includes elements which work to counter this prejudice.

Looking closely at Woolf's narrative technique and her use of free indirect discourse in the 'Time Passes' section, a different and more positive class perspective can be seen as Mrs McNab's thoughts, words and memories are included in the narrative. As Anna Snaith suggests, this narrative technique 'allows for two points of view' (2000: 78) so that the authority of the middle-class narrator is challenged and undermined by the reader's access to Mrs McNab's perspective. For example, the narrative reveals aspects of Mrs McNab's personality – her fondness for flowers and her attitude to waste – as well as her critical attitude to the middle-class neglect of the house: 'Mrs. McNab stooped and picked a bunch of flowers to take home with her. She laid them on the table while she dusted. She was fond of flowers. It was a pity to let them waste. Suppose the house were sold (she stood arms akimbo in front of the looking-glass) it would want seeing to – it would' (*TTL* 129). With what seems a wilful ignorance about the working woman, the narrator can only relate external details – the way Mrs McNab stands – but Woolf's use of free indirect discourse reveals an active mind and sensual response to the world which is far from witless (see Snaith 2000 for further discussion). The flowers she picks for her own pleasure from Mrs Ramsay's garden also trigger her memories of Mrs Ramsay's kindness to her in the past and prompts her vision of Mrs Ramsay, of 'a lady in a grey cloak, stooping over her flowers' (*TTL* 130). The power of her personal memory and Mrs McNab's particular association of Mrs Ramsay with flowers and positive emotion ensures that her vision is not merely a structural element, preparing for Lily's more important vision, but that her vision is as valid and significant as that of Lily.

While this complicated representation of the lower and working classes in this and other novels lays Woolf open to accusation of class prejudice, it also acknowledges the anxieties that political and social changes entail. As she summed up in her essay, 'Mr Bennett and Mrs Brown': 'All human relations have shifted – those between masters and servants, husbands and wives, parents and children' (*E3* 422). It is important that this novel and many of her other works make space for different class views to be voiced – even if Tansley's views meet with silence and incomprehension from some of those around him and reinforce the sense of his not belonging, and even if Mrs McNab's labour in restoring house and nation can be readily subsumed into the middle-class success of Lily and the Ramsay family as they finally make the journey to the lighthouse.

CHAPTER SIX

Empire and Jewishness

For twenty-first-century readers, the co-existence of strong anti-imperialist views alongside antisemitic and racist attitudes in Woolf's writing seems to be incongruous and contradictory. Our frame of reference in relation to these issues has been shaped as a result of powerful twentieth-century political movements and legislation that exposes and challenges racism. In terms of literary analysis, our reading has been informed by postcolonial critical perspectives which not only reveal the brutal history of colonialism and the oppressive effects of imperialism, but also assume a critical stance which challenges power hierarchies of all kinds and opens up questions about the complexity of identity. Whilst we find the racist and antisemitic attitudes in Woolf's work unacceptable, in Woolf's cultural milieu racism and antisemitism were, to a certain extent, habitualized and only semi-conscious, creating a certain acceptance of such prejudices. The extent to which Woolf was aware of her prejudices and the fluctuation of her views – veering from offensive antisemitism to a sense of identification with Jewish people, for example – is very troubling and critics have both taken her to task for the offensive views expressed in her writing, as well as arguing that in including these views she sought to expose the racism of her day. This chapter will examine these issues in relation to Woolf's novels, particularly *The Voyage Out* (1915), *The Years* (1938) and *Between the Acts* (1941), as well as the short story, 'The Duchess and the Jeweller' (1938), and the essay *Three Guineas* (1938).

Empire and imperialism

Issues of empire and imperial dominance permeate Woolf's work from her earliest novel to her last, as well as forming the specific focus of a number of her essays, reviews and personal writings. As a writer and publisher, Woolf was immersed in and helped to shape an environment critical of empire. Working alongside Leonard Woolf and amongst other radical thinkers and writers at the Hogarth Press, she played a key role in exposing the violence and incoherence of imperialism. She also revealed its perpetuation through domestic and wider social structures via the cultural institutions of family, education, religion, government, politics and the military. Her engagement with these ideas raises questions about Britishness and Western identities, nationality and nationalism, civilization and the primitive, cosmopolitanism, globalization and colonial economics, as well as race and racism. References to empire find their way into Woolf's writing in a number of different ways, some more obvious and explicit than others. There are references to 'colonial' places, such as India, Africa, South America and Australia, to non-European characters, to the 'spoils' of empire and also reference to literal objects transplanted from other countries into British life. Less obvious are the references to non-European art, culture and philosophy, for example, the echoes of Hindu prayers in the interludes in *The Waves* (see Marcus 1992: 155), reference to colonial wars and the First World War, and to political controversies and challenges to Britain's colonial rule, such as the rise of mass protests and Ghandi's campaign for Indian independence in *Mrs Dalloway*, and the establishment of the Irish Free State *The Years*. Monuments to the heroes of empire and war are also regularly included in Woolf's descriptions of London, reminding the reader of European imperial rivalries. As these examples show, Woolf's writing demonstrates an awareness of how imperialist ideologies are insidiously present in all areas of life, informing ideas about the self, place (home and abroad), relations (domestic and international) and cultural values. These persistent reminders work to expose and undermine the power and authority of empire (see Introduction).

Woolf's political stance on imperialism is informed in different ways by her cultural and personal experience of empire. Although the British Empire began to lose its status as an unrivalled political and economic power in the early twentieth century, the ideological underpinnings of the cultural institutions through which Woolf's experience, ideas and perspectives were filtered prioritized the belief in White British superiority. This historical and cultural context inevitably informed Woolf's sense of herself, the world and others. In addition, belonging to a family that had for centuries played significant roles in shaping the British Empire and its ideological frameworks complicates her critical political perspective further: her ancestry places her in an 'insider' position, yet she repeatedly assumes the role of 'outsider', critical of imperialist practices, beliefs and values. This complicated position leads to a number of conflicting critical interpretations of Woolf's writing and attitudes. Kathy J. Phillips, for example, points out that although Woolf 'condemns racism explicitly in *A Room of One's Own*... and *Three Guineas*... she never entirely escapes a coolness derived from her early training to feel "superior"' (1994: xxxv). She notes Woolf's 'residual insensitivity to colonized people and her lack of first-hand knowledge of the colonies' (1994: xxxv) and argues that Woolf's representations of non-Europeans are not entirely free of racism: 'she does presume, from time to time, to label people of color with all the unpleasant prejudice of her contemporaries' (1994: xxxiv). Urmila Seshagiri, on the other hand, argues that 'Virginia Woolf's fiction reflects the racial diversity that characterizes the aesthetic, political, and social discourses of her lifetime... Woolf neither reduces racial identities to stereotypes nor self-righteously subverts reductive racism' (2009: 303).

The Dreadnought hoax

Woolf is undoubtedly critical of notions of British superiority and was prepared to challenge the status quo *and* her family connections through her writing and also through her actions. This is well illustrated by her participation in what has become known as the 'Dreadnought hoax' of 1910. The H.M.S. Dreadnought was the newly developed battleship and pride of the British Military. Woolf, Virginia Stephen as she was then, her brother Adrian, sister Vanessa and friends posed as a party of Abyssinian royalty, boarded the ship and demanded a formal tour. For this they blacked up, dressed in flowing robes and turbans and communicated using a made-up 'language' of Swahili, ancient Greek and nonsense words (see Lee 1996: 282–7). The Stephens' cousin, flagship commander William Fisher, unwittingly escorted them on their tour, offering them refreshments and a twenty-one-gun salute (both of which they declined). This incident was a cause of public scandal and personal humiliation for their cousin, and it serves to indicate the extent to which Woolf was prepared to exploit her 'insider' privilege to expose the ignorance of the British military, effectively ridiculing and undermining the belief in an innate British superiority. As Snaith argues, 'Abyssinia's history of resistance to colonization adds another level of subversion the escapade' (2012: 209).

The range of responses that this event has provoked makes clear the complicated and contradictory ways in which Woolf engages with empire, race and imperialism, and gives a sense of the on-going critical debates about these issues. Whereas, Mark Wollaeger asserts that 'if the dubious image of Woolf in blackface during the Dreadnought hoax is any gauge, racial masquerade for her was simply a masquerade, a prank rather than a strategic racial repositioning in relation to dominant society' (2001: 68), Phillips reads this stunt as evidence of Woolf's 'insipient sense of solidarity with oppressed groups', particularly through 'the parallels between the positions of women and colonized peoples' (1994: 248). Seshagiri suggests the contradictory nature of this hoax as both 'an insult to governmental authority and institutional bureaucracy', but also as 'rife with cultural distortions that replicated imperialist racial hegemonies' (2009: 305). For her, the participants' gleeful pleasure in the fancy dress and blacking up, as well as in the performance of their 'cobble[d] together' language not only 'revealed the Navy's ignorance of the nations they dominated', but also suggests the participants' disrespect for real cultural differences given their reductive and nonsensical creation of the racial other, leading to a complicity in an 'imperial violence' (2009: 306). This concept of the 'other' is useful in discussing the ways in which imperialism works to subordinate groups of people. The 'other' is a person or group perceived and treated as if essentially different from, and alien to, oneself. In racist and imperialist discourse the other is also perceived and treated as inferior and incomprehensible.

The Dreadnought hoax episode is often read as an example of Woolf's rebellion against patriarchal structures as well as an exposure of military folly and cultural ignorance. For her part, Woolf cross-dressed as a man, wore a false moustache and beard to take on the identity of 'Prince Mendax'. Her convincing performance in this role works to destabilize both fixed notions of racial identity – British or 'foreigners' – as well as undermining the so-called natural gender identities constructed around binary oppositions. As is evident in Woolf's writing and political critique, she saw feminism and anti-imperialism as interconnected and informing one another. This conjunction of Woolf's anti-imperialist politics and her feminist critique of women's position in a patriarchal society is one of the most radical and controversial aspects of Woolf's politics. At the time of the hoax, Woolf was revising the scene in *The Voyage Out* where the British characters visit the native village (Wollaeger 2001: 75, n. 54) and the contradictory facets of the hoax can help our understanding of Woolf's attitudes to empire and imperial politics in her fiction (discussed in detail below). As Wollaeger also suggests, the visit to the village is the key moment in the novel that exemplifies British women's potential for complicity in imperial systems and empire: '*The Voyage Out* has been understood as a straightforward critique of empire, but Woolf's pivotal scene upriver reveals a more complicated meditation on the potential entanglement of Englishwomen in the norms of gender, sex, and race that empire underwrites' (2001: 44).

The Voyage Out

With its colonial setting extensively exposes the mechanisms of empire and the imperial workings of power – literally, economically, ideologically and symbolically. But it also provides a good example of the many and conflicting possibilities for interpreting Woolf's critical stance on empire and her anti-imperialist politics. As with her later fictions and essays, Woolf's novel engages with the messiness and complexity of imperialism and its legacy; however, her criticism is sometimes compromised by a seeming complicity with imperialist or racist attitudes and values. The novel narrates the story of a group of middle-class English characters (tourists, politicians, artists and businessmen) who travel by boat to South America. Almost immediately, the novel offers a reassessment of assumed British superiority via a satirical perspective. As the cargo boat, the *Euphrosyne*, pulls away from the port, the new perspective from the sea reveals that the imperial centre and the heart of the British Empire is merely 'a very small island…a shrinking island in which people were imprisoned', 'swarming about like aimless ants' (*VO* 24). This is one of many moments in the novel which reassess and undermine the notion of imperial superiority, destabilizing the power hierarchies that help to maintain the Empire's position. The novel has been read as a feminist revision of Joseph Conrad's *Heart of Darkness* in which European civilization is exposed as merely a veneer. Through a satirical approach, Woolf's novel opens up the long history of Western colonization from the Roman Empire and the Renaissance, to the nineteenth-century orchestrators and 'heroes' of the British Empire in order to cast a scathingly light on the colonial enterprise of her present day via representations of the commercial entrepreneur, Willoughby Vinrace, and the conservative M. P., Richard Dalloway, who is on tour to view manufacturing centres, warships and guns. The imperial values and ambitions they champion as part of 'civilized' society are synonymous with their greed for wealth, territory and political power, for dominance over others, and for a fierce drawing and defending of boundaries, geographical, social, racial and sexual. Politics, trade and military force are central to their roles as men of the British Empire and they are depicted as brutish, bullying, egotistical, competitive and belligerent. The veneer of civilization is thinly applied and their barbarism is easily visible.

Yet, Woolf is keen to insist that none of the characters are innocent of an involvement in empire – however knowingly or not. Mrs Flushing deliberately exploits the indigenous people, buying their fabrics and ornaments cheaply to sell them for a profit in London, but others benefit more indirectly. Rachel, although not motivated by the voracious imperialist capitalism that sustains the Empire, is also fundamentally implicated in this brutal system. As she expresses her pity for the cargo of 'Poor little goats' that are going to be traded abroad, her father bluntly reminds she is a beneficiary of this commercial system and that the pleasures of her own life are a direct result of this trade: '"If it weren't for the goats there'd be no music, my dear; music depends upon goats"' (*VO* 16). Rachel is complicit with the colonizers and benefits from the exploitation of the goats and indigenous people involved in her father Willoughby's 'empire'. As Phillips states, 'Although she has no desire to harm any creature, her pampered lifestyle depends on slaughtering animals for their hides and exploiting workers in foreign lands who, by Willoughby's own admission, must be kept "beggars"' (1994: 66).

Woolf's novel also points out a more indirect and yet crucial way in which women support empire, which is through their ignorance of colonial and imperial practices and through the unquestioning respect and admiration they have for the men who are privy to this knowledge. In Conrad's novel, European women are deliberately *kept* in ignorance about the brutal truths of empire, but Woolf's novel suggests and criticizes a seemingly willed ignorance on the part of women, with their unquestioning belief in empire and its practices revealed as ridiculous as well as dangerous. A good example of this is St John Hirst's discussion of the international political situation with Helen. St John shows off his knowledge to attract Helen's attention and she accepts and respects his views and arguments 'without always listening to them, much as she respected a solid brick wall' (*VO* 288). His masculine 'display' not only helps to contextualize the novel in relation to the mounting tensions and rivalries between European imperial powers that finally erupted in the First World War, but also demonstrates Woolf's own understanding of the current imperial crises, and her sense of the ways in which men and women, seemingly detached from direct interests in imperial trade and power structures, are complicit in empire building as they enact their gendered roles (see Phillips for detailed discussion). Women's ignorance, willed or otherwise, works to facilitate the continuation of empire and imperial rivalries which, by the time *The Voyage Out* was published, had resulted in the horrors of the First World War. This sense of connection between women's social and political position and imperialism is also made apparent in other ways in this novel. The patriarchal gender inequalities embedded in domestic arrangements and personal relationships between men and women – in family relations, love, courtship and marriage – are seen in parallel with, and inextricable from, relations of commerce, politics and militarism (as Phillips explores). As Rachel expresses her pity for the goats, what is also made apparent is that she is, similarly, in many ways a resource to be exploited: her father wants Helen to train her to be a competent hostess to further his own political ambitions and, as the plot progresses, she also finds herself to be an object of exchange on the marriage market.

Colonial encounters

The pivotal event in the novel is undoubtedly the expedition that the six English tourists undertake to the native village in the jungle, not least because this is both the point at which Rachel and Terence become engaged and, most likely, when Rachel contracts the fever which leads to her death. As the wide range of critical analyses of this part of the novel suggest, it is also a key event because of the various possibilities it opens up for how to read the relationships between self and other, colonizers and colonized. It also raises issues about the literal, geographical places as well as the social and ideological places that the different groups occupy. The visitors assume their Western cultural and economic superiority as they view the indigenous people as passive objects – in fact, as objects on display to satisfy their curiosity. This scene also demonstrates how imperial relations are firmly enmeshed with the gender politics of Western patriarchal structures.

The journey to the indigenous village begins the process of unsettling the distinctions between 'us' and 'them' on which imperial discourses and power hierarchies rely. The repeated references to 'the darkness', 'the heart of the night', '[t]he great darkness', the 'deep gloom on the banks [of the river]' (VO 251), 'the black water beneath them', 'the darkness', the 'unbroken darkness' (VO 252) builds up the sense of the unknown typical of colonial narratives. Terence's sense of being 'drawn on and on away from all he knew, slipping over barriers and past landmarks into unknown waters as the boat glided over the smooth surface of the river' (VO 252) conveys the sense of the momentousness of this encounter with the racial 'other'. However, the deliberate repetition of words and phrases associated with darkness ironically deflates the idea of unknown territory as something awe-inspiring through over emphasis. The recurrent reference to the English group's proximity to civilization and the likening of this new territory to more familiar settings, and specifically to an English landscape, contributes to this: the forest 'resembled a drive in an English forest' with the addition of 'tropical bushes' (VO 256) and is likened to the grounds and wooded parks of English stately homes, such as Arundel Castle in West Sussex and the Great Park at Windsor.

One explanation for Woolf's depiction of this forest in South America as resembling a quintessentially English landscape could be her lack of experience of such landscapes. Wollaeger points out that 'Woolf never set foot in South America' and suggests that her descriptions may be based on 'colonial postcards and imperial exhibitions' (2001: 44, 43), both of which are forms of display that reinforce ideas of empire as a source of ownership and British pride. However, the insistent likening of the indigenous landscape to England in this novel can also be seen as part of Woolf's anti-imperialist attack. It seems to suggest the ways in which colonizers and imperialists are wilfully blind to the real, authentic differences of new places and cultures. Their perceptions reflect their particular cultural mind-set and likening new territories to something familiar defuses any sense of threat of difference. Imposing an interpretation on a landscape (and the people in it) is a way of metaphorically laying claim to new territories and cultures, reabsorbing them into what is familiar. Woolf's emphasis on this perception of the 'new' world in relation to an English landscape in effect makes it British, creating the 'logical' notion of it being a 'natural' extension of British territory. This way of perceiving others through a particular imperialist ideological frame of reference is also a way of *constructing* other places and cultures rather than seeing them as they really are. Postcolonial theorist, Edward Said, refers to this process of representation as 'textual attitude' (2003: 83) and we can see how the imperial gaze literally constructs the vision of the world.

The suggestion that Woolf's fictional indigenous village may have been based on the 'fictions' that exhibitions, such as the Imperial International Exhibition in London (1909) and the British Empire Exhibition (1924), created raises interesting questions about authenticity that are also implicit in Woolf's novel. For example, the authenticity of her tourists' encounter with the indigenous people is questioned in a number of ways. The journey itself seems to be experienced as a kind of dream: the repeated reference to their drowsiness could be attributed to the heat and exercise, but it also suggests a kind of suspension of reality and rational thought. Terence and Rachel move 'as people walking in their sleep', Terence speaking 'as if he were talking in his sleep' (*VO* 258). This suggests that the colonial other is merely a fantasy, a product of imperialist ideology, speculation and imagination. There is also a clear sense that their 'expedition' is actually a tourist package and the village itself a showpiece or exhibit as part of this tourist experience: 'The tired little horses' carrying the tourists expose the routine as they 'stopped automatically, and the English dismounted' at the village (*VO* 251). The disinterested response of the villagers also suggests that groups of European visitors are simply part of their daily routine.

For Rachel, one of the most significant and shocking aspects of her visit to the village is the similarity she perceives between the indigenous women and her own experience of gendered roles: the men do business, selling objects made by the women, and the women care for and feed their families. It is by comparing herself to these racial 'others' that Rachel discovers the parameters of her own gendered identity. In evoking the gender politics of this indigenous village as a mirror for Rachel's narrowly defined future role as a wife and mother confirms Woolf's political analysis of imperialism as an extension of patriarchal domestic structures. This coincidence of women's experience across the racial divide exposes the power politics at work in both patriarchal and colonial systems, unsettling distinctions between self and other and troubling the hierarchies of power so fundamental to the operation of imperialism. That Woolf's novel derails the romance plot so that Rachel does not fulfil this expectation stands as a scathing indictment of this interconnected patriarchal and imperial system.

Importantly, Woolf's novel positions the indigenous women as challengers to patriarchal and imperialist power dynamics. In a subtle but significant reversal of the imperial and gendered power dynamic, the indigenous women refuse to be simply the objects of the tourists' gaze with all the connotations of colonial and gender inferiority this implies. Instead, the women stare back at the tourists with some hostility, regarding *their* bodies as objects to gaze on:

> The women took no notice of the strangers, except that their hands paused for a moment and their long narrow eyes slid round and fixed upon them with the motionless inexpressive gaze of those removed from each other far far beyond the plunge of speech. Their hands moved again, but the stare continued ... As they sauntered about, the stare followed them, passing over their legs, their bodies, their heads, curiously, not without hostility, like the crawl of a winter fly. (*VO* 269)

This reversal of the gaze raises some contradictory possibilities for interpretation. On the one hand, the women are constructed in racist terms: they are 'far far' beyond communication with the tourists, as if beyond human speech and communication, and their stare is incomprehensible. The sensation this stare creates – 'like the crawl of a winter fly' – evokes a sense of the revulsion this reversed gaze generates, suggesting that this is 'unnatural', just as a fly crawling in winter seems at odds with natural, seasonal cycles. The profoundly unsettling effect of being stared at, of being an object of the women's appraising gaze, also perhaps hints at the psychological effects of being subject to colonization as the tourists' mood is seemingly affected by the experience, leaving them feeling isolated, anxious and miserable (they feel 'alone' and 'insignificant' and have 'bitter and unhappy' thoughts, VO 270). That 'they had become absorbed into it ['the life of the village']' (VO 269) seems to confirm this levelling of distinctions between the colonizers and the colonized. This reversal of the imperialist power dynamic continues also in Woolf's description of the tourists as brutal and monstrous, rather than civilized and superior, even in the most everyday gestures. Accepting hospitality from the villagers at the end of the visit, the English tourists reach for the sweetmeats with 'great red hands' and their interaction with the 'soft instinctive people' of the village is inept as they 'felt themselves treading cumbrously like tight-coated soldiers' (VO 269). This simile associates the tourists with military force, suggesting that even 'innocent' tourist exploration carries with it the connotations of imperialist violence. The gun incongruously placed amongst the indigenous bowls and rushes in one of the huts also suggests the infiltration of colonial violence as well as other European influences.

This detailed analysis of this one event in the novel gives a sense of the varied ways in which Woolf's response to and representation of empire has been interpreted. There are elements of this novel that seem to be complicit in racist discourses. Rachel seems to contract her fatal illness during her journey up the river where she comes into contact with, and is suggestively contaminated by, the 'native' others, as well as by the landscape, flora and fauna. The only indigenous character in the novel is Dr Rodriguez whose misdiagnosis of Rachel leads to her death and who is described in terms of racist stereotypes. Importantly, however, Woolf's novel also makes clear that Rachel's illness is closely bound up with a psychological disturbance and anxiety provoked by the actions of English men. It is the kiss that Richard Dalloway forces on Rachel earlier in the novel, having impressed her with his knowledge of empire (*VO* 66), that triggers Rachel's nightmares which revolve around enclosed spaces and a feeling of being trapped and pursued. Terence's proprietorial behaviour once they have become engaged seems to heighten Rachel's psychological distress and her nightmares become more feverish. Woolf's novel engages in complex ways with the issues of imperialism and colonization, drawing parallels between domestic and marital relations and the oppressions enacted abroad in a way which is deeply challenging and controversial.

Feminist critiques

In her polemical essays, *A Room of One's Own* and *Three Guineas*, Woolf brings a deliberately gendered perspective to her engagement with empire and forces of empire and her feminist political perspective is enmeshed with her attacks on imperialism. However, even in her boldest and seemingly most straightforward declarations of her political position there is a sense of ambivalence towards, or even complicity in, the systems and institutions she is criticizing. In *A Room of One's Own*, for example, she asserts a white woman's difference in her response to black women: 'It is one of the great advantages of being a woman that one can pass even a very fine negress without wishing to make an Englishwoman of her' (*AROO* 49–50). Here, she asserts a feminist anti-imperialist stance in suggesting that women do not feel compelled, unlike men, to possess others, women or colonial subjects or both. While on the one hand this offers a radical gendered critique of the imperialist urge for conquest and colonial greed, distancing women from such imperialist ideologies and practices, it also implies an exclusion of black women from the category of 'woman' and from English society. Similarly, in *Three Guineas* Woolf asserts her freedom as an outsider: she feels free from the pressures of belonging to a country and nation, and distant from the patriotism she sees as fuelling European rivalries for territorial possession and bolstering oppressive power dynamics in the domestic sphere. She states, 'as a woman I have no country. As a woman I want no country. As a woman my country is the whole world' (*TG* 125). However, although this outsider status allows her to disengage from fascist ideologies and violence which have been shaped by imperialism and racism, her ability to stand back is also premised on her privilege as a white middle-class woman. She can refute the need for a country because she still has 'a room of her own' in which to develop and articulate her ideas, a room, as she admits, in large part made possible by the legacy from her Aunt Caroline Emilia and derived from colonial activities.

What is clear as we look across the range of Woolf's writing is a life-long critical engagement with empire and the institutions, ideologies and political and economic systems that maintain it. Her anti-imperialist politics are evident in her direct criticism of empire, but also in the reversals of commonly held beliefs about British and European civilization and the imperial mission. Her feminist perspective is a central component of her anti-imperialist critique and her writing illuminates the complex ways in which imperialism affects experience and shapes national *and* gendered identity. Her later fiction registers the shifts in the global imperial dynamics in the interwar period, with the rise of newer industrial powers, America and Germany, becoming powerful rivals to the outmoded industries of Britain. It also considers the shifts in women's social and political positions with reference to imperial power structures.

Critique of empire

As in *The Voyage Out*, Woolf's later novels also focus on characters whose lives are cut short or their anticipated experience derailed as a result of the interconnections of patriarchal and imperialist systems. In *Jacob's Room*, Woolf criticizes the British social institutions (the class system, university education and the church) that insist on a patriarchal masculine ideal which inculcates imperialist attitudes in young men, fostering militaristic attitudes and actions. Jacob is a product of such institutions and is killed in a war supposedly intended to defend them. From the opening scene on the beach, Jacob's sense of himself as 'heroic' as he explores this territory on a quest for a crab to collect is equated with his conquest, possession (and neglect) of other creatures, such as his collection of beetles and butterflies. This sense of heroism here is overtly linked to death. Naming Jacob 'Flanders' recalls 'Flanders Fields' and can be seen as another element of Woolf's satirical attack. Not only does this name prefigure Jacob's death, but also sets up a sense of inevitability about this, an inevitability attributed to the imperial tensions mounting in Europe from the beginning of the century.

From the beginning of *Orlando* it is apparent that Orlando's sense of his manhood is premised on the violent conquest of racial others and the assertion of dominance – his first act in the novel is to slice the head off a mummified Moor. This is an ideal of masculinity in keeping with this first period of colonial expansion and political and economic dominance. However, although Orlando becomes a colonial adventurer and an agent of Empire in his role as a diplomat and Ambassador Extraordinary to Constantinople, the expected trajectory of his life is derailed by his sudden change of sex. As a woman, Orlando is disenfranchised: she is denied the inheritance of her family estate and becomes increasingly aware of her disempowered social and political status. The novel demonstrates clearly how Orlando *learns* to be feminine through a process that can be seen as one of the cultural colonization of mind and body. Certain assumptions are imposed on her because she is a woman and she learns to see herself and the world through the beliefs and values of a heterosexual, patriarchal culture. This cultural construction of femininity as passive, vulnerable and in need of masculine protection also works to 'justify' war and conquest in the face of perceived threats to this domestic social structure. The location of Orlando's transformation in Constantinople (now Istanbul) also seems to insist on an imperial focus for interpretation. On the geographical and cultural border between East and West, this city has long been a site of intense European rivalries and vying for power, as Leonard Woolf demonstrates in *The Future of Constantinople* (1917) (Phillips 1994: 134–5). While Woolf's depictions of the 'exotic' East echo racist stereotypes, the gypsies that Orlando lives with for a while overtly challenge British imperialist values and domineering practices as well as domestic hierarchies of power and symbols of status: 'a Duke...was nothing but a profiteer or robber who snatched land and money from people who rated these things of little worth, and could think of nothing better to do than build three hundred and sixty-five bedrooms when one was enough, and none was even better than one' (*O* 92–3). Like the village women in *The Voyage Out*, the gypsies offer a reversed gaze on the values of the imperial centre and undermine its assumed superiority.

Other novels also savagely satirize characters directly involved in empire – colonial administrators, military men, and those making their fortune from imperialist ventures. In *The Years*, Abel, Martin and North Pargiter represent three generations of military and commercial involvements in India and Africa, extending 'civilization' across the globe. Yet, these aspects of their lives are dull, monotonous and empty of meaningful values and humanity, based as they are on what Phillips calls an 'impoverished civilization' and ideology (1994: 36). The novel's preoccupation with Ireland and Home Rule brings debates about the struggles of colonies to free themselves from British colonial control closer to home and literally into the home of the Pargiter family. In *Between the Acts*, Bart Oliver, formerly a successful member of the India Civil Service, is now satirically diminished in his authority and views of the world, not least by his sister, Lucy Swithin. Miss La Trobe's pageant, which maps out the historical roots of the tensions about to erupt into the Second World War, also offers a powerful indictment of the masculinist and imperialist values which led to the brutal policing of citizens at home and colonial subjects abroad. In his role as a policeman in the Victorian part of the pageant, Budge enacts the bloody-minded arrogance and coercion used to keep order and to maintain the rule of empire which is exercised through the violent '*Rule of [his] truncheon*' and is, unquestionably, '*a whole-time, white man's job*' (*BTA* 97).

In *Mrs Dalloway*, Peter Walsh, returning briefly from his role as a colonial administrator in India, is also a focus for Woolf's critique of empire. His habit of fingering his pocket knife is suggestive of a predatory sexuality underlying his seemingly civilized identity, as well as, perhaps, his capacity for violence in his colonial role in India. Peter is impressed by the 'progress' Britain has made since he was last there and, specifically, he admires the military troops of young men marching in procession, as well as the monuments which act as symbols of British military and imperial power. The fact that his admiration also includes an ambulance rushing by (in all likelihood carrying Septimus, the traumatized war veteran who has committed suicide) severely undermines Peter's worship of 'civilisation' (*MD* 167). His fantasy of himself as a 'romantic buccaneer', which entails his pursuit of an unknown woman through the city's streets, is inspired by his reflection in a shop window. His inflated self-image is endorsed by a sense of his own colonial power, 'All India lay behind him' (*MD* 54), and by his sense of himself as 'an adventurer, reckless... (landed as he was last night from India)'

(*MD* 60). However, as with other incidents of imperial display, his sexual 'conquest' comes to nothing, his energy dissipates and his 'quarry' is lost. Here again we see the way in which ideologically endorsed notions of masculinity and patriarchal social structures legitimize men's objectification and possession of women and that desires to dominate (sexually) are inextricably linked to men's status as an agents of empire.

The Waves, though the most highly figurative and rhythmic of Woolf's fiction, has been read as both an indictment and an endorsement of empire. Critics argue that its characters are formed by and help to perpetuate imperial politics and Percival in particular, the silent hero of empire, is seen as the relational centre around which all the other characters revolve. For some critics his importance is such that 'when Percival dies...empire dramatically falters' (Doyle 2009: 372). Critics read this novel as illuminating the contradictions and complexities of Woolf's political stance and also as revealing empire as highly problematic in itself.

Contradiction, complicity and ambiguity are recurrent aspects of Woolf's anti-imperialist attacks on empire, but so too is a determination to engage with what was a complex and contradictory set of values and practices at the heart of empire itself. The ambivalence in her position and complicity in certain ways serves as an indication of the impossibility of putting forward an unproblematic, straightforward critique of imperialism and empire, so enmeshed as these structures and practices are in British history and lived experience.

Jewishness and antisemitism

Some of what has already been discussed in relation to Woolf's complex and critical engagements with issues of empire and imperialism is also relevant when we consider the representations of Jewish identity and culture in Woolf's writing. The instances of antisemitism in her fiction and other writings seem at odds with her feminist, pacifist and socialist politics. Woolf's antisemitism is particularly confusing since Woolf was happily married to a secular Jew, Leonard Woolf, for almost thirty years. Although their marriage seems to have been one that was mutually supportive and based on respect and love, her early references to Leonard announcing her marriage describe him as a 'penniless Jew' (L1 500, 501). In fact, the most overtly offensive antisemitic comments and views are found in her diaries and letters. In a letter to her friend, Ethyl Smyth, for example, she says, 'How I hated marrying a Jew – how I hated their nasal voices, and their oriental jewellery, and their noses and their wattles' (L4 195). Her personal writings are most explicitly racist when discussing her Jewish friends and acquaintances, and especially when describing her feelings towards Leonard's family. In part, Woolf's criticism of the Woolf family stems from her class prejudice. Woolf's criticism of what she saw as their showy ostentation, the vulgarity of their elaborate behaviour, and the emptiness of their conversation – 'chatter' – can be related to her different class values. But her attacks are also, as in the letter above, specifically anti-Jewish. Her short story, 'Lappin and Lapinova' (1939) could perhaps be read as a scathing representation of the Woolf family, especially given Woolf's intense dislike of the large family gatherings held by the Woolfs which she found so irritating and distasteful (see Lee 1996: 314). The story revolves around a large party held to celebrate the golden wedding anniversary of Mr and Mrs Thorburn. Unsurprisingly, it focusses on the golden gifts the couple receive but in doing so it also suggests their excessive greed for gold and acquisitions – all of which resonate with the stereotype of the greedy Jew. The character, Rosalind, who marries into the Thorburn family, feels isolated and overwhelmed at this party. Involved as she is in creating fictional scenarios and with the gift she gives of a sand caster (associated with the writing process), Rosalind could (in an autobiographical reading of this story) be seen as a figure representative of Woolf herself (see Simpson 2014).

What is also clear from Woolf's writing, though, is that she was highly conscious of her own prejudices and snobbery, as the letter she sends to Smyth goes on to make clear: 'what a snob I was: for they have immense vitality, and I think I like that quality best of all' (L4 195–6). Time and again we also see Woolf's more positive responses: her affectionate and joking references to Leonard as 'my Jew', her admiration for Jews in general, and her acceptance of a symbolic Jewish identity as a result of her marriage as fascist tensions rose in the 1930s. Incredibly, she and Leonard journeyed through Nazi Germany in 1935 and, in a letter to her friend Violet Dickinson, Woolf refers to the dangers they risk. Her explanation draws on offensive stereotypes – it is because 'Leonards (sic) nose is so long and hooked[,] [that] we rather suspect that we shall be flayed alive' (*L5* 385) — but she accepts the risk they share (articulated in this horrifically prescient image). Other letters about their trip signal her acceptance of a Jewish identity – it is 'our Jewishness [that] is said to be a danger' (*L5* 386). In fact, as Britain entered the war, both she and Leonard were on the Gestapo Arrest List.

Whilst such contradictory attitudes are in keeping with the many other contradictions at work in Woolf's writing and thinking in general, her shifting and unstable responses towards Jews can be seen, in part at least, as symptomatic of a wider cultural confusion about the figure of the Jew in this period. At the turn of the twentieth century there were a number of conflicting ideas about Jewish identity and the dramatic increase in immigration of Jews into London between 1880 and 1914 complicated this picture still further, giving rise to the perceived sense of the 'problem' of the Jew in British society. This immigration disrupted the already established Anglo-Jewish community in London and intensified the perceived sense of threat to British culture that these 'foreign others' represented. The governments of the day responded to these issues and their policies on immigration can be seen to have been shaped by concerns around immigration and commonly held prejudices about Jews in Britain as being dangerously powerful and as having a corrupting influence. Yet, Jews were also perceived as the 'fittest' to survive and adapt to the newly modern world. In particular, given the long-term association of Jews with financial matters and commerce, they were also seen to be able to adjust to the new economic climate which involved an intensification of capitalism and which had an impact on all aspects of life.

Jewish characters can be found in a number Woolf's fictional texts, sometimes drawing on negative Jewish stereotypes but also demonstrating a more positive and respectful approach to Jewish culture (see Bradshaw 1999; Sutton 2013). In Woolf's writing of the mid-late 1930s, we see a more complex and contradictory engagement with these issues in relation to antisemitic attitudes, as well as attacks on fascism. In this period, there was a renewed public awareness of Jewishness as the European crisis mounted and Woolf was increasingly aware of the rise in power and popularity of fascism in Germany, Spain and Italy and of violence towards

Jews. She was also well aware of the rise of fascism at home as the activities of Oswald Mosley's British Union of Fascists (B.U.F., founded in 1932) reached a peak in the period 1934–6. These activities culminated in the issuing of a Public Order Act in 1936 which banned political marches and which aimed to protect East End Jews from the B.U.F.

Three Guineas

Woolf's long polemical essay, *Three Guineas* (1938), engages directly with this political context. She draws together a feminist attack on the patriarchal family with an attack on the rise of fascism in Europe, arguing that there is a direct connection between domestic tyranny and the fascist thinking that leads to war. One solution she proposes to this frightening situation is the formation of an 'anonymous and secret Society of Outsiders' (*TG* 126) comprising those excluded and silenced ('shut out' and 'shut up') by current social and political forces. These outsiders include women and Jews since both, she argues, are oppressed by '[t]he whole iniquity of dictatorship' (*TG* 118). This essay provoked mixed responses from her contemporary critics as well as from friends and family who felt her arguments were unconvincing. More recently, critics have pointed out that Woolf's analogy between patriarchy and fascism and her argument that the two systems are mutually supporting is highly problematic. This is because this critical perspective conflates two very different forms of oppression, with fascism being generally viewed as far more overt, aggressive and violent (Spiro 2013: 95–6). It is also seen to offer a simplistic idea of women's relationship to this complex and conflicted context. As Phyllis Lassner puts it, Woolf suggests that 'women are only passive war victims, war protestors, or complicit with the power of a masculinist war machine' (1998: 4). Woolf's sustained pacifist position in this context, when other staunch pacifists were accepting the necessity of war to halt Hitler's brutality, is also seen by some as untenable. Woolf felt increasingly personally and politically isolated in this period, distanced not only from the patriotic fervour growing in Britain, but also from her intimate relationships with Leonard, family members and friends as they gradually came to support the process of military rearmament in the struggle against Hitler.

That Woolf's thinking in *Three Guineas* is seen to be problematic is also relevant to her representations of Jewishness. While Woolf's essay criticizes tyranny in the form of fascism, patriarchy and the ever-powerful capitalist system, in her fiction she produces some of the most disturbingly antisemitic representations, including that of the greedy Jewish jeweller, Oliver Bacon, in 'The Duchess and the Jeweller' and Abrahamson, the greasy tallow worker, in *The Years* (discussed below). However, it is important not to take apparently antisemitic or racist views at face value, nor to assume that these views are simply Woolf's own views. We can see this from considering the way in which the successful Jewish businessman, Ralph Manresa, in *Between the Acts* is represented.

Between the Acts

Ralph is not literally present in the novel but antisemitism seems to underlie the ways in which he is perceived. He is stereotypically associated with money (reportedly he has 'tons of money' (*BTA* 27) and this economic success (and what it allows him to do) seems to represent a threat to certain members of this fictional village community (which can be read as a microcosm for British society). Money enables him to buy a home in the village and to modernize it, which villagers associate with a despoiling of the English countryside (Linett 2007: 91). More troubling seems to be his attempts to assimilate into English society and to erase his racial difference (see Mia Spiro 2013 for discussion of the associations of the name Manresa with Jewish history). He is 'got up to look the very spit and image of the landed gentry' (*BTA* 26), adopts an English first name (or 'Christian' name as it would have been referred to in 1930s) and perhaps also a surname that connects him with Manresa Street in Chelsea and so with the heart of British wealth and power in London. He has married an English woman, although her heritage is also problematic and suggestive of an intrusion in to British society which Ralph is repeating. It is rumoured that Mrs Manresa originates in Tasmania and that her grandfather was a convict (*BTA* 26), a detail pointing back to Britain's colonization of the antipodes as well as to the more general anxieties about ancestry, racial and ethnic identities, and notions of belonging in this novel. Woolf's novel is steeped in ideas of 'Englishness' and the

English literary tradition and this can be seen to both endorse and celebrate this cultural identity. However, her novel also shows how commonly held beliefs about Englishness are premised on the fierce exclusion of 'alien others' and the imperative to highlight difference and maintain clear boundaries of identity.

Ralph adorns his expensive and showily painted car with his initials, 'twisted so as to look at a distance like a coronet' (*BTA* 30). These pretentions to English aristocratic status trouble ideas of family lineage and racial ancestry. As Linett remarks, 'The word "twisted" emphasizes the distortion inherent in this attempt to appear what he is not' (2007: 90; see also Spiro 2013). However, whether this is an indication of Woolf's antisemitism, or a representation of the antisemitism underlying British society in general is in question. This description of Ralph's car is focalized through one of the characters, Giles Oliver, a stockbroker (and so involved in Ralph's financial 'world') but who, unlike Ralph, is not a success: Giles has 'no capital' (*BTA* 30). Unlike the freedom Ralph seems to have, Giles also feels an overwhelming sense of entrapment in his career and dissatisfaction with his life: 'the conglomeration of things pressed you flat; held you fast, like a fish in water' (*BTA* 31). He sees the Manresas' car as he returns home for the weekend, full of rage about the news he has been reading confirming the imminence of war (of which his family are ignorant) and angry about the obligation to participate in the communal village celebrations. Seemingly in an effort to fit in (or to pretend to), and perhaps to assert his 'legitimate' place in this English society, his change of clothes aligns him with a quintessentially 'English' identity: he 'look[s] like a cricketer, in flannels, wearing a blue coat with brass buttons' (*BTA* 30). All of these details indicate the complexity of Giles's seemingly antisemitic response to Ralph: it is bound up with his conflicted feelings about his national identity and the imminent war; it is perhaps an envious response to Ralph's success and freedom; it also suggests an anger that a Jew, a racial other, could inveigle his way into English society; and finally, Giles is also strongly attracted to Mrs Manresa. His views of Ralph, then, can be seen to be informed by conflicted personal feelings and Ralph, again in a stereotypically 'Jewish' role, acts as a scapegoat for Giles's negative emotions. Designated as an 'outsider', Ralph also shores up Giles's sense of belonging, of being an 'insider' to this community.

As this discussion of *Between the Acts* indicates, antisemitism is closely bound up with racism more generally. In the context of 1930s fascism, racial and ethnic identities were seen as synonymous with monolithic notions of national identity that Woolf attacked for fuelling the drive towards war. As discussed in relation to *The Voyage Out* above, issues of identity, of boundaries between 'us' and 'them', self and other, are highly problematic in relation to racial categories. Racist discourses and ways of understanding the world are premised on the existence of clear distinctions between racial groups, 'evidenced' by bodily or facial features as an indication of 'natural' differences. However, these perceived distinctions are not innate but culturally constructed: racial identity is never 'pure' in a genetic sense and racist discourse works to exaggerate bodily markers of racial difference and to denigrate features perceived to be signs of otherness. Woolf's representation of Jewish characters readily makes use of antisemitic stereotypes relating to so-called 'Jewish' bodily features, notably the 'Jewish' nose. However, her antisemitic depictions are also very self-consciously created and show an awareness of the ways in which the *idea* or *image* of the 'other' provokes a negative response. This is chimes with current notions, as expressed in Valentin Hugo's newspaper article, 'The Challenge to Jewry: A Paradox of Persecution' which states: '"it is not the Jews who are hated but an imaginary image of them"' (in Linett 2007: 3, 190, n. 5). As a writer, Woolf is very aware of the power of words to create images and constructions that can inform but also manipulate the reader's thinking, as propaganda during this period makes blatantly clear. Woolf's antisemitic representations expose the deliberate construction of Jewish identity as alien and other and, in doing so, reveal the cultural and personal fears that underlie this form of prejudice. Her representations also point out the ways in which hard and fast distinctions between groups are not natural and unequivocal, but culturally constructed and always subject to disruption and change. 'Nothing', as Woolf repeatedly demonstrates, 'was simply one thing' (*TTL* 177).

Critics have approached the antisemitism in Woolf's writings in a number of ways. It has been seen as evidence of Woolf's insipient racism and part of her cultural milieu and also as a means of exposing racist intolerance in her society. It has been seen as a 'blind spot' in her political stance as a feminist, socialist, pacifist and anti-imperialist, and as an indication of the limitations of her democratic tolerance. More complex still, Woolf's antisemitism has been interpreted metaphorically as a vehicle for her characters' insecurities and for her own personal and professional anxieties.

The Years

Given that antisemitism is present throughout *The Years*, this novel serves as a good example through which to explore the complexity of Woolf's representation of Jews and Jewishness. The antisemitism in this novel is particularly confusing given that it was originally conceived to work in harmony with the antifascist arguments articulated in *Three Guineas*: it was to be a single work taking the innovative form of 'an Essay-Novel, called the Pargiters' (*D4* 129). The novel takes a 'realist' approach in that it engages more explicitly and directly than most of Woolf's fiction with social and political issues as it charts the declining fortunes of the Pargiter family from the 1880s to the 'Present Day' of the 1930s. It also draws attention to the history of a Jewish presence in London so as to emphasize the rightful place of Jews in Britain, as well as registering the racism inherent in British society alongside the rise of antisemitism and the troubling increase in strength of the British Union of Fascists in the mid-1930s (see Bradshaw 1999). However, the novel also contains one of the most overtly antisemitic moments in any of Woolf's texts in the discussion of the two cousins, Sara and North, in the 'Present Time' section of the novel as they offensively deride Sara's Jewish neighbour, Abrahamson.

Newly returned from his farm in Africa, North is keen to refamiliarize himself with his family and with London life. He drives to Sara's flat to take her to a family party. When he arrives, he and Sara share a meal and discuss Sara's Jewish neighbour, Abrahamson, with whom she shares a bathroom. The sound of Abrahamson entering the bathroom interrupts North's recital of Andrew Marvell's poem, 'The Garden' and, as the two cousins eavesdrop on the sounds of Abrahamson bathing, they articulate their anger and racist prejudice. Although this seems to be obviously racist, a closer examination of this scene reveals some of the alternative ways that Jewish figures function in Woolf's writing. As we will see, Abrahamson is more than simply an alien outsider and the more subtle connections that Woolf's writing implies bring underlying anxieties into focus.

A racist representation?

There is no doubt that this exchange is antisemitic as Sara and North express their blatant prejudice. Their discussion of Abrahamson clearly aligns him with dirt, grease and all that is sordid. Sara complains that he leaves a greasy line and hair in the bath after he has bathed. This complaint also implies contamination since his attempts to clean himself only lead to a lack of hygiene for others. Sara's complaints about his coughing and snorting confirm this suggestion. Through his name, Woolf obviously signals his Jewish lineage and connects her character symbolically to Abraham in the Old Testament from whom the Jewish nation descended. This intensifies Sara's racism here since, as David Bradshaw points out, 'In denigrating a figurative scion of the first Hebrew patriarch, Sara defames all Jews' (Bradshaw 1999: 185).

Rather than considering this scene to be an expression of Woolf's own racist prejudices, we can read it as her exposure of the racism prevalent in Britain at the time through the direct speech of her characters. This interpretation fits with Woolf's more overt and direct engagement with social and political issues in this period. Sara tells North a story of her visit to a newspaper office, seemingly to contribute a story to fuel antisemitism in the press. If this is so, the fact that she assumes the newspaper would be interested in publishing her views suggests that such racist stories were already in circulation and finding a level of acceptance. She recalls her interview at the newspaper office and her explanation of what had brought her there: '"But the Jew's in my bath, I said – the Jew…the Jew …"' (*TY* 298). Her inability to move beyond this opening to explain further suggests that her response is far from rational: she seems to be unnerved and confused and her response to Jewishness borders on the phobic. Woolf's representation Sara's antisemitism here may allude Woolf's concerns about the distortions and sensationalizing of information produced in the mass media, as well as pointing to the irrationality and exaggeration underlying British racism and antisemitism.

One of the key motivations underlying racism is the need to assert clear boundaries between self and other, insider and outsider and, in this situation, British and foreigner. The racial other is seen and treated also a repository of all the characteristics, doubts and negative associations that insiders do not want to acknowledge about themselves. The other is a fantasy projection rather than having any basis in reality. As we never encounter Abrahamson directly, only through his representation by Sara and North, we can see that he is in some ways their imaginary construction and, as such, reveals what underlies their antisemitism. As a racial other, Abrahamson functions as an outsider figure against which others can define themselves in order to assert their position as insiders, to strengthen connections and sense of belonging to the group from which the 'alien' other is excluded. But Sara and North also treat Abrahamson as a scapegoat here. The scapegoat is an archetypal Jewish role, a figure of blame for what is perceived to be wrong in society. As a racial other and scapegoat, Abrahamson also works as a metaphor for Sara's and North's underlying anxieties about their own identities and sense of belonging (or not) to British middle-class society. Sara and North are both social outsiders in different ways and their hostility towards Abrahamson serves to confirm their family bond and secure their sense of their insider status. However, what is most apparent is the ways in which they resemble Abrahamson.

Sara – insider/outsider

Although Sara is a member of a British middle-class family, a fall in the Pargiter family fortunes has led to her living in reduced circumstances. She lives in what North describes as a '"sordid"' flat in a '"low-down street"' in the East End of London (*TY* 271). Without domestic servants, her room is 'untidy' and she offers North a badly cooked and unappealing meal, clumsily served by the 'lodging-house skivvy' with only 'a dish of rather fly-blown fruit' to follow pudding (*TY* 273, 274, 281). This positions Sara as an 'outsider' to middle-class norms and her attitude towards Abrahamson seems to be motivated by the need to counter the sense of exclusion her fall in class status and privilege represents. In addition, she is unmarried and has a deformed shoulder, both of which mark her difference from heterosexual social norms and ideals of feminine beauty. She also lives in part of the East End of London which has specific Jewish associations: it is near to where the 'Battle of Cable Street' took place – a violent clash between fascists and Jews in 1936. It is also an area literally marked as Jewish, as North notices some houses are marked with the BUF symbol 'a circle … with a jagged line in it', a symbol that resembles the swastika symbol, appropriated by the Nazis, and indicating where Jews live (*TY* 270).

At a surface level, Sara's antisemitism enables her to see herself as different from her Jewish neighbour and to distance herself from a figure who is an embodiment of the social outsider. Yet, the more subtle elements of Woolf's novel suggest parallels between Sara's and Abrahamson's circumstances and experience, undermining ideas of distinct identities. Sara's response to Abrahamson can be read as her attempt to fend off unsettling feelings of her own status as a social outsider. As Bradshaw also notes, in renaming her character from 'Elvira' to 'Sara' Woolf also reinforces this sense of connection between them, Sara being the name of Abraham's wife in the Bible (1999: 185).

North – insider/outsider

Similarly, North's antisemitism can also be seen as symptomatic of his own uncertainty about his sense of place and feelings of alienation from British society. He has just returned after many years of being a colonial farmer in Africa and, having sold his farm there, he is in a state of social and financial limbo. He struggles to adjust to the pace and modernity of London and feels 'confused' by the social whirl of his experience as he renews acquaintance with family and friends. Although he is now 'home', he feels displaced: 'He had a feeling that he was no one and nowhere in particular' and, left alone in Sara's room, feels 'an outsider' (*TY* 272, 277). In his collusion with Sara's antisemitic views, articulated in his angry outburst, ' "Damn the Jew!" ' (*TY* 296), he attempts to distance himself from the Jewish outsider, yet other aspects of this scene suggest connection between North and Abrahamson and, as with Sara, boundaries of identity blur as distinctions and differences are undermined. North's recital of Andrew Marvell's poem, 'The Garden', is interrupted by Sara's gesture indicating that Abrahamson had entered the bathroom. The fact that North knows this canonical poem by heart affirms that he belongs to British culture: his insider status is indicated by how deeply embedded this aspect of the English literary tradition is in his memory and emotional life. North identifies so closely with poem as to feel its 'words' as 'actual presences, hard and independent' (*TY* 296). The fact that North does not immediately recognize the sound of Abrahamson as an interruption – 'he heard a sound. Was it in the poem or outside of it, he wondered? Inside, he thought' (*TY* 296) – raises questions about the cultural distinctions upon which he and Sara insist. That Marvell's words give way to the sounds of Abrahamson in the bath suggest that the boundaries of the English literary tradition (and British identity) are not watertight – they cannot fully exclude 'others', nor can they symbolically guarantee insider identity and a sense of belonging.

A metaphor for Woolf's anxieties?

Critics have suggested that the figure of the Jew in modernist writing can be read as a metaphorical representation for the writers' own anxieties and fears, and this can open up other ways of reading this passage (Freedman 1996; Rodríguez 2001–2; Linnet 2007; Leick 2010). In essays written around this time, for example, 'Why Art Today Follows Politics' (1936) and 'Reviewing' (1939), it is clear that Woolf was preoccupied with and anxious about the increasing commercialization of literary writing. She felt that market forces compromised literary quality and the integrity of the artist, turning literature into a mere commodity. In *Three Guineas*, she puts her argument strongly and suggests the 'money-motive' can actually corrupt literature so that it becomes a form of 'brain prostitution' (*TG* 108). However, Woolf *did* want to make money from her work and her sales were always a marker of success for her. The contradiction between her desire to protect literature as an art form separate from the market and her own deliberate participation in the market seems to have given rise to a profound anxiety. Her antisemitic representations, particularly drawing on the racist stereotype of the greedy Jew, can be read as metaphors for Woolf's self-criticism. There is a notable coincidence of Jews, antisemitism and money-making in Woolf's writing, and as critic, Karen Leick, observes, 'Woolf's anti-Semitic characterizations of Jews consistently appear in works where she was most consciously concerned with her mainstream reception and the income she might earn as a result of this success' (2010: 122–3). One of Woolf's most overtly antisemitic short stories, 'The Duchess and the Jeweller', is also one that she wrote and published deliberately to make money, vowing not to 'put pen to paper without a cheque' from the literary agent (*L6* 177). From the outset Woolf's representation of her central character caused offence and she made concessions by removing explicit references to his Jewish identity to maintain the sale of her story. Even so, her story remains controversial and offensive in many ways.

Oliver Bacon has achieved great success, starting life in Whitechapel, an area associated with criminal activity as well as with Jewish communities, to become 'the richest jeweller in England', famous throughout Europe and America, and now based at the heart of British society in Mayfair (*CSF* 249). He is represented as a composite of negative Jewish stereotypes and his insatiable greed, social climbing, conspicuous consumption and success in the commercial world as a jeweller, alongside his physical attributes (an 'elephantine' nose and swaying gait) create a caricature. However, what he most covets is acceptance and assimilation: having achieved great wealth, he now wants to belong to the upper echelons of English society and, for this, he is prepared to enter into a deal with the Duchess of Lambourne. He agrees to pay £20,000 for a string of pearls he knows to be fake in order to gain an introduction the Duchess's daughter, Diana, and so a way into the British aristocracy.

Many of the anxieties revealed in relation to Ralph Manresa's attempts to belong to British society in *Between the Acts* can also apply here and the overtly racist construction of Oliver can similarly be read as a metaphor for wider cultural prejudice. But we can also read this representation of Oliver as a metaphor for Woolf's anxieties and, as we saw with Sara and North in relation to Abrahamson in *The Years*, there are unexpected parallels between Woolf and her character that offer another way of understanding her motivation for creating such an overtly antisemitic representation. Oliver is a professional who compromises his talent as a skilled jeweller able to recognize a fake to satisfy his greedy desires and achieve his social ambition. Woolf's hostile attitude to the commercialization of literature and her desire to make money from this story and to consolidate her reputation on the competitive literary market are in conflict – just as Oliver's desire to consolidate his position in British society is in conflict with his professional judgement. Just as Oliver turns a blind eye to the Duchess's trick to satisfy his greedy social aspirations, so Woolf also compromises her professional and political values by participating in a social, political and economic system she finds increasingly despicable and inhuman. The antagonistic responses towards Oliver her story seems to deliberately provoke in the reader could be seen as a means of self-accusation. However, her story could also be seen as self-protection – she creates a character who is 'other' and who becomes a scapegoat for Woolf's profound sense of unease and anxiety about her contradictory behaviour.

In Woolf's engagements with empire, race, imperialism and Jewishness we see a confusing range of contradictory and conflicting ideas and views. At times Woolf's writing seems to challenge imperialist and racist views, championing an attack on empire and the patriarchal oppressions she associates with it. Conversely, her writing sometimes seems to be complicit with racist and antisemitic prejudice. While some critics perceive positive, if subtle, reference to Jewish culture, there are no positive Jewish (or non-White) characters in Woolf's writing to counter the negative and problematic representations of racial others. Whilst not excusing these 'failings', it is important to remember that Woolf lived through fraught and dramatically changing times – the British Empire was in decline and European tensions erupted into war twice in relatively quick succession, drawing heightened attention to issues of national and racial identities. Woolf was, of course, immersed in this context and so not able to fully stand back to offer an objective or stable perspective. Her own personal, political and professional perspectives were also shaped and altered by changing circumstances and her responses to them. Nonetheless, it would be a mistake to consider her representations of racial others as merely racist and antisemitic. The views expressed in her fictions are not obviously or simply her own. Rather, she often sought to expose the racism and antisemitism prevalent in her own society as sources of oppression which not only had a damaging effect on those victims of such attitudes, but also had a negative effect on society as a whole. She confronts wider cultural prejudice and examines what lies behind British conceptions of the racial other and the Jew. Fear of difference and the perceived threat that Jews in particular represented to British culture and identity resulted in the anxious construction of distinct cultural and national identities, with clear boundaries marking belonging or unbelonging. Woolf's fictions repeatedly indicate the falsity of such distinctions and, as we see in other aspects of her writing, she privileges ideas of connection and association, seeing the self and communities as shaped by others. For all the contradictions and sometimes troublingly offensive representations of racial others in Woolf's writing, what her engagements with empire, imperialism, race and antisemitism reveal is her willingness to think through these complex and entangled issues and to provoke her readers to do the same – however difficult that might be.

ENDNOTES

Introduction

1 Woolf's image has been extensively used to market commodities from mugs, pens and jewellery to golf balls, deck chairs and English beer. See Jane Garrity for discussion of the Bass Ale campaign and Woolf's involvement with commodity culture.
2 See Susan Sellers (2000).
3 First published in *The Times Literary Supplement* in 1923, Woolf slightly revised her essay for inclusion in *The Common Reader, First Series* (1925).

Chapter 1

1 This essay was also published with the title, 'Poetry, Fiction and the Future' in the *New York Herald Tribune* and grew out of a paper Woolf gave to the Oxford University English Club in May 1927.
2 First given as a talk to Hayes Court School (girls) in January 1926, Woolf revised her essay for publication in the *Yale Review* October 1926. She substantially revised it again for inclusion in her collection of essays, *The Second Common Reader* (1932).
3 First published as 'Modern Novels' in 1919, Woolf revised her essay for inclusion in the *Common Reader, First Series* (1925).
4 It began as a shorter essay, 'Mr Bennett and Mrs Brown' published in the *New York Evening Post* (November 1923) and was reprinted in the *Nation and Athenaeum* in December 1923. This first essay then formed the basis of a paper called 'Character in Fiction' that Woolf read to a group of Cambridge academics (the Cambridge Heretics Society) in May 1924. This was then published as 'Character in Fiction' in the *Criterion* in July 1924 and as 'Mr Bennett and Mrs Brown' as the first publication of the Hogarth Essays Series (October 1924). It is best known under this latter title.

Chapter 2

1   Woolf experiments in this way in longer works as well, notably in *Flush* (1933), where the narrative is focalized through a fictionalized representation of Elizabeth Barratt Browning's spaniel. Exploration of the significance of non-human life in Woolf's writing represents a relatively new area of critical study and, alongside a focus on dogs, includes a focus on moths, snails, birds, fish, rabbits and hares. See Ryan (2013 and 2014) and Dubino (2014).

Chapter 4

1   See Julia Kristeva, *Revolution in Poetic Language* (1984).
2   See Bergson's *Matter and Memory* (1896), first translated in 1911.
3   Like Septimus, Rhoda feels unable to survive the sense of alienation she feels: '"The world is entire, and I am outside of it"' (*TW* 18); she feels constrained in her '"ill-fitting body"' (TW 84) and longs to break free of her environment, but she finds the sense of her metaphysical dispersal overwhelming and she too commits suicide.

Chapter 5

1   See Gill Lowe (2005) for further discussion.

REFERENCES

Alt, C. (2010), *Virginia Woolf and the Study of Nature*, Cambridge: Cambridge University Press.

Beauvoir, S. de ([1949] 1988), *The Second Sex*, London: Picador.

Beer, G. (1996), *Virginia Woolf: The Common Ground*, Edinburgh: Edinburgh University Press.

Bell, C. ([1914] 1931), *Art*, London: Chatto and Windus.

Bell, Q. ([1972] 1996), *Virginia Woolf: A Biography, Volume 2*, London: Random House.

Bennett, A. ([1923] 1975), 'Is the Novel Decaying', in R. Majumdar and A. McLaurin (eds), *Virginia Woolf: The Critical Heritage*, Boston: Routledge and Kegan Paul.

Benzel, K. N. and Hoberman, R., eds (2004), 'Introduction', in *Trespassing Boundaries: Virginia Woolf's Short Fiction*, 1–13, Basingstoke and New York: Palgrave Macmillan.

Blair, E. (2007), *Virginia Woolf and the Nineteenth-Century Domestic Novel*, Albany: State University of New York Press.

Bowlby, R. ([1988] 1997), *Feminist Destinations and Further Essays on Virginia Woolf*, Edinburgh: Edinburgh University Press.

Bradshaw, D. (1999), 'Hyams Place: *The Years*, the Jews and the British Union of Fascists', in M. Joannou (ed.), *Women Writers of the 1930s: Gender, Politics and History*, 179–91, Edinburgh: Edinburgh University Press.

Carey, J. (1992), *The Intellectuals and the Masses: Pride and Prejudice Among the Literary Intelligentsia, 1880–1939*, London: Faber and Faber.

Case, A. and Shaw, H. E. (2008), *Reading the Nineteenth-Century Novel*, Oxford: Blackwell.

Caughie, P. L. (1991), *Virginia Woolf & Postmodernism: Literature in Quest & Question of Itself*, Urbana: University of Illinois.

Caughie, P. L. (1992), 'Virginia Woolf and Postmodernism: Returning to the Lighthouse', in K. J. H. Dettmar (ed.), *Rereading the New: A Backward Glance at Modernism*, 297–323, Ann Arbor: University of Michigan Press.

Clements, E. (2005), 'Transforming Musical Sounds into Words: Narrative Method in Virginia Woolf's *The Waves*', *Narrative* 13.2: 160–81.

Clewell, T. ([2004] 2009), 'Consolidation Refused: Virginia Woolf, the Great War, and Modernist Mourning', in M. Linett (ed.), *Virginia Woolf: A MFS Reader*, 171–97, Baltimore: Johns Hopkins Press.

Cramer, P. (1997), 'Introduction', in E. Barrett and P. Cramer (eds), *Virginia Woolf: Lesbian Readings*, 117–27, New York and London: New York University Press.

Cuddy-Keane, M. (2003), *Virginia Woolf, the Intellectual, and the Public Sphere*, Cambridge: Cambridge University Press.

Dick, S., ed. (1983), *Virginia Woolf, 'To the Lighthouse': The Original Holograph Draft*, London: Hogarth Press.

Doyle, L. ([1996] 2009), 'Sublime Barbarians in the Narrative of Empire; or Longinus as Sea', in M. Linett (ed.), *Virginia Woolf: A MFS Reader*, 355–77, Baltimore: Johns Hopkins Press.

Dubino, J. (2014), 'The Bispecies Environment, Coevolution, and Flush', in J. Dubino, G. Lowe, V. Neverow, and K. Simpson (eds), *Virginia Woolf: Twenty-first Century Approaches*, 131–47, Edinburgh: Edinburgh University Press.

Ellis, S. (2007), *Virginia Woolf and the Victorians*, Cambridge: Cambridge University Press.

Emery, M. L. (1992), '"Robbed of Meaning": The Work at the Center of *To the Lighthouse*', *Modern Fiction Studies* 38 (1): 217–34.

Esty, J. (2003), *A Shrinking Island: Modernism and National Culture in England*, Princeton: Princeton University Press.

Fernald, A. (1994), '*A Room of One's Own*, Personal Criticism, and the Essay', *Twentieth-Century Literature* 40 (2): 165–89.

Freedman, J. (1996), 'Henry James and the Discourses of Antisemitism', in B. Cheyette (ed.), *Between 'Race' and Culture: Representations of 'the jew' in English and American Literature*, 62–83, Stanford: Stanford University Press.

Fry, R. ([1920] 1981), *Vision and Design*, J. B. Bullen (ed.), Oxford: Oxford University Press.

Garrity, J. (2000), 'Virginia Woolf, Intellectual Harlotry and 1920s British *Vogue*', in P. L. Caughie (ed.), *Virginia Woolf and the Age of Mechanical Reproduction*, 185–218, Oxon and New York: Garland Publishing.

Gay, J. de (1999), 'Behind the Purple Triangle: Art and Iconography in *To the Lighthouse*', *Woolf Studies Annual* 5: 1–23. New York: Pace University Press.

Gay, J. de (2006), *Virginia Woolf's Novels and the Literary Past*, Edinburgh: Edinburgh University Press.

Gillespie, D. F. (1988), *The Sisters' Arts: The Writing and Painting of Virginia Woolf and Vanessa Bell*, Syracuse, New York: Syracuse University Press.

Gillies, M. A. (2003), 'Bergsonism: "Time out of mind"', in D. Bradshaw (ed.), *A Concise Companion to Modernism*, 95–115, Oxford: Blackwell.

Goldman, J. (1998), *The Feminist Aesthetics of Virginia Woolf: Modernism, Post-Impressionism, and the Politics of the Visual*, Cambridge: Cambridge University Press.

Goldman, J. (2004), *Modernism, 1910–1945: Image to Apocalypse*, Basingstoke: Palgrave Macmillan.

Haller, E. (2010), 'Virginia Woolf and Dance', in M. Humm (ed.), *The Edinburgh Companion to Virginia Woolf and the Arts*, 455–74, Edinburgh: Edinburgh University Press.

Henry, H. (2003), *Virginia Woolf and the Discourse of Science: The Aesthetics of Astronomy*, Cambridge: Cambridge University Press.

Holtby, W. ([1932] 1978), *Virginia Woolf: A Critical Memoir*, Chicago: Academy Press Ltd.

Humm, M. (2012), 'Cinema and Photography', in B. Randall and J. Goldman (eds), *Woolf in Context*, 291–301, Cambridge: Cambridge University Press.

James, H. (1914), *Notes on Novelists: With Some Other Notes*, New York: Charles Scribner's Sons. https://archive.org/details/notesonnovelist02jamegoog (accessed 16 February 2015).

Jones, S. (2009), 'Diaghilev and British Writing', *The Journal for the Society of Dance Research* 27 (1): 65–92.

Kelley, J. E. (2010), 'Virginia Woolf and Music', in M. Humm (ed.), *The Edinburgh Companion to Virginia Woolf and the Arts*, 415–36, Edinburgh: Edinburgh University Press.

Kern, S. ([1983] 2003), *The Culture of Time and Space, 1880–1918*, Massachusetts: Harvard University Press.

Kristeva, J. (1984), *Revolution in Poetic Language*, Margaret Waller (trans.), Leon S. Roudiez (intro.), New York: Columbia University Press.

Lassner, P. (1998), *British Women Writers in World War II: Battlegrounds of Their Own*, London: Macmillan.

Lassner, P. and Spiro, M. (2013), 'A Tale of Two Cities: Virginia Woolf's Imagined Jewish Spaces and London's East End Jewish Culture', *Woolf Studies Annual* 19: 59–82.

Lee, H. (1996), *Virginia Woolf*, London: Chatto and Windus.

Lee, H. (2000), 'Virginia Woolf's essays', in S. Roe and S. Sellers (eds), *The Cambridge Companion to Virginia Woolf*, 91–108, Cambridge: Cambridge University Press.

Leick, K. (2010), 'Virginia Woolf and Gertrude Stein: Commerce, Bestsellers and the Jew', in J. Dubino (ed.), *Virginia Woolf and the Literary Marketplace*, 121–36, New York and London: Palgrave.

Levenback, K. L. (1999), *Virginia Woolf and the Great War*, New York: Syracuse University Press.

Light, A. (2007), *Mrs Woolf and the Servants: The Hidden Heart of Domestic Service*, London: Penguin.

Linett, M. T. (2007), *Modernism, Feminism, and Jewishness*, Cambridge: Cambridge University Press.

Lowe, G. (2005), *Versions of Julia: Five Biographical Constructions of Julia Stephen*, London: Cecil Woolf Publishers.

Majumdar, R. and McLaurin, A., eds (1975), *Virginia Woolf: The Critical Heritage*, Boston: Routledge and Kegan Paul.

Marcus, J. (1987), 'Sapphistry: Narration as Lesbian Seduction' in *A Room of One's Own*, in J. Marcus (ed.), *Virginia Woolf and the Languages of Patriarchy*, 163–87, Bloomington and Indianapolis: Indiana University Press.

Marcus, J. (1992), 'Britannia Rules *The Waves*', in K. R. Lawrence (ed.), *Decolonizing Tradition: New Views of Twentieth-Century "British" Literary Canons*, 137–62, Urbana and Chicago: University of Illinois Press.

Marcus, L. (2004), *Virginia Woolf* (2nd edn), Tavistock, Devon: Northcote House Publishers.

Marshik, C. (2006), *British Modernism and Censorship*, Cambridge: Cambridge University Press.

McClintock, A. (1995), *Imperial Leather: Race, Gender and Sexuality in the Colonial Contest*, New York and London: Routledge.

McGee, Patrick ([1992] 2009), 'The Politics of Modernist Form; Or, Who Rules the Waves?', in M. Linett (ed.), *Virginia Woolf: A MFS Reader*, 378–99, Baltimore: Johns Hopkins Press.

Moorcroft Wilson, J. (1987), *Virginia Woolf, Life and London: A Biography of Place*, London: Cecil Woolf Publishers.

Park, S. (2005), 'Suffrage and Virginia Woolf: "The Mass Behind the Single Voice"', *Review of English Studies* 56 (223): 119–34.

Phillips, K. J. (1994), *Virginia Woolf Against Empire*, Knoxville: The University of Tennessee Press.

Prince, G. (1987), *A Dictionary of Narratology*, Lincoln: University of Nebraska Press.

Protopopova, D. (2012), 'Woolf and Russian Literature', in B. Randall and J. Goldman (eds), *Woolf in Context*, 386–97, Cambridge: Cambridge University Press.

Rodríguez, L. M. Lojo (2001–2), 'Contradiction and Ambivalence: Virginia Woolf and the Aesthetic Experience in "The Duchess and the Jeweller"', *Journal of English Studies* 3: 115–29.

Rosenburg, B. C. and Dubino, J., eds (1997), *Virginia Woolf and the Essay*, Basingstoke and London: Macmillan.

Ryan, D. (2013), *Virginia Woolf and the Materiality of Theory: Sex, Animal, Life*, Edinburgh: Edinburgh University Press.

Ryan, D. (2014), Posthumanist Interludes: Ecology and Ethology in *The Waves*', in J. Dubino, G. Lowe, V. Neverow, and K. Simpson (eds), *Virginia Woolf: Twenty-first Century Approaches*, 148–66, Edinburgh: Edinburgh University Press.

Said, E. ([1978] 2003), *Orientalism*, London: Penguin.

Seshagiri, U. ([2004] 2009), 'Orienting Virginia Woolf: Race, Aesthetics, and Politics in *To the Lighthouse*', in M. Linett (ed.), *Virginia Woolf: A MFS Reader*, 301–26, Baltimore: Johns Hopkins Press.

Scott, B. K., ed. (1990), *The Gender of Modernism: A Critical Anthology*, Bloomington and Indianapolis: Indiana University Press

Schröder, L. K. (2003), 'Tales of Abjection and Miscegenation: Virginia Woolf's and Leonard Woolf's "Jewish" Stories', *Twentieth-Century Literature* 49 (3); 298–327.

Sellers, S. (2000), 'Virginia Woolf's diaries and letters', in S. Roe and S. Sellers (eds), *The Cambridge Companion to Virginia Woolf*, 109–26, Cambridge: Cambridge University Press.

Showalter, E. (1977), 'Virginia Woolf and the Flight into Androgyny', in *A Literature of Their Own: British Women Novelists from Brontë to Lessing*, 263–97, Princeton, NJ: Princeton University Press.

Silver, B. R. (1999), *Virginia Woolf Icon*, Chicago: University of Chicago Press.

Simpson, K. (2012), 'Woolf's Bloomsbury', in B. Randall and J. Goldman (eds), *Virginia Woolf in Context*, 170–82, Cambridge: Cambridge University Press.

Simpson, K. (2014), '"Am I a Jew?": Woolf's 1930's Political and Economic Peregrinations', in J. Dubino, G. Lowe, V. Neverow, and K. Simpson (eds), *Virginia Woolf: Twenty-first Century Approaches*, 111–28, Edinburgh: Edinburgh University Press.

Sinclair, M. ([1918] 1990), 'The Novels of Dorothy Richardson' in *The Egoist*, in B. K. Scott (ed.), *The Gender of Modernism: A Critical Anthology*, 442–8, Bloomington and Indianapolis: Indiana University Press.

Skrbic, N. (2004), '"Excursions into the literature of a foreign country": Crossing Cultural Boundaries in the Short Fiction', in K. N. Benzel and R. Hoberman (eds), *Trespassing Boundaries: Virginia Woolf's Short Fiction*, 25–38, Basingstoke and New York: Palgrave Macmillan.

Smith, A. (1999), *Katherine Mansfield and Virginia Woolf: A Public of Two*, Oxford: Clarendon Press.

Snaith, A. (2000), *Virginia Woolf: Public and Private Negotiations*. Basingstoke and London: Macmillan Press.

Snaith, A. (2003), '"Stray Guineas": Virginia Woolf and the Fawcett Library', *Literature and History* 12 (2): 16–35.

Snaith, A. (2012), 'Race, Empire and Ireland', in B. Randall and J.
   Goldman (eds), *Virginia Woolf in Context*, 206–18, Cambridge:
   Cambridge University Press.
Southworth, H., ed. (2010), *Leonard and Virginia Woolf: The Hogarth
   Press and the Networks of Modernism*, Edinburgh: Edinburgh
   University Press.
Spiro, M. (2013), *Anti-Nazi Modernism: The Challenges of Resistance in
   1930s Fiction*, Evanston, IL: Northwestern University Press.
Sutton, E. (2012), 'Music', in B. Randall and J. Goldman (eds), *Virginia
   Woolf in Context*, 178–290, Cambridge: Cambridge University Press.
Sutton, E. (2013), *Virginia Woolf and Classical Music: Politics, Aesthetics,
   Form*, Edinburgh: Edinburgh University Press.
Tratner, M. (1995), *Modernism and Mass Politics: Joyce, Woolf, Eliot, and
   Yeats*, Stanford: Stanford University Press.
'The Unconventional Novel' ([1922] 2002), *Jacob's Room* reviewed in the
   Guardian, 20 July.
Vanita, R. (1997), 'Bringing Buried Things to Light: Homoerotic Alliances
   in *To the Lighthouse*', in E. Barratt and P. Cramer (eds), Press *Virginia
   Woolf: Lesbian Readings*, 165–79, New York and London: New York
   University Press.
Wells, H. G. (1912), 'The Contemporary Novel', *The Atlantic Monthly*,
   January http://www.unz.org/Pub/AtlanticMonthly-1912jan-00001
   (accessed 17 February 2015).
Whitworth, M. (2001), *Einstein's Wake: Relativity, Metaphor, and
   Modernist Literature*, Oxford: Oxford University Press.
Whitworth, Michael (2005), *Virginia Woolf: Authors in Context*, Oxford:
   Oxford University Press.
Winkiel, L. (2008), *Modernism, Race and Manifestos*, Cambridge:
   Cambridge University Press.
Wollaeger, M. (2001), 'Woolf, Postcards, and the Elision of Race:
   Colonizing Women in *The Voyage Out*', *Modernism/Modernity* 8 (1):
   43–75.
Woolf, L. (1967), *Downhill All the Way: An Autobiography of the Years
   1919 to 1939*, London: Hogarth Press.
Woolf, V. ([1925] 1974), *Mrs Dalloway*, London: Penguin.
Woolf, V. (1974–84), *The Diary of Virginia Woolf*, 5 vols, A. O. Bell (ed.),
   New York and London: Harcourt Brace Jovanovich.
Woolf, V. (1975–80), *The Letters of Virginia Woolf*, 6 vols, N. Nicolson
   and J. Trautmann (eds), New York and London: Harcourt Brace
   Jovanovich.
Woolf, V. ([1931] 1977), 'Introductory Letter', in M. Llewelyn Davies
   (ed.), *Life as We Have Known It*, xvii–xxxxi, London: Virago.
Woolf, V. ([1940] 1979). *Roger Fry*, London: Penguin.

Woolf, V. (1986–2010), *The Essays of Virginia Woolf*, 6 vols, A. McNeillie (ed.) (vols 1–4); A. McNeillie and S. N. Clarke (eds) (vols 5–6), London: Hogarth Press.

Woolf, V. ([1928] 1989), *Orlando: A Biography*, London: Triad Grafton Books.

Woolf, V. ([1929] 1989), *A Room of One's Own*, London: Triad Grafton Books.

Woolf, V. (1990), *Moments of Being* (2nd edn), J. Schulkind (ed.), London: Triad Grafton Books.

Woolf, V. ([1938] 1991), *Three Guineas*, London: Hogarth Press

Woolf, V. (1991), *Virginia Woolf: The Complete Shorter Fiction*, S. Dick (ed.), London: Triad Grafton Books.

Woolf, V. ([1915] 1992), *The Voyage Out*, London: Penguin.

Woolf, V. ([1922] 1992), *Jacob's Room*, London: Penguin.

Woolf, V. ([1927] 1992), *To the Lighthouse*, London: Vintage.

Woolf, V. ([1937] 1992), *The Years*, London: Vintage.

Woolf, V. ([1941] 1992), *Between the Acts*, London: Penguin.

Woolf, V. ([1931] 1994), *The Waves*, London: HarperCollins Publishers.

Wussow, H. (1994), 'Virginia Woolf and the Problematic Nature of the Photographic Image', in *Twentieth-Century Literature* 40 (1): 1–14.

Zimring, R. (2013), *Social Dance and the Modernist Imagination*, Surrey and Burlington: Ashgate.

Zwerdling, A. (1986), *Virginia Woolf and the Real World*, Berkley: University of California Press.

FURTHER READING

All of Woolf's novels and many of her essays and short stories are available online at https://ebooks.adelaide.edu.au/w/woolf/virginia/

Animal studies
Czarneki, K. and Neverow, V., eds (2013), *Virginia Woolf Miscellany, Woolf and Animals* (issue 84). https://virginiawoolfmiscellany.files.wordpress.com/2014/06/vwm84fall2013.pdf

Goldman, J. (2007), 'Ce Chien est Moi: Virginia Woolf and the Signifying Dog', *Woolf Studies Annual* 13: 49–86.

Snaith, A. (2002), 'Of Fanciers, Footnotes, and Fascism: Virginia Woolf's *Flush*', *Modern Fiction Studies* 48 (3): 614–36.

Characterization/subjectivity
Bowlby, R. (2011), 'Untold Stories in *Mrs Dalloway*', *Textual Practice* 25 (3), 397–415.

Edmondson, A. (2012), 'Narrativising Characters in *Mrs. Dalloway*', *Journal of Modern Literature* 36 (1): 17–36.

Gorsky, Susan Rabinow ([1972] 2009), '"The Central Shadow": Characterisation in *The Waves*', in M. Linett (ed.), *Virginia Woolf: A MFS Reader*, 220–37, Baltimore: Johns Hopkins Press.

Minow-Pinkney, M. (1987), *Virginia Woolf and the Problem of the Subject*, Brighton: Harvester.

Cinema
Humm, Maggie (2003), *Modernist Women and Visual Cultures: Virginia Woolf, Vanessa Bell, Photography and Cinema*, New Brunswick, NJ: Rutgers University Press.

Marcus, Laura (2007), *The Tenth Muse: Writing about Cinema in the Modernist Period*, Oxford: Oxford University Press.

Trotter, David (2007), *Cinema and Modernism*, Oxford: Blackwell Publishing.

Class

Childers, M. M. (1992), 'Virginia Woolf on the Outside Looking Down: Reflections on the Class of Women', *Modern Fiction Studies* 38 (1): 61–79.

Flint, K. (1986), 'Virginia Woolf and the General Strike', *Essays in Criticism* 319–34.

Simpson, K. (2015) 'Social Class in *To the Lighthouse*', in A. Pease (ed), *The Cambridge Companion to To the Lighthouse*, 110–21, Cambridge: Cambridge University Press.

Empire/race

Booth, H. J. and Rigby, N. (2000), *Modernism and Empire: Writing and British Coloniality 1890–1940*, Manchester: Manchester University Press.

Jameson, F. (1990), 'Modernism and Imperialism', in S. Deane (intro), *Nationalism, Colonialism and Literature, Terry Eagleton, Fredric Jameson and Edward W. Said*, Minneapolis: Minnesota University Press.

Kennard, J. E. (1996), 'Power and Sexual Ambiguity: *The Dreadnought Hoax, The Voyage Out, Mrs. Dalloway* and *Orlando*', *Journal of Modern Literature* 20 (2): 149–64.

Seshagiri, U. (2010), *Race and the Modernist Imagination*. Ithaca and London: Cornell University Press.

Winston, J. (1996), '"Something Out of Harmony": *To the Lighthouse* and the Subject(s) of Empire', *Woolf Studies Annual* 2: 39–70.

Feminism and gender

Allen, Judith (2012), 'Feminist Politics: "Repetition" and "Burning" in *Three Guineas* (Making It New)', in B. Randall and J. Goldman (eds), *Woolf in Context*, 193–205, Cambridge: Cambridge University Press.

DeKoven, M. (1991), *Rich and Strange: Gender, History, Modernism*, Princeton: Princeton University Press.

Felski, R. (1995), *The Gender of Modernity*, Cambridge, MA: Harvard University Press.

Jewishness, antisemitism and anti-fascism

Cheyette, B., ed. (1996), *Between 'Race' and Culture: Representations of 'the Jew' in English and American Literature*, Stanford, CA: Stanford University Press.

Rosenfeld, N. (2000), *Outsiders Together: Virginia and Leonard Woolf*, Princeton: Princeton University Press.

Schröder, L. K. (2013), '"A question is asked which is never answered": Virginia Woolf, Englishness and Antisemitism', *Woolf Studies Annual* 19: 27–57.

Suh, J. (2009), *Fascism and Anti-Fascism in Twentieth-Century British Fiction*, Basingstoke: Palgrave Macmillan.

Music

Crapoulet, E. (2009) *Virginia Woolf: A Musical Life*, Bloomsbury Heritage Series 50, London: Cecil Woolf Publishers.

Sutton, E. (2013), 'Simple Songs: Virginia Woolf and Music', The Public Domain Review, http://publicdomainreview.org/2013/01/09/simple -songs-virginia-woolf-and-music/

Realism

Jakobson, R. ([1921] 1987), 'On Realism in Art' [1921], in K. Pomorska and S. Rudy (eds), *Language in Literature*, 19–27, Massachusetts, MA: Harvard University Press.

Lodge, David (1991), 'The Language of Modernist Fiction: Metaphor and Metonymy' in M. Bradbury and J. McFarlane (eds), *Modernism: A Guide to European Literature 1890–1930*, London: Penguin.

Morris, P. (2003), *Realism* (The New Critical Idiom series), London: Routledge.

Sexuality

Doan, L. L. and Garrity, J., eds (2007), *Sapphic Modernities: Sexuality, Women, and English Culture*, Basingstoke: Palgrave Macmillan.

Short fictions

Hanson, C. (1985), *Short Stories and Short Fictions, 1880–1980*, Basingstoke: Macmillan.

Head, Dominic (1992), *The Modernist Short Story: A Study in Theory and Practice*, Cambridge: Cambridge University Press.

Time and the everyday

Olsen, L. (2009), *Modernism and the Ordinary*, Oxford: Oxford University Press.

Randall, B. (2007), *Modernism, Daily Time and Everyday Life*, Cambridge: Cambridge University Press.

Sheehan, P. (2015) 'Time as Protagonist in *To the Lighthouse*', in A. Pease (ed), *The Cambridge Companion to To the Lighthouse*, 47–57, Cambridge: Cambridge University Press.

War

Hussey, M., ed. (1991), *Virginia Woolf and War: Fiction, Reality, and Myth*, Syracuse, NY: Syracuse University Press.

Tate, T. (1998), *Modernism, History and the First World War*, Manchester and New York: Manchester University Press.

Tylee, C. M. (1990), *The Great War and Women's Consciousness: Images of Militarism and Womanhood in Women's Writings, 1914–64*, Iowa City: University of Iowa Press.

INDEX

locators in **bold** indicate main references; locators followed by n refer to notes.